# Palgrave Studies in Gender and Education

**Series Editor**
Yvette Taylor
School of Education
University of Strathclyde
Glasgow, UK

This Series aims to provide a comprehensive space for an increasingly diverse and complex area of interdisciplinary social science research: gender and education. Because the field of women and gender studies is developing rapidly and becoming 'internationalised' – as are traditional social science disciplines such as sociology, educational studies, social geography, and so on – there is a greater need for this dynamic, global Series that plots emerging definitions and debates and monitors critical complexities of gender and education. This Series has an explicitly feminist approach and orientation and attends to key theoretical and methodological debates, ensuring a continued conversation and relevance within the well-established, inter-disciplinary field of gender and education.

The Series combines renewed and revitalised feminist research methods and theories with emergent and salient public policy issues. These include pre-compulsory and post-compulsory education; 'early years' and 'lifelong' education; educational (dis)engagements of pupils, students and staff; trajectories and intersectional inequalities including race, class, sexuality, age and disability; policy and practice across educational landscapes; diversity and difference, including institutional (schools, colleges, universities), locational and embodied (in 'teacher'–'learner' positions); varied global activism in and beyond the classroom and the 'public university'; educational technologies and transitions and the (ir)relevance of (in)formal educational settings; and emergent educational mainstreams and margins. In using a critical approach to gender and education, the Series recognises the importance of probing beyond the boundaries of specific territorial-legislative domains in order to develop a more international, intersectional focus. In addressing varied conceptual and methodological questions, the Series combines an intersectional focus on competing – and sometimes colliding – strands of educational provisioning and equality and 'diversity', and provides insightful reflections on the continuing critical shift of gender and feminism within (and beyond) the academy.

Rachel Handforth

# Belonging, Gender and Identity in the Doctoral Years

## Across Time and Space

Rachel Handforth
The Careers Research and Advisory Centre (CRAC)
Cambridge, UK

ISSN 2524-6445　　　　　ISSN 2524-6453　(electronic)
Palgrave Studies in Gender and Education
ISBN 978-3-031-11949-1　　ISBN 978-3-031-11950-7　(eBook)
https://doi.org/10.1007/978-3-031-11950-7

© The Editor(s) (if applicable) and The Author(s), under exclusive licence to Springer Nature Switzerland AG 2022

This work is subject to copyright. All rights are solely and exclusively licensed by the Publisher, whether the whole or part of the material is concerned, specifically the rights of translation, reprinting, reuse of illustrations, recitation, broadcasting, reproduction on microfilms or in any other physical way, and transmission or information storage and retrieval, electronic adaptation, computer software, or by similar or dissimilar methodology now known or hereafter developed.

The use of general descriptive names, registered names, trademarks, service marks, etc. in this publication does not imply, even in the absence of a specific statement, that such names are exempt from the relevant protective laws and regulations and therefore free for general use.

The publisher, the authors, and the editors are safe to assume that the advice and information in this book are believed to be true and accurate at the date of publication. Neither the publisher nor the authors or the editors give a warranty, expressed or implied, with respect to the material contained herein or for any errors or omissions that may have been made. The publisher remains neutral with regard to jurisdictional claims in published maps and institutional affiliations.

Cover illustration: Klaus Vedfelt © Getty Images

This Palgrave Macmillan imprint is published by the registered company Springer Nature Switzerland AG.
The registered company address is: Gewerbestrasse 11, 6330 Cham, Switzerland

# Foreword

Belonging is an issue and experience (or lack of experience), familiar and crucial to every doctoral student. This has been never more so than in 2022, in the post-pandemic era of growing austerity when historical practices to encourage doctoral communities and belonging and the postdoctoral job market are stretched and struggling. This book is more topical than ever at a moment when (in social media) many women doctoral students in particular report the stress, when researching, writing and operating alone often in an intellectually, emotionally and physically demanding vacuum of non-belonging.

The book opens by explaining that beyond exposing problems, it uses its research base, partly through interviews, to explore how women can and do participate and belong in HE and doctoral studies, affected as this is by the predominance of white men in the professorial (and other hierarchical) layers of higher education and so in the culture which upholds their interests. With the current timely concern with diversity, inclusivity and decolonising in the higher education curriculum at every level, the noted emphasis on the lack of diversity affecting the likelihood and experience of belonging throughout doctoral study and gaining and thriving in academic roles is extremely topical.

This well-written book will be very useful and informative for anyone studying for a doctorate degree across STEM, social sciences and arts/humanities, and also for supervisors supervising such doctoral students.

One of its strengths is its breadth and focus on the issues concerning belonging, an experience common yet differently and intersectionally nuanced across disciplines. This focus allows the book to home in on relationships with colleagues and supervisor(s), how time during the doctoral period is spent, as well as how time beyond graduation is envisaged. The book explores how these factors influence perceptions of joining the academic workforce (and individuals' wider job market potential), while keeping the concepts of gender and belonging at the core, thinking of both the actual research and writing period and the time planned after graduation, of joining the academic workforce or other parts of the world of work.

Cambridge and Bath, UK  Gina Wisker
2022

# Acknowledgments

With many thanks to Professor Gina Wisker and Dr Robin Mellors-Bourne for your support in making this book a reality. Thanks also to Professor Sandra Acker for your valuable insights.

This research was funded by Sheffield Hallam University's Faculty of Development and Society, and ethical approval was granted by the research ethics committee at Sheffield Hallam University.

Writing this book would not have been possible without the women who participated in this research, who were willing to give up their time and share their stories with me. I hope this does them justice.

This book is dedicated to Ed, and Ivy—my two favourite people.

# Contents

1 **Academic Identities and Imagined Futures: Women's Doctoral Journeys**    1
   Introduction    1
   The Doctorate as an Inherently Gendered Experience    7
   Developing Academic Identities    9
   The PhD and Beyond: Imagining Post-doctoral Careers    10
   Introducing the Study: Approach to Research    14
   Why Belonging?    16
   Structure of the Book    18
   Introducing the Participants    20
   References    23

2 **Theorising Gender and Belonging in the (Early Career) Academy**    33
   Women in the Academy: Still Outsiders?    34
   Theorising Belonging and Considering Legitimacy    39
   Belonging to Academic Communities: The Role of Disciplines and Departments    42
   Belonging Within Academic Cultures    44
   Belonging as Doctoral Students    48

| | | |
|---|---|---|
| | Feeling 'Other' in the Academy: Considering the Implications of Not Belonging | 51 |
| | References | 52 |
| | Women in STEM: Restoryings of Participants' Doctoral Journeys | 67 |
| |   Harriet | 67 |
| |   Jane | 68 |
| |   Antonia | 70 |
| |   Pepper | 72 |
| **3** | **Contesting Power Structures: Encountering Gatekeepers to Belonging in STEM** | **75** |
| | Studying for a Doctorate in STEM | 77 |
| | Gendered Disciplines: Perceptions of Women Engineers | 79 |
| | Being Positioned as 'Other': Gendered Academic Cultures and Belonging | 84 |
| | Power in Supervisory Relationships: Negotiating and Resisting Expectations | 100 |
| | Navigating Academic STEM Culture: Imagining Non-academic Futures | 109 |
| | Summary | 116 |
| | References | 118 |
| | Women in Health and Related Sciences: Restoryings of Participants' Doctoral Journeys | 129 |
| |   Jessie | 129 |
| |   Sally | 130 |
| |   Liz | 132 |
| **4** | **Negotiating Legitimacy: Struggles and Strategies for Feeling Belonging in Health and Related Sciences** | **135** |
| | Studying for a Doctorate in Health and Related Sciences | 136 |
| | Struggling to Belong: The Liminal Status of Doctoral Students | 138 |
| | Gendered Experiences of Supervision | 149 |
| | Conflicting Personal and Academic Values | 153 |

| | |
|---|---|
| Resisting the Pressure to Publish: Implications for Well-Being | 158 |
| Summary | 167 |
| References | 169 |
| Women in the Humanities and Social Sciences: Restoryings of Participants' Doctoral Journeys | 176 |
|    Martina | 176 |
|    Chloe | 177 |
|    Freija | 178 |
|    Bella | 180 |
|    Eleanor | 181 |

**5 Navigating Belonging Within Academic Spaces: Traversing Territories in the Humanities and Social Sciences**    183

| | |
|---|---|
| Studying for a Doctorate in the Humanities and Social Sciences | 184 |
| Access to Institutional Workspaces and Feeling Belonging | 186 |
| Negotiating Belonging Within Physical Workspaces | 197 |
| Imagining Future Belonging: Witnessing Gendered Careers | 206 |
| Summary | 216 |
| References | 218 |

**6 Reflecting on Women Doctoral Students' Belonging: Struggles, Strategies and Successes**    227

| | |
|---|---|
| Sites of Belonging for Women Doctoral Students | 228 |
|    Belonging Within Institutional Spaces | 228 |
|    Belonging Within Disciplines | 231 |
|    Belonging within Departmental Communities | 233 |
|    Belonging in Everyday Academic Spaces | 235 |
| Claiming Legitimacy and Developing Strategies for Belonging | 237 |
| Post-PhD Futures: Considering Long-Term Belonging in Academia | 240 |
| Implications of (Not) Belonging for Individuals, Identities, Institutions and the Sector | 244 |
| References | 251 |

7 **Facilitating Belonging and Academic Identities: Addressing Barriers Faced by Women Doctoral Students** 259
   Addressing Barriers to Belonging: Institutional Responsibilities 260
   Facilitating Academic Identities: Creating Inclusive Academic Cultures 263
   Thinking to the Future: Disciplinary and Departmental Strategies to Support Belonging 268
     Final Thoughts 272
   References 272

**Index** 279

# 1

# Academic Identities and Imagined Futures: Women's Doctoral Journeys

## Introduction

This book is a product of my own doctoral journey, which began in 2014. My decision to apply for a PhD was simply a result of happenstance; I was unhappy in my job and was motivated by a love of research which I had rediscovered in my part-time degree. I had started a master's in social science research methods whilst working full-time in a related field, and had begun undertaking qualitative research exploring the career experiences of senior women academics. Whilst this research was interesting, I became conscious that the experiences of women further down what has been called the 'leaky pipeline' (Barinaga, 1993), were likely to determine whether or not they became senior academics, or academics at all.

In my working life, further observations fuelled my interest; when a colleague completed her PhD but decided not to pursue an academic career, I was curious about her decision. I had thought that an academic career was what doing a PhD was *for*, and couldn't understand why anyone would embark upon such a long and difficult path only to then leave academia. I wondered what it could be about doing a doctorate that could be so off-putting. I wondered if women experienced doctoral study differently to men, and whether their subsequent careers were similar or not. During my PhD, I interviewed women doctoral students in the UK who had started their doctorate at the same time as me. I was keen to understand how these women, studying across a range of academic disciplines, imagined their futures beyond the PhD, and how their identities and imagined futures shifted during the course of their doctorate. This book is based on their experiences and, to some extent, mine too—whilst I do not view myself as a participant, evidently my own experiences of studying for a doctorate at the same time as the participants have shaped the ways in which I view and write about women doctoral students.

In reviewing literature on women academics' experiences of higher education, I found that the focus was often on the low proportion of women working in traditionally male-dominated science, technology, engineering and mathematics (STEM) disciplines, and the challenges women face while attempting to enter the professoriate and other senior academic roles (see Acker, 1980; Ceci et al., 2014; Deem, 2003; Howe-Walsh & Turnbull, 2016; Kulis et al., 2002; Morley, 2013; O'Connor, 2015; Read & Kehm, 2016; Thanacoody et al., 2006). These bodies of literature often drew attention to the barriers women face in progressing their academic career, either implicitly or explicitly referring to the 'leaky pipeline' whereby fewer women are found at increasingly senior levels of academia (see Barinaga, 1993; Hatchell & Aveling, 2008; Soe & Yakura, 2008).

Yet despite ongoing concerns about the low representation of women in STEM disciplines and in senior positions, little attention has been paid to the day-to-day experiences of women in the early stages of academic life. There are relatively few studies of how women doctoral students experience the academy and construct their career ambitions, despite the PhD being a prerequisite for an academic career,[1] and this being the period within which academic identities and aspirations are often forged (Carter et al., 2021; Mantai, 2017, 2019; McAlpine et al., 2010; 2013; Rao et al., 2021; Szelényi et al., 2016).

In this book, I contend that individuals' experiences during their time as doctoral students (arguably too, during previous degrees) and the early career stage—the bottom of the 'leaky pipeline'—have a considerable

---

[1] Here, the phrase 'academic career' refers to the long-term participation of individuals in academic roles, specifically, research and teaching within universities.

impact on who progresses in academia. Many texts on doctoral education attest to the importance of students becoming 'encultured' into the academic environment during their studies to avoid isolation, feel part of their disciplinary community and ultimately succeed as doctoral candidates (Delamont et al., 2000; Parry, 2007). Yet this is not a straightforward process; doing so involves negotiating gendered academic cultures and attempting to establish a sense of belonging and legitimacy within an environment where women continue to be positioned as outsiders (Ahmed, 2021; Aiston, 2015; Anderson & Williams, 2001; Savigny, 2014). Despite the increase in women's participation in higher education over the past few decades, women continue to experience marginalisation within academic spaces, which at its most extreme may be manifested in sexual harassment and assault (Page et al., 2019; Phipps, 2018; Whitley & Page, 2015).

Participation in the academy still remains far from equal. Whilst in the UK and other higher education sectors initiatives such as Athena SWAN[2] have aimed to address gender inequalities by increasing the representation of women and supporting women's career progression, significant differences persist. Just over a quarter of professors [3] in the UK are women (Advance HE, 2021a)—an inequality which is considerably more pronounced for women of colour. Recent figures highlight that only 2.7% of UK professors are women of Black Asian and Minority Ethnic (BAME) backgrounds, compared with 63.5% who are white men (Advance HE, 2021a). Though there has been increased focus on racial inequalities within UK higher education in recent years, notably in relation to addressing the degree attainment gap between white and BAME undergraduates (Richardson, 2018), the movement towards decolonising the curriculum (Arday & Mirza, 2018) and the introduction of the Race Equality Charter,[4] racial inequalities are often overlooked in favour of gender inequalities (see Bhopal & Henderson, 2019). I am conscious that due to the sample of participants with whom data were collected, my

---

[2] https://www.advance-he.ac.uk/equality-charters/transformed-uk-athena-swan-charter
[3] The UK definition of the term 'professor' is used here (and throughout the book) to refer to those employed at the highest academic grade—equivalent to what in North America may be known as a 'full professorship'.
[4] https://www.advance-he.ac.uk/equality-charters/race-equality-charter

analysis within this book largely focuses on the experiences of white women, with only one participant from an ethnic minority background. I recognise that the issues of belonging and academic identity discussed here are compounded for women from ethnic minority backgrounds, especially given their under-representation within the doctoral student population (Bradbury, 2013; Mattocks & Briscoe-Palmer, 2016).

The research on which this book is based was conducted between 2014 and 2017, with 12 PhD students at several points during their doctorate. Participants, including myself, were undertaking a traditional, full-time PhD across a range of different subject areas, and were based at two different UK institutions (see Table 1.1). During data collection, it became apparent that issues relating to belonging were central to the way in which participants experienced the doctorate, but also to the ways in which they imagined their post-PhD futures. Whilst academics, too, may also struggle to establish belonging to their academic communities at times, these early experiences of belonging (and not belonging) seemed to shape the extent to which women doctoral students were able to construct viable, long-term academic identities. Thus, belonging is one of the central thematic concepts utilised within this book, used as a lens through which to understand women doctoral students' experiences of the gendered cultures of higher education institutions. In this book, I present a new theorisation of belonging in relation to the doctoral experience, which has relevance across academic disciplines.

This book aims to bring the lived experiences of women doctoral students to the fore, exploring how individuals' experiences during the PhD shaped how far they felt they belonged in academia, and the extent to which they were able to construct viable academic identities. It understands the doctorate as a crucial 'phase' (Araújo, 2005) wherein career possibilities are developed and internalised, and argues that regardless of the range of careers potentially open to doctoral graduates, for many, the doctorate acts as a litmus test for a career in academia. This book attempts to address gaps in knowledge by providing rich, qualitative understandings of how women doctoral students from a range of disciplines experienced and negotiated different academic cultures and how this shaped the post-PhD futures they imagined. I illuminate the ways in which participants imagined their future careers in response to their experiences of

Table 1.1 Overview of demographic details about participants

| Institution | Name | Discipline and category | Fee status | Ethnicity | Marital status | Care commitments |
|---|---|---|---|---|---|---|
| Modern University | Antonia | Engineering (STEM) | International | Other white | In a relationship (distance) | None |
| | Sally | Sport psychology (Health and related science) | Home | White British | In a relationship (distance) | None |
| | Jessie | Public Health (Health and related science) | Home | White British | Married | 2 children |
| | Liz | Health sciences (Health and related science) | Home | White British | Married | None |
| | Bella | Psychology (Social science) | Home | White British | Single | None |
| | Chloe | Social policy (Social Science) | Home | Other mixed | Cohabiting | Older parents |
| Redbrick University | Harriet | Biology (STEM) | Home | White British | In a relationship | None |
| | Jane | Conservation (STEM) | Home | White British | Cohabiting | None |
| | Pepper | Engineering (STEM) | Home | White British | Single | None |
| | Freija | Geography (Social science) | Home | Other white | Engaged | None |
| | Martina | Politics (Social science) | International | Other White | Cohabiting | None |
| | Eleanor | English (Humanities) | Home | White British | Cohabiting | None |

belonging within the academic environment, examining the implications of this for individuals, the higher education sector and for the future of the academic workforce. This book is necessary, timely and significant, given the lack of studies attending to the gendered nature of the doctoral experience across disciplines, the impact on women doctoral students' career aspirations and identities and, ultimately, the implications for the academic sector of women choosing to leave academia after the PhD.

It is important to note that emerging research on the impact of the Covid-19 pandemic indicates that the pandemic, and subsequent national lockdowns, have exacerbated many of the challenges to belonging for women doctoral students. Literature highlights how the pressure of negotiating family and professional lives had a disproportionately negative impact on women academics' research productivity (Ribarovska et al., 2021) and well-being (Higginbotham & Dahlberg, 2021), with international findings showing that women academics were more likely than men to take on the additional household burden generated by the stay-at-home orders issued during the pandemic (Yildirim & Eslen-Ziya, 2021).

Emerging findings from research with early career researchers and doctoral students highlight how, during the Covid-19 pandemic, women faced additional struggles in attempting to participate in their academic communities due to the lack of academic conferences, other demands on supervisors' time and getting feedback on work (Jackman et al., 2021; Levine et al., 2021). Alongside practical concerns regarding access to funding extensions (see Munro & Heath, 2021), and the shift to online modes of delivery for those with teaching responsibilities (Levine et al., 2021), the increased dislocation from academic spaces in many cases exacerbated the isolation often experienced in doctoral study, due to the negative impact of lockdowns and working from home on access to peer communities (Wang & DeLaquil, 2020). There is some evidence to suggest that students who are parents, who have disabilities or study part-time have been particularly disadvantaged during the pandemic (Papageorgiou et al., 2020). Further, there were concerns about completion of the doctorate and the long-term impact of the pandemic on career progression opportunities, particularly for women doctoral students with children (Bender et al., 2022).

Whilst the research reported in this book was undertaken pre-pandemic, it is evident that many of the challenges that women doctoral students faced in belonging within their academic communities will have been compounded by the pandemic and related lockdowns. It is not clear what the longer-term impacts of this will be, and this would be worthy of further exploration and research.

## The Doctorate as an Inherently Gendered Experience

In order to understand how studying for a doctorate influences the career aspirations of women, it is important to first acknowledge the gendered historical context of the qualification itself (Carter et al., 2021). A number of assumptions persist within higher education policy and practice about the nature of the doctoral student population, and their motivations and intentions. McCulloch and Stokes (2008, p3) argue that there remains a stereotype of the traditional PhD student, which is inherently gendered:

> he (and it is implicitly a 'he') is a young, full-time, funded student who is geographically mobile, without dependants, studying in a metropolitan area and intending to pursue a career as a full-time researcher or academic.

This traditional view of doctoral students as young, male and free from caring responsibilities, echoes the stereotype of the 'ideal academic' that Lynch (2010) describes as being carefree and therefore able to dedicate themselves entirely to their academic career. Thus, this gendered stereotype of doctoral students informs conceptions about who an ideal academic might be. In this way, studying for a doctorate requires women to 'step into an authority symbolically and historically gendered masculine' (Carter et al., 2013, p. 342). There is evidence that this remains a challenge for some; despite the increase in women around the world participating in higher education in recent decades, women are still under-represented amongst doctoral students. In the UK, women students make up 63.7% of undergraduates, but just 49.5% of doctoral students (Advance HE, 2021b); women remain under-represented at the doctoral level within STEM disciplines, with the lowest numbers in engineering, computing and physical sciences (Advance HE, 2021b).

Beyond lower participation in doctoral degrees, though, it has been argued that women experience the academy differently from the outset, starting at PhD level and perhaps even prior to this (Birch, 2011). Firstly, women are more likely to undertake doctoral study later in life than men (Bagilhole & White, 2013), which has implications for subsequent academic career progression. Even when the doctoral candidacy has commenced, women often have a less straightforward path through the doctorate than men, particularly if they have caring responsibilities (see Brown & Watson, 2010). Studies show that women are more likely to report encountering mental health issues (Levecque et al., 2017), and to struggle with imposter syndrome during their studies compared with their male counterparts (Collett & Avelis, 2013). Further, women doctoral students continue to encounter sexist attitudes, facing direct and indirect discrimination which contributes to feelings of marginalisation and otherness (De Welde & Laursen, 2011; Hughes et al., 2017). These inequalities are further compounded for women students with disabilities and those from ethnic minorities, who face multiple forms of discrimination (Mattocks & Briscoe-Palmer, 2016). Perhaps unsurprisingly, these experiences during doctoral study can discourage women from pursuing an academic career (Guest et al., 2013; Hatchell & Aveling, 2008).

It is evident from existing research that experiencing discrimination during the doctorate has longer-term career impacts. For example, a longitudinal study examining gender differences in post-PhD employment in Australian universities found that women had been less likely than men to be encouraged to engage in activities related to developing an academic career during the PhD (Dever et al., 2008). Further, in the UK, studies conducted by the Royal Society of Chemistry (2008) and the Wellcome Trust (2013) highlighted that women were far more likely than their male peers to become discouraged from pursuing an academic career during their PhD.

As I have argued elsewhere (Handforth, 2022), the doctorate can therefore be understood as a gendered experience. Yet other than the studies in STEM subjects such as those conducted by the Royal Society of Chemistry (2008) and Wellcome Trust (2013), little work has been done to understand the aspects of academic culture which discourage women from remaining in academia after the PhD. Attending to the ways in which women are supported—or not—to develop a sense of belonging to their academic communities during the doctorate is therefore crucial in understanding women's post-PhD career aspirations. This book explores this question across disciplines, addressing this gap in knowledge and making it a valuable and timely piece of research.

## Developing Academic Identities

In this book, I present an understanding of post-PhD career aspirations as bound up with academic identity development, exploring the extent to which participants were able to form viable academic identities during the doctorate. It has been argued that scholarly identity emerges during the PhD experience (Baker & Lattuca, 2010). However, this process is not straightforward, as becoming a doctoral candidate requires identity shifts (Carter et al., 2013; Gravett, 2021; Mantai, 2019; McAlpine & Turner, 2012), as individuals become encultured into the academic environment. Drawing on data gathered from participants at different stages of their studies, I highlight how, during the PhD, individuals' academic identities were formulated, renegotiated and in some cases abandoned altogether.

Defining academic identities is complex because they are continually in flux, highly individualised and often contested (Clegg, 2008). However, the understanding of academic identity used throughout this book views identities as multiple, socially formed and potentially conflicting (Stets & Burke, 2000). Further, it holds that identities involve 'issues about who we are and what we want to be and become' (Weeks, 1990, p. 89). This understanding views identities as narratively constructed; stories which are constantly under revision (McAdams, 1993; Polkinghorne, 1998; Woodward, 2003). Recognising literature which attests to the significant influence of disciplinary cultures on doctoral experiences (see Delamont, Atkinson, et al., 1997; Delamont et al., 2000; Delamont, Parry, et al., 1997), in Chaps. 4, 5 and 6, I explore the ways in which participants' academic identities were shaped by their particular disciplinary cultures. In doing so, I draw on Henkel's (2005) framing of academic identity, arguing that participants developed identities in relation to how able they were to identify with what they viewed as the values of being an academic.

During their doctorate, participants learned about the structural aspects of academic careers through a process of observational learning (Rossiter, 2004) and came to understand the implications of what taking on an academic identity might mean for their future. A number of challenges encountered in developing long-term academic identities related to factors such as the competition for academic jobs, and the pressure to publish, derived from a culture of performativity (Ball, 2003). This cultural shift in academic working conditions has been linked to what has been described as the neoliberalisation of the academy, with a focus on measuring individual productivity and performance as indicators of success (Ball, 2012; Brooks, 2001; Collini, 2012). Neoliberal understandings of academic labour therefore pervaded participants' conceptions of what taking on academic identities beyond the doctorate might require. Drawing on discourses of academic identity development, legitimacy and validity, I argue that doctoral experiences challenged the participants' ability to belong to their academic communities not only as PhD students, but also their capacity to envisage themselves belonging in the future, as academics.

## The PhD and Beyond: Imagining Post-doctoral Careers

Given that the focus of this book is on experiences of the UK doctorate, it is useful to briefly set out how the PhD model in the UK differs from those found in other parts of the world. There are significant international variations in the structure of the PhD. In the UK, Australia and New Zealand, a PhD broadly takes the same form, with expectations that full-time study will result in a written thesis after 3 years, with some funding options available through national research councils and individual university bursaries. Most students will have more than one supervisor and, depending on the discipline, will either apply for advertised doctoral opportunities where the research programme is set (more common in STEM and science-related subjects) or design their own research project. There may be some options to take on teaching and research opportunities, but these are fairly limited in comparison to other countries.

In Canada, many PhD students—often referred to as 'graduate' students—work at their institutions in teaching and/or research roles to help support the funding of their doctoral research, and part-time study is increasingly common (Acker & Haque, 2015). Whilst in the USA, doctoral students are expected to complete coursework alongside examinations over a longer period of time (often between 6 and 9 years), the structure of the doctorate means that there is more capacity for working alongside peers and academic staff, with less reliance on the supervisory relationship, which is critical for the success of a doctoral student within the UK model. Yet again, doctoral study elsewhere in northern Europe, for example Finland, is structured quite differently than in the UK. Doctoral education is publicly funded, and students receive a stipend, also often working at their university during the doctorate, which usually takes 4–5 years to complete on a full-time basis (Pyhältö et al., 2019). These aspects of doctoral study means that the role of doctoral student is much more akin to that of an academic than in the UK; in countries like the Netherlands and Finland, as well as other Scandinavian countries, they are viewed as junior members of academic staff with duties, rights and a regular salary (Kehm, 2006).

Beyond these international differences, conceptions of the purpose of the doctorate have changed significantly in recent decades. McAlpine and Emmioğlu (2014, p. 1) note that 'while the doctorate was once perceived as preparation for an academic position, internationally more than half of all graduates leave the higher education sector, whether by choice or lack of opportunity'. In the UK, even a decade ago, statistics indicated that few who aspire to an academic career would be successful, with just 38% of doctoral graduates in 2010 working in either teaching or research in higher education (Vitae, 2013). This knowledge of the career destinations of many doctoral students counters the traditional view of the PhD purely as an academic apprenticeship. Despite the fact that most PhD graduates will not pursue academic careers, institutional policies often maintain assumptions about the doctorate simply as preparation for an academic career (see Neumann & Tan, 2011), which can lead to a lack of advice for doctoral students about careers outside of academia (Vitae, 2017; Wellcome Trust, 2013). Further, some PhD supervisors may still consider that they are training apprentice researchers (Park, 2005), and many feel unqualified to provide any other type of career guidance (UKCGE, 2021).

Yet the ongoing assumption that PhD candidates are often motivated by the prospect of an academic career is not unfounded. There has been a significant increase in competition for academic jobs in recent decades (Royal Society, 2010), which has been linked to the expansion of doctoral education (Wolff, 2015). Internationally, there has been a considerable rise in the number of individuals enrolling on doctoral programmes (OECD, 2014), and in the UK, 20% more students enrolled in doctoral programmes in 2016–7 than in 2007–8 (Universities UK, 2017). A recent national Postgraduate Research Experience Survey—a national survey undertaken in the UK—highlighted that 38% of respondents envisaged an academic career after completing their doctorate (Advance HE, 2020). Thus, it seems that though a significant proportion of doctoral students imagine an academic future after the PhD, they are unlikely to realise this aspiration, and concurrently are not fully informed about the range of other career options available to them after the doctorate.

Significantly, however, studies have found that those who pursued academic research careers after their PhD were actually less satisfied than those working in other sectors. A report undertaken by Research Councils UK in 2014 found that of various occupational groups, those working in research in higher education were least satisfied with their role, with individuals expressing 'particular concern over job security and career prospects' (Diamond et al., 2014, p. 23). A significant challenge for those aspiring to become academics is the instability of employment within the higher education sector, complicated by a changing economic context and an uncertain political landscape (UK Council for Science and Technology, 2007). There has been an increase in the number of short-term, temporary academic research roles advertised by universities (Vitae, 2019), indicative of the 'casualisation' of academic labour (Lopes & Dewan, 2014). Some argue that the early academic career stage is becoming increasingly characterised by precariousness, often placing individuals under significant financial pressure (The Res-Sisters, 2016; UCU, 2016). Women and ethnic minority academics are over-represented in these insecure academic positions (UCU, 2021).

International research has illuminated that the ways in which doctoral students perceive the lives of academics have a significant impact upon their own career aspirations. Research on students in the US who left their doctorates before completing the PhD found that a significant factor influencing attrition was the perception that being an academic was incompatible with a healthy work/life balance (Golde, 2005). Further, a study based on a survey of 8000 male and female doctoral students in California found that academic posts in research-intensive institutions were perceived particularly negatively as post-PhD career options (Mason et al., 2009). In the same study, it was noted that women doctoral students in particular were reluctant to pursue careers which would mean replicating the career experiences of their supervisors, who were perceived as not being able to successfully combine the demands of their work with family life.

This book explores how the career aspirations of women doctoral students are informed by, and reflect, these changing conceptions of the purpose of doctoral study, and perceptions of academic careers. It also examines the impact of the doctoral experience on women's sense of belonging within the academic environment. Previous UK studies have identified gendered shifts in doctoral students' career intentions during the PhD. For example, the Royal Society of Chemistry (2008) found that at the beginning of their PhD, 72% of women and 61% of men wanted to pursue careers in research. By their third year, just 37% of women had the same aspiration, compared with 59% of men. Findings indicated that this was largely due to the isolation perceived in academic research careers, along with a perception of a career in academic science as incompatible with family life. Similarly, the Wellcome Trust (2013) conducted a qualitative study with men and women who studied science PhDs, and found that most of the women who left academia did so immediately after their PhD, 'suggesting that their experience during the PhD, and/or their perception of what post-doctoral academic work might be like, influenced their decision' (*ibid,* p. 6). One of the few empirical studies of gender differences in career progression outside of STEM, *Gender and Career Progression in Theology and Religious Studies*, found that:

> For many women, the process of doing an MA or PhD will often determine whether they pursue a career in academia or not. It is on the basis of this experience that they begin to see the rewards and costs of being an academic.
> (Guest et al., 2013, p. 6)

The doctorate can therefore be viewed as a key formative experience for women, who use their cumulative experiences and knowledge to decide whether or not they want to pursue academic careers in the future. I argue in this book that this decision, conscious or not, is largely based on whether or not they can envisage themselves belonging in academia. The empirical studies discussed above, whilst identifying links between women's experiences of the doctorate and leaving academia, are often limited to particular academic subjects or are based on data collected on a single occasion, thus representing a single point within the doctoral journey rather than enabling insight into how different stages of doctoral study may shape career aspirations. This book attempts to provide detailed insight of individuals' lived experiences of doctoral study and illustrate the impact of academic cultures on women's' career aspirations.

## Introducing the Study: Approach to Research

Thirteen participants were recruited from two UK institutions, which I have named 'Redbrick University' and 'Modern University'. Redbrick University has a large population of doctoral students and significant funding provision for doctoral education, whereas Modern University has a smaller proportion of doctoral students and receives less funding for doctoral research. Calls for participants were circulated by central university administrators with responsibility for doctoral student support at each institution. Participants were recruited from across disciplines, as I was interested in whether women's experiences of doctoral study differed across subject areas and how disciplinary cultures shaped career aspirations. No incentives were offered for participation.

A qualitative approach to the research allowed insight into how the different stages of doctoral study shaped participants' aspirations during the PhD, noting that most existing studies on doctoral students' aspirations only collect data at a single point during the PhD (see Birch, 2011; Brailsford, 2010). The approach taken in this research involved interviewing each participant twice during their studies—once during their first year of study, and again part way through their second year—and collecting online research diaries kept by participants over the duration of the PhD. For practical reasons, including the timely completion of my own doctoral thesis, interviews were not undertaken in the final year of participants' degrees, and diaries were kept on an ad hoc basis by participants throughout their studies. The combination of qualitative methods used in this research enabled understandings of how career aspirations could be shaped by cumulative experiences of doctoral study, as well as rich, detailed insight into participants' day-to-day attempts to belong within their academic communities.

This research utilised a narrative inquiry framework wherein participants' experiences were understood as narratives, which I then reconstructed—or 're-storied' (Clandinin & Connelly, 2000)—in the writing up process. This perspective conceptualises participants as narrators of their own lives (Chase, 2005), emphasising individual agency in identity construction (McAdams, 1993; Polkinghorne, 1988; Woodward, 2003) while recognising the power dynamics inherent in presenting the voices of other women (Handforth & Taylor, 2016). My status as a woman PhD student at the time influenced the stories that participants told me, and the way in which they were conveyed; narratives are always told differently depending on the audience (Sfard & Prusak, 2005). Yet, I acknowledge the inherent tension in viewing participants as narrators, when the writing of this book has necessitated the narration of their stories through my own perspective.

Whilst analysing participants' experiences collectively, and according to their broad disciplinary area, I have drawn on Clandinin and Connelly's (2000) narrative analytical process of 'restorying' in order to try and maintain individual, anonymised accounts of individuals' experiences ahead of each main chapter. These anonymised, restored accounts represent my understanding and reconstruction of participants' stories. Creating these accounts allowed me to attend to the contexts within which stories were constructed (Plummer, 1983) and create a more linear understanding of participants' doctoral journeys. My approach to analysis in the following chapters of this book attempts to connect the 'small stories' (Bamberg & Georgakopoulou 2008) from participants' day-to-day experiences, to the broader sociological and cultural narratives which inform and shape these individual stories (Riessman, 2008), including narratives of legitimacy, identity and belonging in the academy.

## Why Belonging?

Whilst the 'problem' of women's under-representation in senior academic roles and male-dominated disciplines (the 'leaky pipeline') has been well documented, this phenomenon has never been explored in relation to women doctoral students' ability to belong within the academy. Belonging provides a useful theoretical lens for understanding the ways in which women negotiate gendered academic cultures, not only as doctoral students but also how they imagined the possibility of navigating this as academics. Whilst hoping to avoid what Thomas (2018, p. 27) describes as the 'tempting dazzle of the binary' and viewing experiences simply as being indicative either of 'belonging/not-belonging', I deploy a view of belonging as being relational and highly contextual, depending on the situation. From this perspective, belonging is seen as an ongoing accomplishment (May, 2013), which may be more challenging for some individuals than for others. In this book, I focus on the temporal dimensions of future, imagined belonging and highlight the contexts within which this was, and was not, possible for women doctoral students.

The concept of belonging is under-theorised by social scientists, despite its utility in understanding issues of identity, power and community

(Thomas, 2018). Further, despite belonging being used to understand the experience of undergraduates (see Cashmore et al., 2014; Thomas, 2018), the concept is largely overlooked within literature on doctoral education (see Morris, 2021; White & Nonnamaker, 2008). This seems odd, particularly given the significant attention paid within many studies to the potential for isolation during the doctorate and the impact on retention (Ali et al., 2007; Golde, 2005; Lovitts, 2001; Pifer & Baker, 2014; Tinto, 1993). This book deploys belonging as a theoretical concept to explore how women doctoral students negotiated academia in a highly gendered environment. In Chap. 2, I present a new theoretical understanding of belonging in relation to the doctoral experience.

As I explore fully in Chaps. 3, 4 and 5, institutional, disciplinary and departmental cultures influenced how able participants were to develop a sense of belonging to their academic communities. My analysis focuses on how participants' experiences of these cultures during the doctorate shaped their sense of belonging within academia more widely. I situate their experiences in relation to studies which argue that the culture of academic institutions is inherently masculine (see Acker & Webber, 2006; Parsons & Priola, 2013) and that disciplinary cultures are highly gendered (Becher & Trowler, 2001). This analytical focus also acknowledges the ways in which the structures and practices of individual academic departments produce 'fundamental cultural rules' (Gerholm, 1990, p. 263), which doctoral students must learn how to negotiate, such as accepted working practices and academic publishing conventions.

Beyond simply attending to the ways in which participants attempted to develop a sense of belonging during the doctorate, I explore the impact of this on how participants imagined their futures and constructed career aspirations. I argue that women doctoral students' ability to construct viable academic identities was shaped by the extent to which they were able to develop this sense of belonging within academic communities as doctoral students. Understanding belonging as individual, situational and involving connections with others, I explore how participants' interactions with physical workspaces, supervisors, academics and peers influenced feelings of belonging, contending that these encounters were highly influential in shaping what they considered to be possible, or desirable, in the future. Further, I attend to the ways in which the working practices of others within academic spaces informed participants' ability to feel a sense of belonging, drawing on literature which highlights the increasingly competitive and pressured environment experienced by those working in academia (do Mar Pereira, 2016; Gill & Donaghue, 2015).

Drawing together these different facets of belonging allows me to present new insights into how women experience doctoral study, and show how individuals' observations of academic life informed their identity development and career aspirations. Further, analysing longitudinal data from women students' doctoral experiences allows for new theoretical understandings of the strategies that individuals developed in order to try and establish a sense of belonging in both the short and long terms. This has implications for those researching in the areas of doctoral education and early career academia, particularly for those exploring the experiences of individuals from marginalised groups. It also makes an important contribution to discussions about how to facilitate inclusive doctoral and research communities.

## Structure of the Book

This book consists of three main parts. The first part theorises gender and belonging in the academy, drawing on international literature outlining women's participation and representation across higher education sectors, to provide wider context for this study. In Chap. 2, I draw on research which highlights the ways in which women continue to be marginalised within academic spaces (see De Welde & Laursen, 2011; Savigny, 2014; Thanacoody et al., 2006), presenting a theorisation of belonging within the contemporary academy related to discourses of imposterism, legitimacy and validity. In this chapter, relevant UK policy developments in the area of equality and diversity are drawn on, contextualising the findings of this research.

The second part, Chaps. 3, 4 and 5, is based on my analysis of empirical data, explored by broad disciplinary groupings, in order to attend the specific academic contexts of womens' doctoral experiences. Ahead of each chapter, I provide a brief narrative overview of each participant, summarising their doctoral journeys and career aspirations in restoried narrative accounts.

Chapter 3 focuses on issues of power and academic hierarchies, examining how participants in science and engineering disciplines negotiated disciplinary gatekeepers in attempting to belong within their academic communities. This chapter draws attention to the extent to which participants in STEM were able to challenge the traditional power dynamics of their supervisory relationships and manoeuvre around traditional gatekeepers to develop a sense of belonging. Strategies included establishing strong peer groups and, for some, resisting neoliberalised expectations of working practices.

Chapter 4 explores how participants in health and related sciences struggled to establish a sense of legitimacy within their academic communities, but also the strategies they developed in order to try and create a sense of belonging. This chapter illuminates the ways in which elitist attitudes of senior academics, neoliberal expectations of productivity and lad culture could act as potential barriers to individuals' ability to do so. In this chapter, I explicate the strategies which participants devised to try and establish feelings of legitimacy, validity and, ultimately, belonging.

In Chap. 5, I examine the ways in which participants in humanities and social science disciplines navigated academic spaces and attempted to belong within them. This chapter focuses on the impact of physical workspaces on participants' sense of belonging, as well as the gendered 'micropolitics' (Morley, 1999) of particular academic spaces. I illuminate examples of how and *where* participants did and did not experience belonging and attend to the barriers which they encountered.

The final part of the book brings together the analysis to draw out the implications of feeling a sense of belonging within the academy. Chapter 6 draws together the findings of Chaps. 3, 4 and 5 to reflect on the struggles, strategies and successes that participants faced in trying to establish a sense of belonging within their academic communities. This chapter highlights the various sites where this was more challenging, as well as illuminating the strategies which individuals enacted to try and create this sense of belonging. In it, I draw attention to the impact of their relationship with peers, academics and supervisors on their ability to do so, and consider how these experiences shaped participants' perceptions of an academic career.

Finally, Chap. 7 outlines the ways in which institutions, departments and supervisors can address barriers to belonging and help to facilitate academic identity development. In this chapter, I highlight the structural barriers to belonging that women doctoral students encounter during their studies, and consider how academic institutions can create inclusive academic cultures and develop strategies which facilitate belonging. These insights have international relevance for those considering doctoral study, as well as for current doctoral students, institutions, supervisors and others involved in doctoral education and support.

## Introducing the Participants

Here, I provide some personal details about participants, including biographical details, in order to provide a useful overview of each individual for readers and give some context for their doctoral journey. In doing so, I acknowledge that individuals' personal circumstances often shaped the ways they accessed academic communities (see Acker & Haque, 2015).

Participants and institutions have been given pseudonyms in order to try and preserve individuals' anonymity. Table 1.1 also indicates the type of institution they studied at, as well as their subject area. I have also coded participants' subjects into broad disciplinary categories. The subsequent paragraphs offer insight into their career aspirations as reported to me at the start of the PhD.

Antonia, an international student from Europe, was in her midtwenties when she began studying for her doctorate in engineering at Modern University. Prior to the PhD, she completed her master's in her home country and worked in various part-time jobs for a year before this. She was in a relationship, with no caring responsibilities. Antonia applied for a PhD because she wanted to do further research and hoped to pursue an academic research career afterwards.

Sally was in her mid-thirties when she started her doctorate in sports psychology at Modern University. She had previously worked in the charity sector before later returning to academic study. She completed a full-time master's the year ahead of starting the PhD and committed a significant amount of time, effort and money to her decision to return to study and qualify as a psychologist. Sally applied for a PhD because she had enjoyed studying and had done well in her master's. She was in a relationship, with no caring responsibilities. Sally was unsure of what career she would like to pursue at the end of the PhD but had considered a range of options, including academia and consultancy work.

Jessie was in her mid-thirties when she began her doctorate in public health at Modern University. Prior to the PhD, she had a successful career in the public sector. She quit her job, which necessitated a long commute, in order to pursue a career in public health. She decided to apply for a PhD as it suited her family circumstances; Jessie was married with two children under five. At the start of the PhD, Jessie was not fully sure as to how to take her career forward, but was open to options, including an academic career.

Liz was in her mid-fifties when she began her doctorate in health sciences at Modern University. Before starting the PhD, she studied for her undergraduate and master's degrees at a different university as a mature student. Before this, she had worked in a clinical role in the NHS but had retired due to ill health. Liz was married, with no caring responsibilities. Liz was motivated to do a PhD because she enjoyed doing research. She did not have a fixed career aspiration but considered applying for an academic job at the end of the PhD.

Bella began her doctorate in psychology at Modern University when she was in her early twenties. Prior to the PhD, she studied for her undergraduate degree at another UK university. She was single, with no caring responsibilities. She applied for a PhD because she wanted to study further, and felt that it would enable her to do more independent research than a master's. Bella intended to pursue an academic career after the PhD.

Chloe was in her late twenties when she started her doctorate in social policy at Modern University. Prior to the PhD, she studied for her master's degree. She had worked in marketing whilst studying part-time for her undergraduate degree. She was in a relationship with an academic and did not have caring responsibilities. Chloe applied for a PhD because she had enjoyed her master's and saw an opportunity to apply for a funded PhD which matched her research interests. Chloe was unsure about her long-term career direction but considered a career in academia or public policy.

Harriet was in her early twenties when she began her doctorate in biology at Redbrick University. Before the PhD, she did her undergraduate degree at the same institution. She was in a relationship, with no caring responsibilities. She applied for a PhD because she had enjoyed her undergraduate work, and it allowed her to stay in a city where she enjoyed living. Harriet intended to pursue a postdoctoral research position after her PhD but was unsure about a long-term career in academia.

Jane was in her early twenties when she started her doctorate in conservation at Redbrick University. Prior to beginning the PhD, she worked as an intern for a local conservation organisation for a year, having completed her undergraduate degree before this at an elite UK university. She was motivated to apply for a PhD because she felt it would enable her to make a practical difference in her field, and because she enjoyed doing research. She was in a relationship and cohabiting, with no caring responsibilities. Jane intended to pursue an academic career after completing the PhD.

Pepper was in her early twenties and when she started her doctorate in engineering at Redbrick University. Prior to getting her place to do the PhD, she studied for her undergraduate degree and integrated master's at a different university. She applied for a PhD because she had enjoyed independent project work and was interested in doing research which had practical applications and would give her experience of working in industry. Pepper was in a relationship, with no caring responsibilities. She was not sure what type of career she would pursue after the PhD, but she was interested in developing her skills and experience.

Freija began her doctorate in geography at Redbrick University when she was in her mid-twenties. She completed undergraduate and master's degrees before working in an administrative role in a university after she graduated. Freija was motivated by a desire to conduct research with an emphasis on social justice. She was cohabiting and engaged to her partner, with no caring responsibilities. Freija hoped to pursue an academic career but was not entirely set on this career path.

Martina, an international student from Europe, was in her mid-twenties when she started her doctorate in politics at Redbrick University.

Prior to the PhD, she worked in an administrative role for a European NGO, having previously completed a master's. She was in a relationship, with no caring responsibilities. Martina was motivated to do a PhD because she was interested in her particular topic. After the PhD, she hoped to work either in an academic role which fitted with her interests or for an NGO.

Eleanor was in her mid-twenties when she began her doctorate in English at Redbrick University. After completing her undergraduate degree, she studied for a master's in an area related to her undergraduate degree at an elite UK university. She was motivated by a strong personal interest in her topic. Eleanor was in a relationship and cohabiting, with no caring responsibilities. She hoped to become an academic after the PhD, though she was not completely set on this career path.

# References

Acker, S. (1980). Women, the other academics. *British Journal of Sociology of Education, 1*(1), 81–91.

Acker, S., & Haque, E. (2015). The struggle to make sense of doctoral study. *Higher Education Research & Development, 34*(2), 229–241.

Acker, S., & Webber, M. (2006). *Women working in academe: Approach with care. The Sage handbook of gender and education.* Sage.

Advance HE. (2020). Findings from the 2020 Postgraduate Research Experience Survey. Retrieved from: https://www.advance-he.ac.uk/knowledge-hub/postgraduate-research-experience-survey-2020

Advance HE. (2021a). Equality in higher education: Staff statistical report 2021.

Advance HE. (2021b). Equality in higher education: Student statistical report 2021.

Ahmed, S. (2021). *Complaint!* Duke University Press.

Aiston, S. J. (2015). *Whose academy? gender and higher education. Researching higher education* (pp. 80–96). Routledge.

Ali, A., Kohun, F., & Levy, Y. (2007). Dealing with social isolation to minimize doctoral attrition—A four stage framework. *International Journal of Doctoral Studies, 2*(1), 33–49. https://doi.org/10.28945/3082

Anderson, P., & Williams, J. (2001). *Identity and difference in higher education: Outsiders within.* Ashgate.

Araújo, E. R. (2005). Understanding the PhD as a phase in time. *Time & Society, 14*(2–3), 191–211. https://doi.org/10.1177/0961463X05055133

Arday, J., & Mirza, H. S. (Eds.). (2018). *Dismantling race in higher education: Racism, whiteness and decolonising the academy.* Palgrave Macmillan.

Bagilhole, B., & White, K. (2013). *Generation and gender in academia.* Palgrave Macmillan.

Baker, V. L., & Lattuca, L. R. (2010). Developmental networks and learning: Toward an interdisciplinary perspective on identity development during doctoral study. *Studies in Higher Education, 35*(7), 807–827. https://doi.org/10.1080/03075070903501887

Ball, S. J. (2003). The teacher's soul and the terrors of performativity. *Journal of Education Policy, 18*(2), 215–228. https://doi.org/10.1080/0268093022000043065

Ball, S. J. (2012). Performativity, commodification and commitment: An I-spy guide to the neoliberal university. *British Journal of Educational Studies, 60*(1), 17–28.

Bamberg, M., & Georgakopoulou, A. (2008). Small stories as a new perspective in narrative and identity analysis. *Text & Talk, 28*(3), 377–396.

Barinaga, M. (1993). Science education: The pipeline is leaking women all the way along. *Science, 260*(5106), 409–411. https://doi.org/10.1126/science.260.5106.409

Becher, T., & Trowler, P. (2001). *Academic tribes and territories: Intellectual enquiry and the culture of disciplines.* McGraw-Hill.

Bender, S., Brown, K. S., Hensley Kasitz, D. L., & Vega, O. (2022). Academic women and their children: Parenting during COVID-19 and the impact on scholarly productivity. *Family Relations, 71*(1), 46–67.

Bhopal, K., & Henderson, H. (2019). *Advancing equality in higher education: An exploratory study of the Athena SWAN and Race equality charters.* University of Birmingham.

Birch, L. J. (2011). *Telling stories: A thematic narrative analysis of eight women's experiences.* Doctoral thesis. Retrieved from http://vuir.vu.edu.au/19398/

Bradbury, J. (2013, May 3). Black, female and postgraduate: Why I cannot be the only one. *The Guardian.* Retrieved from https://www.theguardian.com/higher-education-network/blog/2013/may/03/black-postgraduate-university-diversity-recruitment

Brailsford, I. (2010). Motives and aspirations for doctoral study: Career, personal, and interpersonal factors in the decision to embark on a history PhD. *International Journal of Doctoral Studies, 5*, 15–27.

Brooks, A. I. (2001). Restructuring bodies of knowledge. In A. Brooks & A. Mackinnon (Eds.), *Gender and the restructured university* (pp. 15–45). SRHE/Open University Press.

Brown, L., & Watson, P. (2010). Understanding the experiences of female doctoral students. *Journal of Further and Higher Education, 34*(3), 385–404. https://doi.org/10.1080/0309877X.2010.484056

Carter, S., Blumenstein, M., & Cook, C. (2013). Different for women? the challenges of doctoral studies. *Teaching in Higher Education, 18*(4), 339–351. https://doi.org/10.1080/13562517.2012.719159

Carter, S., Smith, K., & Harrison, N. (2021). Working in the borderlands: Critical perspectives on doctoral education. *Teaching in Higher Education, 26*(3), 283–292.

Cashmore, A., Scott, J., Cane, C., Bartle, C., Dorum, K., Jackson, P., & Pennington, M. (2014). "Belonging" and "intimacy" factors in the retention of students—An investigation into the student perceptions of effective practice and how that practice can be replicated. *Evaluation, 3*(6).

Ceci, S. J., Ginther, D. K., Kahn, S., & Williams, W. M. (2014). Women in academic science: A changing landscape. *Psychological Science in the Public Interest, 15*(3), 75–141. https://doi.org/10.1177/1529100614541236

Chase, S. E. (2005). Narrative inquiry: Multiple lenses, approaches, voices. In N. K. Denzin & Y. S. Lincoln (Eds.), *The Sage handbook of qualitative research* (3rd ed., pp. 651–659). Sage.

Clandinin, D. J., & Connelly, F. M. (2000). *Narrative inquiry: Experience and story in qualitative research*. Sage.

Clegg, S. (2008). Academic identities under threat? *British Educational Research Journal, 34*(3), 329–345. https://doi.org/10.1080/01411920701532269

Collett, J. L., & Avelis, J. (2013). *Family-friendliness, fraudulence, and gendered academic career ambitions*. American Sociological Association Annual Meeting.

Collini, S. (2012). *What are universities for?* Penguin UK.

Deem, R. (2003). Gender, organizational cultures and the practices of manager-academics in UK universities. *Gender, Work & Organization, 10*(2), 239–259.

Delamont, S., Atkinson, P., & Parry, O. (1997). *Supervising the PhD: A Guide to Success*. Open University Press.

Delamont, S., Atkinson, P., & Parry, O. (2000). *The doctoral experience: Success and failure in graduate school*. Routledge.

Delamont, S., Parry, O., & Atkinson, P. (1997). Critical mass and pedagogic continuity: Studies in academic habitus. *British Journal of Sociology of Education, 18*(4), 533–549.

Dever, M., Laffan, W., Boreham, P., Behrens, K., Haynes, M., Western, M., & Kubler, M. (2008). *Gender differences in early post-PhD employment in Australian universities: The influence of PhD experience on women's academic careers*. Final report.

De Welde, K., & Laursen, S. (2011). The glass obstacle course: Informal and formal barriers for women PhD students in STEM fields. *International Journal of Gender, Science and Technology, 3*(3), 571–595.

Diamond, A., Roberts, J., Vorley, T., Birkin, G., Evans, J., Sheen, J., & Nathwani, T. (2014). UK Review of the provision of information about higher education: Advisory study and literature review: Report to the UK higher education funding bodies.

do Mar Pereira, M. (2016). Struggling within and beyond the performative university: Articulating activism and work in an "academia without walls". *Women's Studies International Forum, 54*, 100–110. https://doi.org/10.1016/j.wsif.2015.06.008

Gerholm, T. (1990). On tacit knowledge in academia. *European Journal of Education*, 263–271. https://doi.org/10.2307/1503316

Gill, R., & Donaghue, N. (2015). Resilience, apps and reluctant individualism: Technologies of self in the neoliberal academy. *Women's Studies International Forum, 54*, 91–99. https://doi.org/10.1016/j.wsif.2015.06.016

Golde, C. M. (2005). The role of the department and discipline in doctoral student attrition: Lessons from four departments. *The Journal of Higher Education, 76*(6), 669–700.

Gravett, K. (2021). Disrupting the doctoral journey: Re-imagining doctoral pedagogies and temporal practices in higher education. *Teaching in Higher Education, 26*(3), 293–305.

Guest, M., Sharma, S., & Song, R. (2013). *Gender and career progression in theology and religious studies*. Durham University.

Handforth, R. (2022). Feeling "stupid": Considering the affective in women doctoral students' experiences of imposter 'syndrome'. In *The Palgrave handbook of imposter syndrome in higher education* (pp. 293–309). Palgrave Macmillan.

Handforth, R., & Taylor, C. A. (2016). Doing academic writing differently: A feminist bricolage. *Gender and Education, 28*(5), 627–643.

Hatchell, H., & Aveling, N. (2008). Gendered disappearing acts: Women's doctoral experiences in the science workplace. In *Australian Association for Research in Education conference, Brisbane* (Vol. 30).

Henkel, M. (2005). Academic identity and autonomy in a changing policy environment. *Higher Education, 49*(1), 155–176. https://doi.org/10.1007/s10734-004-2919-1

Higginbotham, E. J., & Dahlberg, M. L. (Eds.). (2021). *The impact of COVID-19 on the careers of women in academic sciences, engineering, and medicine*. National Academies Press.

Howe Walsh, L., & Turnbull, S. (2016). Barriers to women leaders in academia: Tales from science and technology. *Studies in Higher Education, 41*(3), 415–428.

Hughes, C. C., Schilt, K., Gorman, B. K., & Bratter, J. L. (2017). Framing the faculty gender gap: A view from STEM doctoral students. *Gender, Work & Organization, 24*(4), 398–416.

Jackman, P. C., Sanderson, R., Haughey, T. J., Brett, C. E., White, N., Zile, A., Tyrrell, K., & Byrom, N. C. (2021). The impact of the first COVID-19 lockdown in the UK for doctoral and early career researchers. *Higher Education*, 1–18.

Kehm, B. M. (2006). Doctoral education in Europe and North America: A comparative analysis. *Wenner Gren International Series, 83*, 67.

Kulis, S., Sicotte, D., & Collins, S. (2002). More than a pipeline problem: Labor supply constraints and gender stratification across academic science disciplines. *Research in Higher Education, 43*(6), 657–691.

Levecque, K., Anseel, F., De Beuckelaer, A., Van der Heyden, J., & Gisle, L. (2017). Work organization and mental health problems in PhD students. *Research Policy, 46*(4), 868–879. https://doi.org/10.1016/j.respol.2017.02.008

Levine, F. J., Nasir, N. I. S., Ríos-Aguilar, C., Gildersleeve, R. E., Rosich, K. J., Bang, M., Bell, N. E., & Holsapple, M. A. (2021). *Voices from the field: The impact of COVID-19 on early career scholars and doctoral students*. American Educational Research Association (AERA).

Lopes, A., & Dewan, I. (2014). Precarious pedagogies? The impact of casual and zero-hour contracts in Higher Education. *Journal of Feminist Scholarship, 7*(8), 28–42.

Lovitts, B. E. (2001). *Leaving the ivory tower: The causes and consequences of departure from doctoral study*. Rowman & Littlefield.

Lynch, K. (2010). Carelessness: A hidden doxa of higher education. *Arts and Humanities in Higher Education, 9*(1), 54–67. https://doi.org/10.1177/1474022209350104

Mantai, L. (2017). Feeling like a researcher: Experiences of early doctoral students in Australia. *Studies in Higher Education, 42*(4), 636–650.

Mantai, L. (2019). "Feeling more academic now": Doctoral stories of becoming an academic. *The Australian Educational Researcher, 46*(1), 137–153.

Mason, M. A., Goulden, M., & Frasch, K. (2009). Why graduate students reject the fast track. *Academe, 95*(1), 11–16.

Mattocks, K., & Briscoe-Palmer, S. (2016). Diversity, inclusion, and doctoral study: Challenges facing minority PhD students in the United Kingdom. *European Political Science, 15*, 476–492.

May, V. (2013). *Connecting self to society: Belonging in a changing world.* Macmillan International Higher Education.

McAdams, D. P. (1993). *The stories we live by: Personal myths and the making of the self.* Guilford Press.

McAlpine, L., Amundsen, C., & Jazvac-Martek, M. (2010). Living and imagining academic identities. In L. McAlpine & G. Akerlind (Eds.), *Becoming an academic: International perspectives* (pp. 129–149). Palgrave Macmillan.

McAlpine, L., Amundsen, C., & Turner, G. (2013). Constructing post-PhD careers: Negotiating opportunities and personal goals. *International Journal for Researcher Development, 4*(1), 39–54. https://doi.org/10.1108/ijrd-01-2013-0002

McAlpine, L., & Emmioğlu, E. (2014). Navigating careers: Perceptions of sciences doctoral students, post-PhD researchers and pre-tenure academics. *Studies in Higher Education,* 1–16. https://doi.org/10.1080/03075079.2014.914908

McAlpine, L., & Turner, G. (2012). Imagined and emerging career patterns: Perceptions of doctoral students and research staff. *Journal of further and Higher Education, 36*(4), 535–548. https://doi.org/10.1080/0309877x.2011.643777

McCulloch, A., & Stokes, P. (2008). The silent majority: Meeting the needs of part-time research students. In A. Martin (Ed.), *Issues in Postgraduate education: Management, teaching and supervision, series 2 no. 5.* Society for Research into Higher Education.

Morley, L. (1999). *Organising feminisms: The micropolitics of the academy.* Palgrave Macmillan.

Morley, L. (2013). The rules of the game: Women and the leaderist turn in higher education. *Gender and Education, 25*(1), 116–131.

Morris, C. (2021). "Peering through the window looking in": Postgraduate experiences of non-belonging and belonging in relation to mental health and wellbeing. *Studies in Graduate and Postdoctoral Education.* https://doi.org/10.1108/SGPE-07-2020-0055

Munro, E., & Heath, S. (2021). Falling short: Response to UKRI's phase 1 and phase 2 support for PhD researchers during the COVID-19 pandemic.

Neumann, R., & Tan, K. K. (2011). From PhD to initial employment: The doctorate in a knowledge economy. *Studies in Higher Education, 36*(5), 601–614. https://doi.org/10.1080/03075079.2011.594596

O'Connor, P. (2015). Good jobs—But places for women? *Gender and Education, 27*(3), 304–319.

OECD. (2014). *Education at a glance 2014: OECD indicators*. OECD. https://doi.org/10.1787/eag-2014-en

Page, T., Bull, A., & Chapman, E. (2019). Making power visible: "Slow activism" to address staff sexual misconduct in higher education. *Violence Against Women, 25*(11), 1309–1330.

Papageorgiou, V., Kendall, W., & Puerta, L. L. (2020). COVID-19 stories: How PhD students are experiencing disruption and uncertainty during the pandemic. Consciously quarantined: A COVID-19 response from the social sciences.

Park, C. (2005). New variant PhD: The changing nature of the doctorate in the UK. *Journal of Higher Education Policy and Management, 27*(2), 189–207. https://doi.org/10.1080/13600800500120068

Parry, S. (2007). *Disciplines and doctorates*. Springer.

Parsons, E., & Priola, V. (2013). Agents for change and changed agents: The Micro-politics of change and feminism in the academy. *Gender, Work & Organization, 20*(5), 580–598. https://doi.org/10.1111/j.1468-0432.2012.00605.x

Phipps, A. (2018). 'Lad culture' and sexual violence against students. In *The Routledge handbook of gender and violence* (pp. 171–182). Routledge.

Pifer, M. J., & Baker, V. L. (2014). "It could be just because I'm different": Otherness and its outcomes in doctoral education. *Journal of Diversity in Higher Education, 7*(1), 14.

Plummer, K. (1983). *Documents of life: An introduction to the problems and literature of a humanistic method*. Allen & Unwin.

Polkinghorne, D. E. (1988). *Narrative knowing and the human sciences*. Suny Press.

Polkinghorne, J. (1998). *Beyond science: The wider human context*. Cambridge University Press.

Pyhältö, K., Peltonen, J., Castelló, M., & McAlpine, L. (2019). What sustains doctoral students' interest? Comparison of Finnish, UK and Spanish doctoral students' perceptions. *Compare: A Journal of Comparative and International Education, 50*, 726–741.

Rao, N., Hosein, A., & Raaper, R. (2021). Doctoral students navigating the borderlands of academic teaching in an era of precarity. *Teaching in Higher Education, 26*(3), 454–470.

Read, B., & Kehm, B. M. (2016). Women as leaders of higher education institutions: A British–German comparison. *Studies in Higher Education, 41*(5), 815–827.

Ribarovska, A. K., Hutchinson, M. R., Pittman, Q. J., Pariante, C., & Spencer, S. J. (2021). Gender inequality in publishing during the COVID-19 pandemic. *Brain, Behavior, and Immunity, 91*, 1.

Richardson, J. T. (2018). Understanding the under-attainment of ethnic minority students in UK higher education: The known knowns and the known unknowns. In *Dismantling race in higher education* (pp. 87–102). Palgrave Macmillan.

Riessman, C. K. (2008). *Narrative methods for the human sciences*. Sage.

Rossiter, M. (2004). Educational relationships and possible selves in the adult undergraduate experience. *The Cyril O'Houle Scholars in Adult and Continuing Education Program Global Research Perspectives, 4*, 138–155. https://doi.org/10.1002/ace.259

Royal Society. (2010). The Scientific Century: Securing our future prosperity. Retrieved from: https://royalsociety.org/-/media/Royal_Society_Content/policy/publications/2010/4294970126.pdf

Royal Society of Chemistry. (2008). *The chemistry PhD: The impact on women's retention*. A report for the UK Resource Centre for Women in SET and the Royal Society of Chemistry, 1–38.

Savigny, H. (2014). Women, know your limits: Cultural sexism in academia. *Gender and Education, 26*(7), 794–809. https://doi.org/10.1080/09540253.2014.970977

Sfard, A., & Prusak, A. (2005). Telling identities: In search of an analytic tool for investigating learning as a culturally shaped activity. *Educational Researcher, 34*(4), 14–22. https://doi.org/10.3102/0013189x034004014

Soe, L., & Yakura, E. K. (2008). What's wrong with the pipeline? Assumptions about gender and culture in IT work. *Women's Studies, 37*(3), 176–201. https://doi.org/10.1080/00497870801917028

Stets, J. E., & Burke, P. J. (2000). Identity theory and social identity theory. *Social Psychology Quarterly*, 224–237.

Szelényi, K., Bresonis, K., & Mars, M. M. (2016). Who am i versus who can i become?: Exploring women's science identities in STEM Ph. D. programs. *The Review of Higher Education, 40*(1), 1–31.

Thanacoody, P. R., Bartram, T., Barker, M., & Jacobs, K. (2006). Career progression among female academics: A comparative study of Australia and Mauritius. *Women in Management Review, 21*(7), 536–553. https://doi.org/10.1108/09649420610692499

The Res-Sisters. (2016). 'I'm an early career feminist academic: Get me out of here?': Encountering and resisting the neoliberal academy. In R. Thwaites &

A. Pressland (Eds.), *Being an early career feminist academic* (pp. 267–284). Palgrave Macmillan.

The Universities and Colleges Union (UCU). (2016). Precarious work in higher education: A snapshot of insecure contracts and institutional attitudes. Retrieved from: https://www.ucu.org.uk/media/7995/Precarious-work-in-higher-education-a-snapshot-of-insecure-contracts-and-institutional-attitudes-Apr-16/pdf/ucu_precariouscontract_hereport_apr16.pdf

The Universities and Colleges Union (UCU). (2021). Precarious work in higher education: Insecure contracts and how they have changed over time. Retrieved from: https://www.ucu.org.uk/media/10899/Precarious-work-in-higher-education-May-20/pdf/ucu_he-precarity-report_may20.pdf

Thomas, K. C. (2018). *Rethinking student belonging in higher education: From bourdieu to borderlands.* Routledge.

Tinto, V. (1993). *Leaving college: Rethinking the causes and cures of student attrition.* University of Chicago Press.

UK Council for Graduate Education (UKCGE). (2021). Research supervision survey 2021 report. Retrieved from: https://ukcge.ac.uk/assets/resources/UK-Research-Supervision-Survey-2021-UK-Council-for-Graduate-Education.pdf

UK Council for Science and Technology. (2007). *Pathways to the future: The early careers of researchers in the UK.* Council for Science and Technology.

Universities UK. (2017). *Patterns and trends in UK higher education.* Universities UK.

Vitae. (2013). *What do researchers do? Early career progression of doctoral graduates.* The Careers Research and Advisory Centre (CRAC) Limited.

Vitae. (2017). *One size does not fit all: Arts and humanities doctoral and early career researchers' professional development survey.* The Careers Research and Advisory Centre (CRAC) Limited.

Vitae. (2019). Do researchers' careers have to be precarious? Retrieved from: https://www.vitae.ac.uk/impact-and-evaluation/what-do-researchers-do/do-researchers-careers-have-to-be-precarious-research-article.pdf/view

Wang, L., & DeLaquil, T. (2020). The isolation of doctoral education in the times of COVID-19: Recommendations for building relationships within person-environment theory. *Higher Education Research & Development, 39*(7), 1346–1350.

Weeks, J. (1990). The values of difference in identity. In J. Rutherford (Ed.), *Identity: Community, culture, difference* (pp. 88–100). Lawrence and Wishart.

Wellcome Trust. (2013). *Risks and rewards: How PhD students choose their careers.* Ipsos MORI.

White, J., & Nonnamaker, J. (2008). Belonging and mattering: How doctoral students experience community. *NASPA Journal, 45*(3), 350–372.

Whitley, L., & Page, T. (2015). Sexism at the centre: Locating the problem of sexual harassment. *New Formations, 86*(86), 34–53.

Wolff, J. (2015, April 21). Doctor, doctor…we're suffering a glut of PhDs who can't find academic jobs. *The Guardian.* Retrieved from https://www.theguardian.com/education/2015/apr/21/phd-cant-find-academic-job-university

Woodward, K. (2003). *Understanding Identity*. Hodder Arnold.

Yildirim, T. M., & Eslen-Ziya, H. (2021). The differential impact of COVID-19 on the work conditions of women and men academics during the lockdown. *Gender, Work & Organization, 28*, 243–249.

# 2

# Theorising Gender and Belonging in the (Early Career) Academy

This chapter sets out the rationale for attending to gender and belonging within the context of early career academia. It views the academy from an international perspective, drawing on literature which shows how women continue to be marginalised within academic institutions, across higher education sectors.

In this chapter I present my theorisation of belonging in the academy, drawing on the work of May (2013) and Miller (2003). Within this, I use the concept of legitimate peripheral participation (Lave & Wenger, 1991) to explore how women doctoral students' experiences of power structures within academic cultures influenced their ability to develop a sense of belonging within academia. Further, I examine the unique status of doctoral students, who occupy a liminal position within the academic hierarchy (Delamont et al., 2000), and consider how this influenced individuals' sense of belonging to their academic communities. Reflecting on contemporary work on imposterism in the academy (see Addison et al., 2022; Breeze, 2018; Vaughn et al., 2020), I draw attention to the ways in which factors such as age, disability and ethnicity may compound feelings of marginalisation within the academy.

In order to theorise gender and belonging within early career academia, this chapter first provides a brief account of women's participation in higher education across the globe, offering a historical context for how gender continues to influence feelings of belonging within the contemporary academy.

## Women in the Academy: Still Outsiders?

Globally, women remain relative newcomers to higher education (Delamont, 2006). Though a small number of wealthy women managed to obtain degrees during the seventeenth and eighteenth centuries in European countries, it was not until the mid-late nineteenth century that women began to gain entry to higher education institutions in any considerable numbers. Only in 1947 did all UK universities award women degrees with equal status to men, with significant opposition from male students and academics (see Dyhouse, 2016). Yet recent decades have seen a large increase in women's participation in higher education; now, in the majority of developed countries, there are more women than men in higher education (Parvazian et al., 2017), and in OECD countries, the proportions of women participating in higher education have increased from 33% in 1970, to 54% in 2012 (UNESCO, 2016). This rise in women's participation, along with the increase in women achieving higher-grade degrees than men in the UK (see Thompson & Bekhradnia, 2009), has been termed 'feminization' by some (see Burke et al., 2013), leading to 'moral panics' (Morley, 2011, p. 224) about women taking over the academy. However, as Leathwood and Read (2009, p. 48) contend, 'for eight centuries, men totally dominated higher education in the UK; for just one decade, women have constituted a slightly higher proportion of the graduate population. This, in itself, puts the feminization thesis into context'.

Feminist researchers continue to refer to universities as masculine institutions (see Letherby, 2003; Stanley, 1997), observing how the male origins of these institutions have shaped academic disciplines, processes and even terminology (Bagilhole, 2007). This perspective understands higher education institutions not only as gendered, but also as racialised and classed institutions which marginalise certain groups, as Anderson and Williams (2001, p. 2) observe: 'higher education has traditionally been the preserve of white, middle class, male academics. Those who do not possess these racial, class and gender identities are…constituted as 'other' '. Morley and David (2009, p. 2) go further, arguing that women's academic identities are 'forged in otherness, as strangers in opposition to (privileged) men's belonging and entitlement'.

Higher education institutions have been described as gendered institutions, where 'gender is present in the processes, practices, images and ideologies, and distributions of power in the various sectors of social life' (Acker, 1992, p. 567). The history of these institutions shapes these processes, practices and ideologies, and within the context of academic institutions, traditional academics were men with wives who took on the domestic workload (see Baker, 2012; Ward & Wolf-Wendel, 2016). These traditional academics have been described as 'ideal workers' (Williams, 2000), because they were able to dedicate themselves fully to their work due to this domestic support (see Ollilainen & Solomon, 2014; Probert, 2005). Woman academics thus operate in opposition to this traditional, male conception of the academic worker, attempting to work in institutions designed for and created by men (Acker & Webber, 2006).

Understanding universities as 'greedy institutions' (Coser, 1974) which demand exclusive and undivided loyalty, particularly in the contemporary, neoliberal academy, highlights that individuals able to fully dedicate themselves to work will be more likely to build successful careers than those with other responsibilities. The demands of contemporary academic careers, shaped by pressure to secure external research grants, deliver excellent teaching and participate in public engagement activities in order to demonstrate the impact and relevance of academic work, are significant. In addition, expectations of academics to participate in activities which demand physical mobility, such as international travel and attending research seminars, as well as to demonstrate online availability in order to be responsive to students even out of office hours, can all be seen as universities becoming increasingly 'greedy'.

Engaging in these activities is expected from those working in the competitive environment of modern-day academia, and individuals' ability to do so may have significant implications for career progression (Leemann, 2010; Lubitow & Zippel, 2014; Savigny, 2014). This increased 'greed' of academic institutions disproportionately disadvantages women, as they remain more likely to have multiple demands on their time outside work, including caring responsibilities (Bagilhole, 2002; Carter et al., 2013; Jöns, 2011; Knights & Richards, 2003; van Anders, 2004). Indeed, despite the increased participation of women in academic life, it has been argued that, 'to be a successful academic is to be unencumbered by caring' (Lynch, 2010, p. 63). The expectations implicit within contemporary academic careers also implicitly discriminate against disabled academics (see Acker & McGinn, 2021; Brown & Leigh, 2018; CRAC, 2020; Sang, 2017).

Despite recent increase in the numbers of women academics—in the UK in 2014–5, women made up 45% of all academics in comparison to 38% in 2001-2 (Higher Education Statistics Agency, 2017)—the careers and experiences of women in the academy remain gendered. Canadian scholar Sandra Acker (1980) was one of the first to note the otherness of women in academic institutions in the UK, commenting on their underrepresentation in senior academic roles and highlighting the lack of research on their lived experiences. Yet, five decades on, researchers continue to observe gendered patterns in the participation of women in academic life, from lack of women in senior roles and STEM disciplines (Morley, 2013; O'Connor et al., 2019; White, 2015), to the types of academic labour undertaken.

Women are more likely to work in teaching roles compared with men (Becher & Trowler, 2001; Cotterill et al., 2007; Dever & Morrison, 2009), a type of labour which has been referred to as the 'institutional housework' (Brabazon, 2014, p. 51) of academia. This pattern can be observed from an early career stage; White (2013) argues that the gendered division of research and teaching is often established during the doctorate and can persist throughout women academics' careers. Women academics are also often given heavier teaching loads than men (Acker & Feuerverger, 1996; Becher & Trowler, 2001; Deem, 1998; Parsons & Priola, 2013), meaning an increased workload with less time available for research. In a recent analysis of national survey data collected from academics across the US, Guarino and Borden (2017) found that women academics were also undertaking a significantly larger amount of administrative work and duties than their male counterparts, again leaving less time for research.

Further, for those working in teaching roles, women are often subject to different expectations than their male counterparts, particularly in relation to providing pastoral care to students (see Eveline & Booth, 2004; Gill & Donaghue, 2015; Henkel, 2000; Parsons & Priola, 2013; Reay, 2004), something which requires considerable emotional labour (Hochschild, 1983). This expectation of women academics to provide nurturing and emotional support to students has been termed 'mom work' (Tierney & Bensimon, 1996, p. 87) and is indicative of how care is expected from women in a way that it is not from men (Letherby & Shiels, 2001). This pressure may contribute to the performance of these gendered expectations by some women academics, such as undertaking a greater proportion of administrative duties and taking more time to ensure the well-being of those around them (see Britton, 2017; Crabtree & Shiel, 2019)—behaviours which have been described as 'smile work' (Tierney & Bensimon, 1996, p. 85).

Gender divisions are clearly visible in the ways in which different types of academic labour are valued. Teaching and research are not equally valued within the academy, and research performance is not only linked with the prestige economy in higher education (Morley, 2014) but is directly associated with individuals' ability to progress their academic career, with winning grants and producing research outputs often being key performance indicators used within promotion processes (see Acker & McGinn, 2021; Wellcome Trust, 2020). Gender disparities exist in access to research funding (Bedi et al., 2012; European Commission, 2021), publication rates (Aiston & Jung, 2015; Nygaard & Bahgat, 2018; Tower et al., 2007) and citations in research papers (Larivière et al., 2013). Further, across academic disciplines, men have been found to cite their own work far more frequently than women (King et al., 2017). Given the significance of metrics which measure research outputs within these promotion processes, there are obvious implications for women academics' careers.

In the UK, despite sector-wide initiatives such as Athena SWAN which aim to address gender stereotypes and reduce inequalities, significant gender differences persist in career experiences. In the early 1980s, Hall and Sandler (1982) described what they termed the 'chilly climate' that women experience within the academy, manifesting in harassment, biased recruitment and promotion processes and discrimination against those with caring responsibilities. They argued that the persistence of this climate works to 'communicate to women that they are not quite first-class citizens in the academic community' (*ibid*, p. 3). More recently, Savigny (2014) has described the cultural norms and organisational structures of academic institutions as being inherently sexist, observing how women continue to be marginalised due to practices such as holding research seminars and conferences in the evenings and on weekends, which make balancing academic work with caring responsibilities challenging.

Thus, whilst some may argue that discussions of women academics' experiences have moved beyond the chilly climate (see Ceci & Williams, 2011; Williams & Ceci, 2015), women academics continue to experience gender discrimination in systemic but also everyday forms. Across higher education sectors, women academics are less likely to progress to senior positions (Santos & Dang Van Phu, 2019) and are paid less (Advance HE, 2021a), but they also receive less positive feedback from student-teaching evaluations (Carson, 2001; Fan et al., 2019; MacNell et al., 2015) and are judged differently than their male counterparts in relation to their clothing and dress (Adams et al., 2022; Tsaousi, 2020). For women from BAME backgrounds, who define themselves as LGBTQ+, or who come from working-class backgrounds, these experiences may be compounded by institutional racism and prejudice (see Hoskins, 2010; Pittman, 2010; Reay, 1998; Rollock, 2019; Valentine & Wood, 2010). These experiences can be understood collectively as cultural sexism, which poses a 'significant, invisible, normalising barrier to women's progression within the academy' (Savigny, 2014, p. 795).

As well as dwelling in less visible processes, cultural sexism in academia also manifests itself in more overt forms. In the mid-1990s, Bagilhole and Woodward (1995) identified the prevalence of sexual harassment in the experiences of women academics, arguing that there was significant under-reporting and underestimation of incidences of sexual harassment in UK universities. More than two decades later, Sara Ahmed (2021) described sexual harassment as part of the culture of universities, arguing that it is enabled by institutions which refuse to acknowledge sexual harassment as a part of wider gender discrimination, because of reputational concerns. This has been reinforced by subsequent studies which have highlighted how universities may seek to conceal the extent of sexual harassment cases and protect their reputations through the use of non-disclosure agreements (see Page et al., 2019; Tutchell & Edmonds, 2020).

Sexual harassment in UK universities has been linked to an increase in the prevalence of 'lad culture' within higher education institutions, defined as a range of behaviours which objectify, demean and in some cases assault women, which are performed by men on campuses (Phipps & Young, 2013). Yet, more than a decade after the publication of *Hidden Marks* report (2010) by the National Union of Students, which found that incidents of sexual violence and harassment were rife at UK universities, women students and staff continue to experience sexual harassment, as recent international media attention has highlighted (see Batty & Bengtsson, 2017; Davies, 2021; Gibbons, 2018; Murray, 2021; Weale & Batty, 2016, 2017). It appears that these experiences are common; a survey conducted by the National Union of Students in 2018 found that over 40% of respondents had experienced at least one experience of sexualised behaviour from staff (NUS, 2018), a figure verified in a larger-scale survey conducted in the US (Cantor et al., 2019). The persistence of sexual harassment in universities is indicative of how women continue to be marginalised in the academy. This sense of being both historically other and subsequently othered in the contemporary academy through different forms of discrimination and harassment can lead to women feeling that they are 'bodies out of place' (Puwar, 2004, p. 68). It is this environment which women doctoral students must negotiate and attempt to develop a sense of belonging within.

## Theorising Belonging and Considering Legitimacy

Belonging is a contested term which has multiple meanings. The understanding of belonging deployed in this book draws from the work of May (2013) and Miller (2003), viewing belonging as affective, involving connections with others and necessitating the continual negotiation of power relations.

Taking the first of these—the understanding of belonging as innately affective—requires attending to the impact of belonging (or not belonging) on individual's well-being. Belonging has been defined as feeling 'a sense of accord with the various physical and social contexts in which our lives are lived out' (Miller, 2003, p. 220). Indeed, belonging 'makes us feel good about our being and our being-in-the-world' (*ibid*, p. 219), and thus is inherently an affective and embodied experience (May, 2013).

Secondly, belonging requires feeling a sense of connection with others, however straightforward or challenging developing these connections may be. Feeling a sense of belonging necessitates feeling connected, whether to a community of people, a particular tradition or a specific locality (Miller, 2003). Thirdly, belonging involves power relations, and whilst individuals exert agency in attempting to belong, their ability to be successful in this is contingent on the recognition of individuals by others within a particular community. This is linked to mattering, where individuals feel accepted and valued (Emmioglu et al., 2017; White & Nonnamaker, 2008) and are able to act in a 'socially significant manner that is recognised by others' (May, 2013, p. 142). Finally, belonging is a process which requires continual negotiation and must be re-accomplished over time (May, 2013).

This four-part theorisation of belonging holds that when individuals are unable to develop a sense of belonging, one or more of these concepts are contested, which may lead to conflict rather than a sense of ease or accord (Miller, 2003). I contend that individuals' ability to feel a sense of belonging within their academic communities is significantly influenced by factors such as gender, age, social class and ethnicity. Feeling at ease, being able to make connections with others and being recognised as a valuable contributor to the academic environment are easier for those who have not been traditionally marginalised within these spaces. As Probyn (1996, p8) observes; 'if you have to think about belonging, perhaps you are already outside'.

Within this book, I use the above theorisation of belonging alongside Lave and Wenger's (1991) concept of legitimate peripheral participation, utilising these concepts as 'a set of thinking tools' (Bourdieu, in Wacquant, 1989, p. 50) with which to explore how women doctoral students negotiate academic spaces and hierarchies. Legitimate peripheral participation, which holds that participation in a particular community can be a way of knowing (Teeuwsen et al., 2014), is particularly useful in reflecting on the process of doctoral study, whereby individuals gradually accrue knowledge, skills and status within their academic communities. The process of developing an academic identity may be understood as 'a question of legitimacy, an assurance of belonging and worth' (*ibid*, p. 691).

For doctoral students to feel a sense of belonging within academia, they need to be recognised as legitimate members of these communities. However, the process of becoming a legitimate contributor to a knowledge community is gradual (Parry, 2007), requiring newcomers 'to move toward full participation in the socio-cultural practices of a community' (Lave & Wenger, 1991, p. 29). This process is not straightforward for those from marginalised groups, for whom working within higher education institutions requires navigating racial and gender discrimination (Bhopal & Henderson, 2019; Mirza, 2009; Rollock, 2019). Thus, establishing legitimacy may be challenging to achieve in practice:

> Legitimate peripherality is a complex notion, implicated in social structures involving relations of power. As a place in which one moves toward more-intensive participation, peripherality is an empowering position. As a place in which one is kept from participating more fully…it is a disempowering position. (Lave & Wenger, 1991, p. 36)

In using legitimate peripheral participation alongside a four-part theorisation of belonging, it is possible to generate a new understanding of how women doctoral students negotiate belonging within their academic communities. This understanding not only attends to individual agency and the strategies that are undertaken to try and establish belonging, but also illuminates the structural power relations inherent within academic spaces. It also highlights the significance of doctoral supervisors as gatekeepers to the academic community; a positive student-supervisor relationship can enable students to imagine themselves in similar roles, and thus identify as future members of the academic community (Rossiter, 2004). In exploring these relationships, I attend to the affective dimensions of women doctoral students' experiences, drawing attention to the ways in which they attempted to develop connections to, and within, their academic communities, whilst navigating multiple power relations.

In my analysis, I highlight the barriers that participants encountered to developing a sense of belonging and the impact on their well-being. This is particularly important in the context of comparatively poor sector understandings of doctoral students' well-being and mental health, compared to undergraduates (see Creaton & Handforth, 2021; Vitae, 2018). In the chapters that follow, I contend that belonging is situated, fluid and contingent on the individuals' ability to negotiate different academic cultures. Finally, I argue that the concepts of belonging and legitimate peripheral participation allow insight into the ways in which, through a process of observational learning (Rossiter, 2004), women doctoral students' understandings about academic life inform their identity development and career aspirations.

## Belonging to Academic Communities: The Role of Disciplines and Departments

The role of academic communities, including individual disciplines and departments, is significant in shaping individuals' feelings of belonging within academia, and particularly for women, considering the gendered nature of disciplinary cultures. Yet it is important first to clarify what is meant by academic community, acknowledging the 'slipperiness' (Kogan, 2000) of the term and the 'danger of cosy ascriptions of community that eschew differentiation and definition' (*ibid*, p. 210). Here, I draw on the work of Parry (2007), understanding academic communities as key disciplinary groups within which there are particular 'modes of enquiry, communication networks, bodies of scholarly traditions and sets of values, beliefs and conceptual structures' (*ibid*, p. 9), which are broadly shared by those who work within them. Within these communities, there are opportunities for individuals to establish a sense of belonging and engage in academic identity development. Indeed, academic communities constitute 'a bounded and defining space within which individuals make their choices, construct their identities and in so doing make their own contribution to those communities' (Henkel, 2004, p. 169). More specifically, viewing academic disciplines and departments as communities of practice (Lave & Wenger, 1991) illuminates the possibilities for shared learning offered by these academic communities. This understanding holds that regardless of the formality of the setting, those taking part in a particular practice or set of practices can engage in social learning through their common participation (see Lave & Wenger, 1991). Yet, as has already been observed, establishing legitimacy within these communities may be more challenging for certain groups.

Attending to the role of disciplinary communities in shaping the belonging of women doctoral students requires an understanding of the ways in which academic disciplines can be viewed as gendered. Each discipline has a different history, tradition and social organisation, which are shaped by gendered patterns of participation (Hearn, 2001). In his historic categorisation of disciplines, Biglan (1973) divided subjects into natural sciences which were 'hard' and traditionally dominated by men, with women clustered in the 'softer' disciplines of the humanities and social sciences. Indeed, in their seminal work, *Academic Tribes and Territories,* Becher and Trowler (2001, p. 55), argue that disciplines 'are not culturally neutral: areas of study are widely held to embody beliefs about masculinity and femininity'. They contend that academic disciplines produce 'disciplinary stereotypes' which pose barriers to women working in traditionally male-dominated disciplines (*ibid*, p. 55).

Despite the fact that in the UK and many developed countries, there are more women undergraduates than men, fewer women study STEM subjects at doctoral level (Advance HE, 2021b). The lack of women working in these disciplines has been well documented (Blickenstaff, 2005; De Welde & Laursen, 2011; Jones, 2005; Kulis et al., 2002; Smith, 2011). Though efforts have been made by the UK governments over recent decades to address the under-representation of women and increase the labour market within scientific and technological industries (Glover & Fielding, 1999; Greenfield et al., 2002; Wynarczyk & Renner, 2006), gendered patterns of participation persist, both in secondary and tertiary education (PWC, 2017; Smith, 2011). Despite the introduction of specific policy initiatives such as Athena SWAN, designed to address gender inequalities within traditionally male-dominated STEM disciplines, gendered stereotypes persist at the heart of many academic disciplines, reinforcing the idea of women academics as 'other'. These stereotypes are manifested in a number of ways which influence women's career experiences in these disciplines, contributing to imposter syndrome (Howe-Walsh & Turnbull, 2016), gender discrimination and harassment (De Welde & Laursen, 2011; Nature, 2019), the persistence of male-dominated networks (Barnard et al., 2010; Fisher & Kinsey, 2014) and unequal opportunities to access training in grant applications and financial management—skills necessary for career progression (Equality Challenge Unit, 2016).

In relation to how disciplinary communities are encountered in the everyday academic environment, an important distinction can be made between how doctoral students experience belonging within disciplinary and departmental communities. Whilst the discipline is 'the intellectual society to which the doctoral student aspires', the department or research group 'is the organisational unit that provides opportunities for socialisation to a specific discipline' (Parry, 2007, p. 22). Indeed, Henkel (2004) observes the importance of departments in enabling individuals to orient themselves to their discipline by undertaking collective activities and engaging in dialogue with colleagues. Thus, the structure of academic departments plays a significant role in the everyday experiences of doctoral students, and thus may facilitate or preclude belonging. Within departments, there are likely also to be a number of research groups, offices, laboratories and social communities within which academics and doctoral students will participate. Considering belonging as 'a sense of accord with the various physical and social contexts in which our lives are lived out' (Miller, 2003, p. 220) requires a focus, too, on the cultures of these everyday academic communities, and an examination of the gendered micropolitics (Morley, 1999) of the interactions which occur within these spaces.

## Belonging Within Academic Cultures

Academic cultures operate at the level of the institution, discipline and department, as well as within specific workspaces, research groups and teaching teams. These cultures have the ability to either foster or preclude a sense of belonging amongst doctoral students, who are often both working and studying within them (see Rao et al., 2021). Defining academic cultures is not straightforward, though amongst the myriad definitions of culture are those which highlight the significance of everyday behaviours and values within particular institutional contexts, which provide a useful starting point. Williams (1961, p. 32) argues that culture is 'a description of a particular way of life which expresses certain meanings and values, not only in art and learning but also in institutions and ordinary behaviour'. This view is supported by Becher and Trowler (2001, p. 23), who attend to the cultures of academic disciplines, defining academic cultures as 'sets of taken-for-granted values, attitudes and ways of behaving…articulated through and reinforced by recurrent practices among a group of people in a given context'. These definitions provide a useful understanding of how cultures can operate within academic contexts, and how particular values and behaviours may become normalised by individuals.

The values, ideals and working practices of the 'contemporary academy' (Gill, 2009) are worthy of exploration here, as they constitute the broader environment within which doctoral students attempt to establish a sense of belonging. Thus, scholarship which is concerned with the impact of marketisation and neoliberalism on the academy, and how these forces have shaped contemporary academic careers, is particularly pertinent. The cultural conditions within which individuals engage in academic labour and the values espoused by academic institutions have shifted with the rise of neoliberalism—defined here as 'a political and economic rationality characterised by increasing individualisation, withdrawal of the state and introduction of market logics and rationality into ever more spheres of life' (Gill & Donaghue, 2015, p. 2), which has created a business-focused, competitive culture within universities (Ball, 2012; Collini, 2012). Academics must acquire research funding, produce research which demonstrates impact and fulfil the increasing requirements of national audits which assess the value of research and teaching in the UK, in the form of the Research Excellence Framework (REF) [1]

---

[1] The UK system for assessing research excellence within universities, used to inform how public funding is allocated to universities.

and the Teaching Excellence Framework (TEF). [2] The pervasive 'publish or perish' culture, particularly within academic STEM, puts individuals under pressure to 'produce and keep producing' (do Mar Pereira, 2016, p. 103). Contemporary academic careers require individuals to continually demonstrate how they are meeting these various demands, creating a culture of performativity (Ball, 2003) which may have a significant negative impact on individuals' mental health and well-being (see Kinman, 2014; Loveday, 2018; Morrish, 2019; Wray & Kinman, 2021). It is this culture within which doctoral students must learn to assimilate if they hope to build successful academic careers, meaning that establishing a sense of belonging—and critically, establishing legitimacy during the doctorate—is of vital importance.

Researchers have likened the process of navigating career success within contemporary academia to playing a kind of 'game', but one with rules which are often covert (Clegg, 2012; Hancock, 2019; Lucas, 2006). Bagilhole and White (2013, p. 189) observe that one of the challenges for women academics is 'to understand the "game" of academia…even if they are not interested in playing it'. They argue that newer generations of early career academics are more aware of the strategies they will need to enact in order to progress their careers, and thus better prepared to play this game. Indeed, a successful contemporary academic career requires individuals to engage in world-class research, publish high-quality publications and undertake public engagement work to promote their research (Thwaites & Pressland, 2016). Yet, with men dominating higher-status research roles, women academics continue to be disadvantaged in playing the research game (Lucas, 2006). Further, there is an implicit expectation of mobility in academic careers (Ackers, 2010), which can be challenging for those trying to balance family commitments with their career (see Bagilhole & White, 2013; Jöns, 2011; Leemann, 2010).

For individuals employed on casual contracts, often at the early career stage, their ability to play this academic career game is compromised by concerns over job security. In a recent report, the UK's Universities and

---

[2] The UK system for assessing universities' excellence in teaching, which is linked to the level of tuition fees which universities can charge.

Colleges Union (UCU, 2016) argued that insecure employment has become the norm rather than the exception for early career academics. In the UK, whilst there are a greater proportion of short-term contracts in research, lecturing roles have also become less secure; whilst in 2010, 80% of doctoral graduates working in these roles were employed on permanent contracts, by 2016 this had fallen to 72% (Vitae, 2019). There is a direct link between the gendered nature of academic careers and the increasing casualisation of academic labour. Recent research by Vitae (2019) in the UK indicates some gender disparity in the use of temporary contracts by universities, with analysis of 2017–8 HESA data showing that a higher proportion of all female academic staff were employed on fixed-term contracts compared with males. Indeed, in a large-scale survey of research staff at higher education institutions across Europe, women, disproportionately to men, reported that they left academic research due to the lack of job security, fixed-term contracts and poor work-life balance (Vitae, 2016). Other studies have highlighted how perceptions of academic work as unstable can discourage doctoral students from this career, and is particularly off-putting to women, compared with men (Guest et al., 2013; Royal Society of Chemistry, 2008; Wellcome Trust, 2013).

Successfully playing 'the game' of academia in an era of increasing casualisation therefore appears to require the embodiment of Williams' (2000) ideal worker—a good neoliberal subject who is able to devote themselves singularly to their work, be highly productive, be geographically mobile and able to withstand sustained periods of precariousness. Yet subscribing to the values underpinning this model of contemporary academic labour may not be appealing, or even possible, for all. As the Res-Sisters (2016, p. 267), a feminist collective of academics, question: 'who is this ideal academic? Who can—and indeed wants to—play this game?'. In this book, I argue that as other discipline-specific studies have shown, women doctoral students may become discouraged from pursuing an academic career because the prospect of taking on an identity which requires the embodiment of these values is either not appealing or not practical, or perhaps both.

## Belonging as Doctoral Students

Establishing a sense of belonging within the academy is inherently challenging for doctoral students due to their uncertain status within the academic hierarchy (Wisker et al., 2010). This challenge is compounded by the expectation of many doctoral candidates to perform academic identities whilst undertaking academic labour, usually in the form of teaching (Jazvac-Martek, 2009; Rao et al., 2021), but without the status or recognition of an academic contract (see Handforth, 2022). It has been argued that doctoral study is a 'liminal experience' wherein students 'stand on the threshold' of an academic career (Delamont et al., 2000, p. 176). The successful doctoral candidate must be able to gain acceptance within the existing culture of their academic environment (Carter et al., 2013), which involves socialisation, or what has been described as 'enculturation' (Delamont et al., 2000; Kamimura, 2006; Parry, 2007) into the disciplinary community.

Research indicates the significance of social integration for doctoral student retention and success (Ali et al., 2007; Lovitts, 2001; Tinto, 1993), and how academic cultures can facilitate well-being through collegiality and valuing of doctoral students and their research (Morris & Wisker, 2011). However, as Acker and Haque (2015) indicate, successful socialisation into the academic community is not the outcome for all doctoral students, and some may spend many years vainly attempting to attain this goal. Instead, I argue that establishing a sense of belonging to an academic community during the doctorate—which involves affective connections with others and the continual negotiation of power relations—is vital, not only for successful individual outcomes and positive experiences of doctoral study but also to make academic identity development a valid possibility.

Yet the structure of contemporary academic careers may challenge doctoral students' ability to develop a sense of belonging within academia, even for those who began their PhD with strong academic career aspirations. The competitive environment of contemporary academia increasingly pressures doctoral students to acquire additional skills and experience, such as experience of publishing work (see Rolf, 2021) and teaching (Rao et al., 2021), in order to have the best chance of obtaining an academic position afterwards. Yet statistics highlight that few doctoral students who aspire to an academic career will be successful (see Vitae, 2012). During the doctorate, many become discouraged from this career path as they learn about what an academic career requires, particularly in relation to the pressure to publish, the expectation of geographical mobility and the competition for posts which are often insecure and temporary (Jones & Oakley, 2018; Lopes & Dewan, 2014; UCU, 2016). These concerns about insecure future employment within academia have been connected to poor mental health and well-being among doctoral student populations (see Levecque et al., 2017; Vitae, 2018), and have implications for individuals' ability to belong to their academic community, if they perceive that they will be unable to sustain in their academic identity in the longer term (Austin, 2002; Jazvac-Martek, 2009).

Thus, the process of developing a sense of belonging as a doctoral student is not straightforward, especially for those from marginalised groups. There is limited research on the lived experiences of BAME doctoral students, LGBTQ+ doctoral students and those with disabilities (though see Arday, 2017; English & Fenby-Hulse, 2019; Hannam-Swain, 2018; Mattocks & Briscoe-Palmer, 2016 for exceptions). Studies of gender in relation to doctoral experiences are more common, and have highlighted that women students have less positive experiences of doctoral study than men, due to direct and indirect gender discrimination (see De Welde & Laursen, 2011; Fisher et al., 2019; White, 2004). Women doctoral students are also more likely to struggle with imposter syndrome than their male counterparts (Collett & Avelis, 2013) and suffer from mental health issues and poor levels of well-being (Gonzalez et al., 2021). Moreover, women doctoral students are less likely than men to be encouraged to engage in activities relevant to building academic careers (Curtin et al., 2016; Dever et al., 2008), and less likely to be introduced to useful networks during their doctorate (Asmar, 1999; Giles et al., 2009; Kemelgor & Etzkowitz, 2001). As women also often study for a PhD later in life than men (Bagilhole & White, 2013), and complete their studies on a part-time rather than full-time basis (Advance HE, 2021b), men have a significant advantage in developing an academic career by being more likely to have a more straightforward doctoral journey, both pragmatically and experientially.

A further barrier to women doctoral students being able to develop a sense of belonging within their academic community is imposter syndrome (see Handforth, 2022). This phenomenon was first identified by psychologists (Clance & Imes, 1978) in a study of high-achieving women staff and students at a university in the USA. They noted that 'despite outstanding academic and professional accomplishments, women who experience the imposter phenomenon persist in believing that they are really not bright and have fooled anyone who thinks otherwise' (*ibid*, p. 1). The imposter phenomenon, with its feelings of fraudulence and implications of 'otherness', has been observed more often, and with greater intensity, in women than in men (Clance, 1985; Collett & Avelis, 2013; Sakulku & Alexander, 2011). It is experienced as a type of marginalisation, which has implications for individuals to feel a sense of belonging. Research has found that particularly marginalised groups of women such as those from BAME backgrounds (Peteet et al., 2015), first-generation students (Gardner & Holley, 2011) and those in the early stages of their careers (Collett & Avelis, 2013; Handforth, 2022; Morris et al., 2022) feel a sense of being fraudulent more intensely than others, which may affect longer-term career aspirations.

These feelings of otherness are compounded by academic cultures which systemically marginalise women. The prevalence of cases of sexual harassment against women students (see NUS, 2018; Page et al., 2019), along with the persistence of lad culture within higher education spaces (see Phipps, 2018; Phipps & Young, 2015), is evidence of how women continue to be marginalised within academic spaces. For doctoral students, the power dynamics inherent in supervisory relationships may be particularly easily exploited by academics, who have considerable influence on individuals' ability to succeed (see Bull & Rye, 2018; Bull & Page, 2021; Lee, 1998). This makes women doctoral students structurally vulnerable to harassment, particularly where their funding is linked to a particular department or academic (see UCU, 2021). Sexual harassment has a range of implications for women in higher education: for individuals' well-being, for their ability to feel a sense of belonging within the academy and ultimately for their careers (Leonard, 2001).

## Feeling 'Other' in the Academy: Considering the Implications of Not Belonging

This chapter has outlined some of the ways in which women academics and doctoral students experience marginalisation within the academy. It has presented an understanding of belonging within academic communities as affective, involving the negotiation of power relations, with the aim of establishing a legitimacy which is recognised by others in the community (May, 2013; Miller, 2003; White & Nonnamaker, 2008). Developing a sense of belonging within academic spaces is a complex endeavour for women due to the existence of gendered cultures which position women as 'other'.

Women working and studying within the academic environment face particular barriers to belonging such as the persistence of 'lad culture' (Phipps, 2018; Phipps & Young, 2015), overt sexism (De Welde & Laursen, 2011; Knights & Richards, 2003) and gendered expectations of their abilities and contributions to academic labour (Crabtree & Shiel, 2019; White, 2013). This is compounded for women doctoral students, who experience further challenges in developing a sense of belonging within their academic communities due to the liminal status of PhD students within the academy, something not fully acknowledged or understood by institutions and those working with doctoral students (Handforth, 2022; Hockey, 1994; White & Nonnamaker, 2008; Wisker et al., 2010).

Given the significant link between belonging and retention (Lovitts, 2001), there are potentially considerable career-related consequences for those who are not able to feel a sense of belonging to the academy as doctoral students. This has clear implications for academic institutions and the higher education sector in terms of the future recruitment and retention of both doctoral students and academics. Research has highlighted that women are more likely than men to leave the academy at the early career stage, particularly in STEM subjects (Royal Society of Chemistry, 2008; Wellcome Trust, 2013). Moreover, this trend is also seen amongst those from minority ethnic backgrounds due to the persistence of racial discrimination within the academy (see Arday, 2017;

Bhopal et al., 2015). The lack of women and BAME individuals within doctoral student populations and in early career positions will have an ongoing impact on the 'leaky pipeline' due to the lack of role models for those considering academic careers, reinforcing already entrenched inequalities. However, as Thomas (2018) warns, it is vital to consider feelings of belonging as important in themselves, rather than simply viewing belonging as a potential solution to issues of retention.

There are a range of possible responses to struggling to belong within academia. In subsequent chapters of this book, I draw on data collected within my doctoral research to explore how participants devised strategies which allowed them to negotiate gendered academic cultures and develop ways of belonging within their academic communities. These included resisting neoliberal expectations of productivity and presenteeism, creating strong peer networks and learning to subvert traditional academic hierarchies—such as the supervisory relationship—in order to pursue their own goals.

# References

Acker, J. (1992). From sex roles to gendered institutions. *Contemporary Sociology: A Journal of Reviews, 565*–569. https://doi.org/10.1177/0011392113479315

Acker, S. (1980). Women, the other academics. *British Journal of Sociology of Education, 1*(1), 81–91.

Acker, S., & Feuerverger, G. (1996). Doing good and feeling bad: The work of women university teachers. *Cambridge Journal of Education, 26*(3), 401–422. https://doi.org/10.1080/0305764960260309

Acker, S., & Haque, E. (2015). The struggle to make sense of doctoral study. *Higher Education Research & Development, 34*(2), 229–241.

Acker, S., & McGinn, M. K. (2021). Fast professors, research funding, and the figured worlds of mid-career Ontario academics. *Brock Education Journal, 30*(2), 79–79.

Acker, S., & Webber, M. (2006). *Women working in academe: Approach with care. The Sage handbook of gender and education.* Sage.

Ackers, L. (2010). Internationalisation and equality: The contribution of short stay mobility to progression in science careers. *Recherches Sociologiques Et Anthropologiques, 41*(1), 83–103. https://doi.org/10.4000/rsa.189

Adams, S., Bekker, S., Fan, Y., Gordon, T., Shepherd, L. J., Slavich, E., & Waters, D. (2022). Gender bias in student evaluations of teaching: 'Punish [ing] those who fail to do their gender right'. *Higher Education, 83*(4), 787–807.

Addison, M., Breeze, M., & Taylor, Y. (2022). *The Palgrave handbook of imposter syndrome in higher education*. Palgrave Macmillan.

Advance HE. (2021a). Equality in higher education: Staff statistical report 2021.

Advance HE. (2021b). Equality in higher education: Student statistical report 2021.

Ahmed, S. (2021). *Complaint!* Duke University Press.

Aiston, S. J., & Jung, J. (2015). Women academics and research productivity: An international comparison. *Gender and Education, 27*(3), 205–220.

Ali, A., Kohun, F., & Levy, Y. (2007). Dealing with social isolation to minimize doctoral attrition—A four stage framework. *International Journal of Doctoral Studies, 2*(1), 33–49. https://doi.org/10.28945/3082

Anderson, P., & Williams, J. (2001). *Identity and difference in higher education: Outsiders within*. Ashgate.

Arday, J. (2017). *Exploring black and minority ethnic (BME) doctoral students' perceptions of an academic career*. Universities and Colleges Union.

Asmar, C. (1999). Is there a gendered agenda in academia? The research experience of female and male PhD graduates in Australian universities. *Higher Education, 38*(3), 255–273.

Austin, A. E. (2002). Preparing the next generation of faculty: Graduate school as socialization to the academic career. *The Journal of Higher Education, 73*(1), 94–122.

Bagilhole, B. (2002). Challenging equal opportunities: Changing and adapting male hegemony in academia. *British Journal of Sociology of Education, 23*(1), 19–33. https://doi.org/10.1080/01425690120102836

Bagilhole, B. (2007). Challenging women in the male academy: Think about draining the swamp. In P. Cotterill, S. Jackson, & G. Letherby (Eds.), *Challenges and negotiations for women in higher education* (pp. 21–32). Springer.

Bagilhole, B., & White, K. (2013). *Generation and gender in academia*. Palgrave Macmillan.

Bagilhole, B., & Woodward, H. (1995). An occupational hazard warning: Academic life can seriously damage your health. An investigation of sexual harassment of women academics in a UK university. *British Journal of Sociology of Education, 16*(1), 37–51. https://doi.org/10.1080/0142569950160103

Baker, M. (2012). *Academic careers and the gender gap*. UBC Press.

Ball, S. J. (2003). The teacher's soul and the terrors of performativity. *Journal of Education Policy, 18*(2), 215–228. https://doi.org/10.1080/0268093022000043065

Ball, S. J. (2012). Performativity, commodification and commitment: An I-spy guide to the neoliberal university. *British Journal of Educational Studies, 60*(1), 17–28.

Barnard, S., Powell, A., Bagilhole, B., & Dainty, A. (2010). Researching UK women professionals in SET: A critical review of current approaches. *International Journal of Gender, Science and Technology, 2*(3).

Batty, D., & Bengtsson, H. (2017, March 5). Why the true scale of university harassment is so hard to uncover. *The Guardian*. Retrieved from https://www.theguardian.com/education/2017/mar/05/why-the-true-scale-of-university-harassment-is-so-hard-to-uncover

Becher, T., & Trowler, P. (2001). *Academic tribes and territories: Intellectual enquiry and the culture of disciplines*. McGraw-Hill.

Bedi, G., Van Dam, N. T., & Munafo, M. (2012). Gender inequality in awarded research grants. *The Lancet, 380*(9840), 474.

Bhopal, K., Brown, H., & Jackson, J. (2015). *Academic flight: How to encourage black and minority ethnic academics to stay in UK higher education*. Equality Challenge Unit.

Bhopal, K., & Henderson, H. (2019). *Advancing equality in higher education: An exploratory study of the Athena SWAN and Race equality charters*. University of Birmingham.

Biglan, A. (1973). Relationships between subject matter characteristics and the structure and output of university departments. *Journal of Applied Psychology, 57*(3), 204.

Blickenstaff, J. C. (2005). Women and science careers: Leaky pipeline or gender filter? *Gender and Education, 17*(4), 369–386. https://doi.org/10.1080/09540250500145072

Brabazon, T. (2014). "Maybe he's just better than you": Generation X women and higher education. *Journal of Women's Entrepreneurship and Education*, (3–4), 48–70.

Breeze, M. (2018). Imposter syndrome as a public feeling. In Y. Taylor & L. Kinneret (Eds.), *Feeling academic in the neoliberal university*. Palgrave Macmillan.

Britton, D. M. (2017). Beyond the chilly climate: The salience of gender in women's academic careers. *Gender & Society, 31*(1), 5–27.

Brown, N., & Leigh, J. (2018). Ableism in academia: Where are the disabled and ill academics? *Disability & Society, 33*(6), 985–989.

Bull, A., & Page, T. (2021). Students' accounts of grooming and boundary-blurring behaviours by academic staff in UK higher education. *Gender and Education, 33*(8), 1057–1072.

Bull, A., & Rye, R. (2018). *Silencing students: Institutional responses to staff sexual misconduct in UK higher education.* The 1752 Group and University of Portsmouth.

Burke, P. J., Crozier, G., Read, B., Hall, J., Peat, J., & Francis, B. (2013). *Formations of gender and higher education pedagogies (GaP).* Higher Education Academy.

Cantor, D., Fisher, B., Chibnall, S., Harps, S., Townsend, R., Thomas, G., Lee, H., Kranz, V., Herbison, R., & Madden, K. (2019). *Report on the AAU campus climate survey on sexual assault and misconduct.* The Association of American Universities.

Carson, L. (2001). Gender relations in higher education: Exploring lecturers' perceptions of student evaluations of teaching. *Research Papers in Education, 16*(4), 337–358.

Carter, S., Blumenstein, M., & Cook, C. (2013). Different for women? the challenges of doctoral studies. *Teaching in Higher Education, 18*(4), 339–351. https://doi.org/10.1080/13562517.2012.719159

Ceci, S. J., & Williams, W. M. (2011). Understanding current causes of women's underrepresentation in science. *Proceedings of the National Academy of Sciences of the United States of America, 108*(8), 3157–3162.

Clance, P. R. (1985). *The impostor phenomenon: Overcoming the fear that haunts your success.* Peachtree.

Clance, P. R., & Imes, S. A. (1978). The imposter phenomenon in high achieving women: Dynamics and therapeutic intervention. *Psychotherapy: Theory, Research and Practice, 15*(3), 241–247. https://doi.org/10.1037/h0086006

Clegg, S. (2012). Conceptualising higher education research and/or academic development as 'fields': A critical analysis. *Higher Education Research & Development, 31*(5), 667–678. https://doi.org/10.1080/07294360.2012.690369

Collett, J. L., & Avelis, J. (2013). *Family-friendliness, fraudulence, and gendered academic career ambitions.* American Sociological Association Annual Meeting.

Collini, S. (2012). *What are universities for?* Penguin UK.

Coser, L. A. (1974). *Greedy institutions; patterns of undivided commitment.* Macmillan Publishing Company.

Cotterill, P., Jackson, S., & Letherby, G. (2007). *Challenges and negotiations for women in higher education.* Springer.

Crabtree, S., & Shiel, C. (2019). "Playing mother": Channeled careers and the construction of gender in academia. *SAGE Open, 9*(3), 2158244019876285.

CRAC. (2020). Qualitative research on barriers to progression for disabled scientists. Retrieved from: https://www.crac.org.uk/Media/Default/files/Qualitative%20research%20on%20barriers%20to%20progression%20of%20disabled%20scientists.pdf

Creaton, J., & Handforth, R. (2021). Considering mental health and wellbeing in postgraduate research: A critical reflection. *Special Issue of Studies in Graduate and Postdoctoral Education, 12*(1).

Curtin, N., Malley, J., & Stewart, A. J. (2016). Mentoring the next generation of faculty: Supporting academic career aspirations among doctoral students. *Research in Higher Education, 57*(6), 714–738.

Davies, D. (2021, October 19). Oxford professors abused position with sexist and drunken conduct. *Al Jazeera*. Retrieved from: https://www.aljazeera.com/news/2021/10/19/oxford-professors-abused-position-with-sexist-and-drunken-conduct

Deem, R. (1998). 'New managerialism' and higher education: The management of performances and cultures in universities in the United Kingdom. *International Studies in Sociology of Education, 8*(1), 47–70. https://doi.org/10.1080/0962021980020014

Delamont, S. (2006). *Gender and higher education. The Sage handbook of gender and education* (pp. 179–189). Sage.

Delamont, S., Atkinson, P., & Parry, O. (2000). *The doctoral experience: Success and failure in graduate school*. Routledge.

Dever, M., Laffan, W., Boreham, P., Behrens, K., Haynes, M., Western, M., & Kubler, M. (2008). *Gender differences in early post-PhD employment in Australian universities: The influence of PhD experience on women's academic careers*. Final report.

Dever, M., & Morrison, Z. (2009). Women, research performance and work context. *Tertiary Education and Management, 15*(1), 49–62. https://doi.org/10.1080/13583880802700107

De Welde, K., & Laursen, S. (2011). The glass obstacle course: Informal and formal barriers for women PhD students in STEM fields. *International Journal of Gender, Science and Technology, 3*(3), 571–595.

do Mar Pereira, M. (2016). Struggling within and beyond the performative university: Articulating activism and work in an "academia without walls". *Women's Studies International Forum, 54*, 100–110. https://doi.org/10.1016/j.wsif.2015.06.008

Dyhouse, C. (2016). *No distinction of sex?: Women in British universities* (pp. 1870–1939). Routledge.

Emmioglu, E., McAlpine, L., & Amundsen, C. (2017). Doctoral students' experiences of feeling (or not) like an academic. *International Journal of Doctoral Studies, 12*, 73–91.

English, R., & Fenby-Hulse, K. (2019). Documenting diversity: The experiences of LGBTQ doctoral researchers in the UK. *International Journal of Doctoral Studies, 14*(1).

Equality Challenge Unit. (2016). Athena Survey of Science, Engineering and Technology (ASSET) 2016 . Accessed from: https://www.advance-he.ac.uk/knowledge-hub/asset-2016

European Commission. (2021). *She figures 2021: Gender in research and innovation | Statistics and indicators. 2021*. European Union.

Eveline, J., & Booth, M. (2004). "Don't write about it" writing "the other" for the ivory basement. *Journal of Organizational Change Management, 17*(3), 243–255. https://doi.org/10.1108/09534810410538306

Fan, Y., Shepherd, L. J., Slavich, E., Waters, D., Stone, M., Abel, R., & Johnston, E. L. (2019). Gender and cultural bias in student evaluations: Why representation matters. *PLoS One, 14*(2), e0209749.

Fisher, A. J., Mendoza-Denton, R., Patt, C., Young, I., Eppig, A., Garrell, R. L., Nelson, T. W., Rees, D., & Richards, M. A. (2019). Structure and belonging: Pathways to success for underrepresented minority and women PhD students in STEM fields. *PLoS One, 14*(1), e0209279.

Fisher, V., & Kinsey, S. (2014). Behind closed doors! Homosocial desire and the academic boys club. *Gender in Management: An International Journal., 29*(1), 44–64.

Gardner, S. K., & Holley, K. A. (2011). "Those invisible barriers are real": The progression of first-generation students through doctoral education. *Equity & Excellence in Education, 44*(1), 77–92.

Gibbons, K. (2018, July 28). Sex harassment victims force University College London to end gagging orders. *The Times*. Retrieved from: https://www.the-times.co.uk/article/sex-harassment-victims-forceuniversity-college-london-to-end-gagging-orders-h9v9v279f

Giles, M., Ski, C., & Vrdoljak, D. (2009). Career pathways of science, engineering and technology research postgraduates. *Australian Journal of Education, 53*(1), 69–86. https://doi.org/10.1177/000494410905300106

Gill, R. (2009). Breaking the silence: The hidden injuries of neo-liberal academia. In R. Ryan-Flood & R. Gill (Eds.), *Secrecy and silence in the research process: Feminist reflections* (pp. 228–244). Routledge.

Gill, R., & Donaghue, N. (2015). Resilience, apps and reluctant individualism: Technologies of self in the neoliberal academy. *Women's Studies International Forum, 54*, 91–99. https://doi.org/10.1016/j.wsif.2015.06.016

Glover, J., & Fielding, J. (1999). Women and the sciences in Britain: Getting in? *Journal of Education and Work, 12*(1), 57–73. https://doi.org/10.1080/1363908990120104

Gonzalez, J. A., Kim, H., & Flaster, A. (2021). Transition points: Well-being and disciplinary identity in the first years of doctoral studies. *Studies in Graduate and Postdoctoral Education.* https://doi.org/10.1108/SGPE-07-2020-0045

Greenfield, S., Peters, J., Lane, N., Rees, T., & Gill, S. (2002). SET fair: A report on women in science, engineering, and technology from the Baroness Greenfield CBE to the Secretary of State for Trade and Industry. Department of Trade and Industry.

Guarino, C. M., & Borden, V. M. (2017). Faculty service loads and gender: Are women taking care of the academic family? *Research in Higher Education, 58*(6), 672–694.

Guest, M., Sharma, S., & Song, R. (2013). *Gender and career progression in theology and religious studies.* Durham University.

Hall, R. M., & Sandler, B. R. (1982). *The classroom climate: A chilly one for women.* Association of American Colleges.

Hancock, S. (2019). A future in the knowledge economy? Analysing the career strategies of doctoral scientists through the principles of game theory. *Higher Education, 78*(1), 33–49.

Handforth, R. (2022). Feeling "stupid": Considering the affective in women doctoral students' experiences of imposter 'syndrome'. In *The Palgrave handbook of imposter syndrome in higher education* (pp. 293–309). Palgrave Macmillan.

Hannam-Swain, S. (2018). The additional labour of a disabled PhD student. *Disability & Society, 33*(1), 138–142.

Hearn, J. (2001). *Academia, management and men: Making the connections, exploring the implications.* SRHE/Open University Press.

Henkel, M. (2000). *Academic identities and policy change in higher education.* Jessica Kingsley Publishers.

Henkel, M. (2004). Current science policies and their implications for the formation and maintenance of academic identity. *Higher Education Policy, 17*(2), 167–182.

Higher Education Statistics Agency. (2017). Staff numbers and characteristics. Retrieved from https://www.hesa.ac.uk/data-and-analysis/staff

Hochschild, A. (1983). *The managed heart: Commercialization of human feeling.* University of California Press.

Hockey, J. (1994). New territory: Problems of adjusting to the first year of a social science PhD. *Studies in Higher Education, 19*(2), 177–190. https://doi.org/10.1080/03075079412331382027

Hoskins, K. (2010, March). The price of success? The experiences of three senior working class female academics in the UK. In *Women's Studies International Forum* (Vol. 33, No. 2, pp. 134–140). Pergamon.

Howe-Walsh, L., & Turnbull, S. (2016). Barriers to women leaders in academia: Tales from science and technology. *Studies in Higher Education, 41*(3), 415–428.

Jazvac-Martek, M. (2009). Oscillating role identities: The academic experiences of education doctoral students. *Innovations in Education and Teaching International, 46*(3), 253–264. https://doi.org/10.1080/14703290903068862

Jones, R. A. (2005). How many female scientists do you know? *Endeavour, 29*(2), 84–88. https://doi.org/10.1016/j.endeavour.2005.03.005

Jones, S., & Oakley, C. (2018). *The precarious postdoc report for working knowledge*. Working Knowledge/Hearing.

Jöns, H. (2011). Transnational academic mobility and gender. *Globalisation, Societies and Education, 9*(2), 183–209. https://doi.org/10.1080/14767724.2011.577199

Kamimura, M. (2006). *Finding my way: Enculturation to the PhD* (pp. 191–198). Stylus.

Kemelgor, C., & Etzkowitz, H. (2001). Overcoming isolation: Women's dilemmas in American academic science. *Minerva, 39*(2), 153–174.

King, M. M., Bergstrom, C. T., Correll, S. J., Jacquet, J., & West, J. D. (2017). Men set their own cites high: Gender and self-citation across fields and over time. *Socius, 3*, 2378023117738903.

Kinman, G. (2014). Doing more with less? work and wellbeing in academics. *Somatechnics, 4*(2), 219–235.

Knights, D., & Richards, W. (2003). Sex discrimination in UK academia. *Gender, Work & Organization, 10*(2), 213–238. https://doi.org/10.1111/1468-0432.t01-1-00012

Kogan, M. (2000). Higher education communities and academic identity. *Higher Education Quarterly, 54*(3), 207–216.

Kulis, S., Sicotte, D., & Collins, S. (2002). More than a pipeline problem: Labor supply constraints and gender stratification across academic science disciplines. *Research in Higher Education, 43*(6), 657–691.

Larivière, V., Ni, C., Gingras, Y., Cronin, B., & Sugimoto, C. R. (2013). Bibliometrics: Global gender disparities in science. *Nature, 504*(7479), 211–213.

Lave, J., & Wenger, E. (1991). *Situated learning: Legitimate peripheral participation*. Cambridge University Press.

Leathwood, C., & Read, B. (2009). *Gender and the changing face of higher education: A feminized future?* Open University Press.

Lee, D. (1998). Sexual harassment in PhD supervision. *Gender and Education, 10*(3), 299–312. https://doi.org/10.1080/09540259820916

Leemann, R. J. (2010). Gender inequalities in transnational academic mobility and the ideal type of academic entrepreneur. *Discourse: Studies in the Cultural Politics of Education, 31*(5), 605–625.

Leonard, D. (2001). *A woman's guide to doctoral studies*. Open University Press.

Letherby, G. (2003). *Feminist research in theory and practice*. Open University Press.

Letherby, G., & Shiels, J. (2001). "Isn't he good, but can we take her seriously?": Gendered expectations in higher education. In P. Anderson & J. Williams (Eds.), *Identity and difference in higher education: Outsiders within* (pp. 121–132). Ashgate.

Levecque, K., Anseel, F., De Beuckelaer, A., Van der Heyden, J., & Gisle, L. (2017). Work organization and mental health problems in PhD students. *Research Policy, 46*(4), 868–879. https://doi.org/10.1016/j.respol.2017.02.008

Lopes, A., & Dewan, I. (2014). Precarious pedagogies? The impact of casual and zero-hour contracts in Higher Education. *Journal of Feminist Scholarship, 7*(8), 28–42.

Loveday, V. (2018). The neurotic academic: Anxiety, casualisation, and governance in the neoliberalising university. *Journal of Cultural Economy, 11*(2), 154–166.

Lovitts, B. E. (2001). *Leaving the ivory tower: The causes and consequences of departure from doctoral study*. Rowman & Littlefield.

Lubitow, A., & Zippel, K. (2014). Strategies of academic parents to manage work-life conflict in research abroad. In V. Demos, C. W. Berheide, & M. T. Segal (Eds.), *Gender transformation in the academy* (pp. 63–84). Emerald.

Lucas, L. (2006). *The research game in academic life*. SRHE/Open University Press.

Lynch, K. (2010). Carelessness: A hidden doxa of higher education. *Arts and Humanities in Higher Education, 9*(1), 54–67. https://doi.org/10.1177/1474022209350104

MacNell, L., Driscoll, A., & Hunt, A. N. (2015). What's in a name: Exposing gender bias in student ratings of teaching. *Innovative Higher Education, 40*(4), 291–303.

Mattocks, K., & Briscoe-Palmer, S. (2016). Diversity, inclusion, and doctoral study: Challenges facing minority PhD students in the united kingdom. *European Political Science, 15*, 476–492.

May, V. (2013). *Connecting self to society: Belonging in a changing world*. Macmillan International Higher Education.

Miller, L. (2003). Belonging to country—A philosophical anthropology. *Journal of Australian Studies, 27*(76), 215–223.

Mirza, H. S. (2009). Chapter 14: Postcolonial subjects, black feminism, and the intersectionality of race and gender in higher education. *Counterpoints, 369*, 233–248.

Morley, L. (1999). *Organising feminisms: The micropolitics of the academy*. Palgrave Macmillan.

Morley, L. (2011). Misogyny posing as measurement: Disrupting the feminisation crisis discourse. *Contemporary Social Science, 6*(2), 223–235.

Morley, L. (2013). The rules of the game: Women and the leaderist turn in higher education. *Gender and education, 25*(1), 116–131.

Morley, L. (2014). Lost leaders: Women in the global academy. *Higher Education Research & Development, 33*(1), 114–128.

Morley, L., & David, M. (2009). Celebrations and challenges: Gender in higher education. *Higher Education Policy, 22*(1), 1. https://doi.org/10.1057/hep.2008.31

Morris, C., Kadiwal, L., Telling, K., Ashall, W., Kirby, J., & Mwale, S. (2022). Restorying imposter syndrome in the Early Career stage: Reflections, recognitions and resistance. In *The Palgrave handbook of imposter syndrome in higher education* (pp. 225–240). Palgrave Macmillan.

Morris, C., & Wisker, G. (2011). *Troublesome encounters: Strategies for managing the wellbeing of master's and doctoral education students during their learning processes*. HEA ESCalate Subject Centre Report.

Morrish, L. (2019). *Pressure vessels: The epidemic of poor mental health among higher education staff*. Higher Education Policy Institute.

Murray, J. (2021, May 16). Universities are failing to tackle rape culture on campus. Retrieved from: https://www.theguardian.com/world/2021/may/16/universities-rape-culture-on-campus-students-protest

National Union of Students (NUS). (2010). *Hidden marks: A study of women students' experiences of harassment, stalking, violence and sexual assault*. NUS.

National Union of Students (NUS). (2018). *Power in the academy: Staff sexual misconduct in UK higher education*. NUS.

Nature. (2019). Nature PhD survey 2019: Report by Shift Learning. Retrieved from: https://figshare.com/s/74a5ea79d76ad66a8af8

Nygaard, L. P., & Bahgat, K. (2018). What's in a number? how (and why) measuring research productivity in different ways changes the gender gap. *Journal of English for Academic Purposes, 32*, 67–79.

O'Connor, P., O'Hagan, C., Myers, E. S., Baisner, L., Apostolov, G., Topuzova, I., & Caglayan, H. (2019). Mentoring and sponsorship in higher education institutions: Men's invisible advantage in STEM? *Higher Education Research & Development*, 1–14.

Ollilainen, M., & Solomon, C. R. (2014). Carving a "Third path": Faculty parents' resistance to the ideal academic worker norm. In V. Demos, C. W. Berheide, & M. T. Segal (Eds.), *Gender transformation in the academy* (pp. 21–39). Emerald Group.

Page, T., Bull, A., & Chapman, E. (2019). Making power visible: "Slow activism" to address staff sexual misconduct in higher education. *Violence Against Women, 25*(11), 1309–1330.

Parry, S. (2007). *Disciplines and doctorates*. Springer.

Parsons, E., & Priola, V. (2013). Agents for change and changed agents: The Micropolitics of change and feminism in the academy. *Gender, Work & Organization, 20*(5), 580–598. https://doi.org/10.1111/j.1468-0432.2012.00605.x

Parvazian, S., Gill, J., & Chiera, B. (2017). Higher education, women, and sociocultural change: A closer look at the statistics. *SAGE Open, 7*(2), 2158244017700230.

Peteet, B. J., Montgomery, L., & Weekes, J. C. (2015). Predictors of imposter phenomenon among talented ethnic minority undergraduate students. *The Journal of Negro Education, 84*(2), 175–186. https://doi.org/10.7709/jnegroeducation.84.2.0175

Phipps, A. (2018). 'Lad culture' and sexual violence against students. In *The Routledge handbook of gender and violence* (pp. 171–182). Routledge.

Phipps, A., & Young, I. (2013). *That's what she said: Women students' experiences of 'lad culture' in higher education*. Project Report. National Union of Students.

Phipps, A., & Young, I. (2015). Neoliberalisation and 'lad cultures' in higher education. *Sociology, 49*(2), 305–322.

Pittman, C. T. (2010). Race and gender oppression in the classroom: The experiences of women faculty of color with white male students. *Teaching Sociology, 38*(3), 183–196.

Probert, B. (2005). 'I just couldn't fit it in': Gender and unequal outcomes in academic careers. *Gender, Work & Organization, 12*(1), 50–72. https://doi.org/10.1111/j.1468-0432.2005.00262.x

Probyn, E. (1996). *Outside belongings*. Routledge.

Puwar, N. (2004). Thinking about making a difference. *The British Journal of Politics & International Relations, 6*(1), 65–80. https://doi.org/10.1111/j.1467-856x.2004.00127.x

PWC. (2017). U.K. women in tech, time to close the gender gap. Retrieved from: https://www.pwc.co.uk/who-we-are/women-in-technology/time-to-close-the-gender-gap.html

Rao, N., Hosein, A., & Raaper, R. (2021). Doctoral students navigating the borderlands of academic teaching in an era of precarity. *Teaching in Higher Education, 26*(3), 454–470.

Reay, D. (1998). Surviving in dangerous places: Working-class women, women's studies and higher education. *Women's Studies International Forum, 21*(1), 11–19. https://doi.org/10.1016/s0277-5395(97)00087-3

Reay, D. (2004). Cultural capitalists and academic habitus: Classed and gendered labour in UK higher education. *Women's Studies International Forum, 27*(1), 31–39. https://doi.org/10.1016/s0277-5395(03)00163-8

Rolf, H. G. (2021). Navigating power in doctoral publishing: A data feminist approach. *Teaching in Higher Education, 26*(3), 488–507.

Rollock, N. (2019). *Staying power: The career experiences and strategies of UK Black female professors*. UCU.

Rossiter, M. (2004). Educational relationships and possible selves in the adult undergraduate experience. *The Cyril O'Houle Scholars in Adult and Continuing Education Program Global Research Perspectives, 4*, 138–155. https://doi.org/10.1002/ace.259

Royal Society of Chemistry. (2008). *The chemistry PhD: The impact on women's retention*. A Report for the UK Resource Centre for Women in SET and the Royal Society of Chemistry, 1–38.

Sakulku, J., & Alexander, J. (2011). The impostor phenomenon. *International Journal of Behavioral Science (IJBS), 6*(1).

Sang, K. (2017). *Disability and academic careers*. Retrieved from: https://migrantacademics.files.wordpress.com/2017/05/disability-sang-may-2017.pdf

Santos, G., & Dang Van Phu, S. (2019). Gender and academic rank in the UK. *Sustainability, 11*(11), 3171.

Savigny, H. (2014). Women, know your limits: Cultural sexism in academia. *Gender and Education, 26*(7), 794–809. https://doi.org/10.1080/09540253.2014.970977

Smith, E. (2011). Women into science and engineering? gendered participation in higher education STEM subjects. *British Educational Research Journal, 37*(6), 993–1014. https://doi.org/10.1080/01411926.2010.515019

Stanley, L. (1997). Methodology matters! In V. Robinson & D. Richardson (Eds.), *Introducing Women's Studies* (2nd ed., pp. 198–219). Macmillan.

Teeuwsen, P., Ratković, S., & Tilley, S. A. (2014). Becoming academics: Experiencing legitimate peripheral participation in part-time doctoral studies. *Studies in Higher Education, 39*(4), 680–694.

The Res-Sisters. (2016). 'I'm an early career feminist academic: Get me out of here?': Encountering and resisting the neoliberal academy. In R. Thwaites & A. Pressland (Eds.), *Being an early career feminist academic* (pp. 267–284). Palgrave Macmillan.

The Universities and Colleges Union (UCU). (2016, April). *Precarious work in higher education: A snapshot of insecure contracts and institutional attitudes*. UCU.

The Universities and Colleges Union (UCU). (2021). Eradicating sexual violence in tertiary education: A report from UCU's sexual violence task group. Retrieved from: https://www.ucu.org.uk/media/12269/UCU-sexual-violence-task-group-report-2021/pdf/UCU_sexual_violence_task_group_report_20211220.pdf

Thomas, K. C. (2018). *Rethinking student belonging in higher education: From Bourdieu to borderlands*. Routledge.

Thompson, J., & Bekhradnia, B. (2009). *Male and female participation and progression in higher education*. Full report. Higher Education Policy Institute (HEPI). Retrieved from https://www.hepi.ac.uk/2009/06/05/male-and-female-participation-and-progression-in-higher-education/

Thwaites, R., & Pressland, A. (2016). *Being an early career feminist academic: Global perspectives, experiences and challenges*. Springer.

Tierney, W. G., & Bensimon, E. M. (1996). *Promotion and tenure: Community and socialization in academe*. Suny Press.

Tinto, V. (1993). *Leaving college: Rethinking the causes and cures of student attrition*. University of Chicago Press.

Tower, G., Plummer, J., & Ridgewell, B. (2007). A multidisciplinary study of gender-based research productivity in the worlds best journals. *Journal of Diversity Management (JDM), 2*(4), 23–32.

Tsaousi, C. (2020). That's funny… you don't look like a lecturer! dress and professional identity of female academics. *Studies in Higher Education, 45*(9), 1809–1820.

Tutchell, E., & Edmonds, J. (2020). *Unsafe spaces: Ending sexual abuse in universities*. Emerald Group.

United Nations Educational, Scientific and Cultural Organization (UNESCO). (2016). UNESCO data centre: UNESCO Institute for Statistics. Retrieved from http://stats.uis.unesco.org/unesco/TableViewer/document.aspx?ReportId=143&IF_Language=eng

Valentine, G., & Wood, N. (2010). The experiences of lesbian, gay and bisexual staff and students in higher education. Equality and Human Rights Commission research summary 39. Retrieved from: https://www.equalityhumanrights.com/sites/default/files/research-summary-39-experiences-of-lesbian-gay-bisexual-higher-education.pdf

van Anders, S. M. (2004). Why the academic pipeline leaks: Fewer men than women perceive barriers to becoming professors. *Sex Roles, 51*(9-10), 511–521. https://doi.org/10.1007/s11199-004-5461-9

Vaughn, A. R., Taasoobshirazi, G., & Johnson, M. I. (2020). Impostor phenomenon and motivation: Women in higher education. *Studies in Higher Education, 45*(4), 780–795.

Vitae. (2012). *What do researchers want to do? The career intentions of doctoral researchers*. The Careers Research and Advisory Centre (CRAC) Limited.

Vitae. (2016). What do research staff do next? Retrieved from: https://www.vitae.ac.uk/vitae-publications/reports/vitae-what-do-research-staff-do-next-2016.pdf

Vitae. (2018). Exploring wellbeing and mental health and associated support services for postgraduate researchers. Retrieved from: https://www.vitae.ac.uk/doing-research/wellbeing-and-mental-health/HEFCE-Report_Exploring-PGR-Mental-health-support/view

Vitae. (2019). Do researchers' careers have to be precarious? Retrieved from: https://www.vitae.ac.uk/impact-and-evaluation/what-do-researchers-do/do-researchers-careers-have-to-be-precarious-research-article.pdf/view

Wacquant, L. J. (1989). Towards a reflexive sociology: A workshop with Pierre Bourdieu. *Sociological theory*, 26–63.

Ward, K., & Wolf-Wendel, L. (2016). Academic motherhood: Mid-Career perspectives and the ideal worker norm. *New Directions for Higher Education, 2016*(176), 11–23. https://doi.org/10.1002/he.20206

Weale, S., & Batty, D. (2016, October 21). University sex abuse report fails to tackle staff attacks on UK students. *The Guardian*. Retrieved from https://www.theguardian.com/society/2016/oct/21/university-sex-abuse-report-fails-staff-attacks-students

Weale, S., & Batty, D. (2017, March 6). Calls for action by universities on 'epidemic' of harassment on campus. *The Guardian*. Retrieved from https://www.theguardian.com/education/2017/mar/06/calls-for-review-into-how-universities-handle-sexual-harassment-allegations

Wellcome Trust. (2013). *Risks and rewards: How PhD students choose their careers*. Ipsos MORI.

Wellcome Trust. (2020). What researchers think about the culture they work in. Retrieved from: https://cms.wellcome.org/sites/default/files/what-researchers-think-about-the-culture-they-work-in.pdf

White, J., & Nonnamaker, J. (2008). Belonging and mattering: How doctoral students experience community. *NASPA Journal, 45*(3), 350–372.

White, K. (2004). The leaking pipeline: Women postgraduate and early career researchers in Australia. *Tertiary Education & Management, 10*(3), 227–241. https://doi.org/10.1023/b:team.0000044828.44536.67

White, K. (2013). An outsider in academia. In B. Bagilhole & K. White (Eds.), *Generation and gender in academia* (pp. 103–126). Palgrave Macmillan.

White, K. (2015). *Keeping women in science*. Melbourne Univ Publishing.

Williams, J. C. (2000). *Unbending gender: Why family and work conflict and what to do about it*. Oxford University Press.

Williams, R. (1961). The analysis of culture. In *The long revolution* (pp. 41–71). Columbia University Press.

Williams, W. M., & Ceci, S. J. (2015). National hiring experiments reveal 2:1 faculty preference for women on STEM tenure track. *Proceedings of the National Academy of Sciences of the United States of America, 112*(17), 5360–5365.

Wisker, G., Morris, C., Cheng, M., Masika, R., Warnes, M., Trafford, V., & Lilly, J. (2010). *Doctoral learning journeys: Final report*. Higher Education Academy. Retrieved https://www.heacademy.ac.uk/system/files/doctoral_learning_journeys_final_report_0.pdf

Wray, S., & Kinman, G. (2021). *Supporting staff wellbeing in higher education*. Project Report. Education Support, London, UK.

Wynarczyk, P., & Renner, C. (2006). The "gender gap" in the scientific labour market: The case of science, engineering and technology-based SMEs in the UK. *Equal Opportunities International, 25*(8), 660–673.

## Women in STEM: Restoryings of Participants' Doctoral Journeys

### Harriet

Harriet was in her early 20s when she started her PhD in Biology at Redbrick University. She was in a relationship, with no caring responsibilities. Her partner was also pursuing a PhD from the same institution and in the same subject area. Harriet chose to pursue a doctorate after her undergraduate degree because she had enjoyed lab work and doing independent research. She had not intended to do a PhD but the opportunity to apply for funding arose in her department and she felt it would have been stupid not to take it. After the PhD she initially planned to pursue a post-doctoral position, though was not completely certain about a career in academic STEM.

During her studies, she became increasingly critical of the culture of academic science which pressurises scientists to constantly publish work and seek funding. In order to pursue an academic career, Harriet recognised that she must develop particular skills and engage in activities beyond her PhD. Though she was not fully committed to a career in academic science, Harriet was keen to ensure that she gains experience outside of her research which she can draw on when she applies for jobs. This awareness developed from conversations with peers and seeing the experiences of doctoral graduates applying for jobs. She recognised that she had many other options after the PhD, including teaching and STEM outreach work. Harriet viewed particular activities such as teaching and presenting her work at conferences as important for her personal development.

The lab where Harriet worked had a huge impact on her experience of the PhD. She worked with post-docs under a huge amount of pressure, and who struggled to balance family life alongside their career. Her fellow students also struggled with stress, and their experiences discouraged them from staying in academia. Senior scientists in her lab, including her supervisor, expected high levels of dedication from doctoral students including expectations of working on evenings, weekends and holidays, which Harriet found challenging to negotiate. Throughout her doctorate, Harriet's lab was under financial strain and staff were under pressure to publish work and attract more funding. She was concerned about the impact of these financial pressures, and particularly about the way this affected the lab's priorities for scientific research. Harriet struggled to imagine herself being able to prioritise securing funding over scientific interest, which she sees as being necessary in academia. The culture of academic science thus has a significant impact on Harriet's career aspirations, as the pressure on individuals to publish results and secure funding within such a competitive environment discourages her from choosing this career.

By her second year, Harriet had become more involved with the postgraduate community through her departmental postgraduate society and gained significant support from her peers. However, by this stage she also began to question whether or not she should pursue a post-doc position because she was unable to visualise herself in a senior lab position. Harriet envisaged various barriers to pursuing a career in academic science such as the intense competition for jobs after the PhD, the pressure to move between institutions in order to accumulate experience of multiple labs, the pressure to publish and the financial constraints involved in working in a lab which requires research funding to be secured on a regular basis. Harriet also observed gender-specific barriers to working in academic science, referring to the gendered roles of women in her department in relation to research and teaching, her experiences of lad culture, the struggles of women with young children to balance caring responsibilities with an academic career and the differential treatment of men and women in her lab. Imagining herself as a parent in the future, she perceived combining an academic career with having a family as difficult, and questioned her level of dedication to developing a career in academic science in the face of challenging personal circumstances.

## Jane

Jane was in her early 20s when she began studying for her doctorate in Conservation at Redbrick University. Prior to getting her place to do the

PhD, she worked as an intern for a local conservation organisation. She had been determined to do a PhD, applying to multiple institutions and eventually moving across the country with her partner to start her doctorate. Jane had strong academic aspirations on starting her studies, and was motivated by the prospect of making an impact in her field. She felt that an academic career would allow her to have this impact, as well as give her freedom to follow her own interests.

However, as she progressed through the doctorate, Jane's perceptions of academia became gradually more negative. Jane found her undergraduate degree at an elite UK university very stressful, which informed her attitude to her doctoral studies, which was based on the need to maintain a healthy work-life balance. Yet during her PhD Jane struggled to resist the culture of over-work in her department, and was influenced by others' work habits. At her previous institution there was a lot of pressure to work very hard and she made significant sacrifices to achieve her degree, including not having a social life which had a negative impact on her wellbeing. Jane tried to maintain a healthier approach to her studies, but found that the culture of her current department encouraged total dedication to academic work which was normalised by the behaviour of the academics. Further, though she had no immediate plans to have children, Jane became increasingly concerned about the issues she might face if she were to start a family whilst developing an academic career, including fears that taking career breaks to have children would be disadvantageous for her promotion prospects.

Jane's experience of the PhD was not what she expected. She became frustrated that PhD students in her department were not treated as members of staff, which made accessing equipment necessary for her fieldwork difficult, and also had financial implications. She also experienced issues within her supervisory relationships; whilst she had expected that supervisors would value her academic abilities and respect her views, she found that her male supervisor was often dismissive. Though her other, female, supervisor was more supportive, both supervisors pressured her to publish papers during her PhD, which she found stressful.

Beyond this, Jane had chosen her particular PhD because it allowed her to do fieldwork in a specific climate, which she had been looking forward to. However, the reality of fieldwork was more difficult and less interesting than she had anticipated, and being away from home and from her partner affected her more than she had anticipated. After returning from fieldwork in her second year, Jane questioned her long-held academic aspirations. She was frustrated that her work was more theoretical than she had wanted, with less practical application than she had hoped.

Though she had initially intended to pursue an academic career, Jane's career aspirations shifted during her PhD towards a career in policy, which she felt would enable her to have a positive and measurable impact in her field. However, she recognised that having an academic reputation would be beneficial for working in the policy sector, and so planned to gain further academic credentials and then transition from academia into policy. During the PhD she sought out experiences which would help her to make this transition, such as doing scientific outreach work. Jane received little career advice during her studies, and perceived that her supervisors would not support her to move out of academia.

The long working hours, pressure to publish and competition for jobs implicit in pursuing a career in academic STEM, as well as Jane's perception that combining academic work with having a family would be challenging, all discouraged her from wanting to pursue this as a career. By her second year, she considered that her life would be easier outside of academia because of these factors, and particularly the long working hours expected in academic STEM.

## Antonia

Antonia, an international student from a European country, was in her mid-20s when she began studying for her doctorate in Engineering at Modern University. Prior to the PhD, she was a master's student at a university in her home country and she worked in various part-time jobs for a year before this. Antonia was frustrated at the lack of opportunities to study in her home country, which meant that she had to leave her family and partner to move to the UK to study. However, she appreciated the opportunity to do her PhD in the UK, as she felt it would be perceived as more prestigious, which would have a positive impact on her subsequent career. She applied for a PhD because she had a passion for her subject and wanted to do further research, with a view to pursuing an academic research career after the PhD and ideally securing a post-doctoral position in her home country.

Antonia's struggles with English were the most challenging aspect of her doctoral experience. She found the language barrier difficult to overcome, and it negatively affected her work because at first, she was not able to understand her supervisor. She often misunderstood what she was instructed to do in the lab, meaning that she had to repeat experiments and do twice the amount of work, which had a negative impact on her wellbeing. Her lack of confidence with the language also impacted on the opportunities she was able to access; though she enjoyed teaching and had experience of doing this in her home country, she did not have the confidence to do any teaching during her PhD. Antonia perceived that her lack of fluent English compromised the progress she was able to make with her research, meaning that she would be likely to take longer to successfully complete her studies.

The opportunity to work with her particular supervisor was one of the main reasons that Antonia applied to do her doctorate at Modern University, as he had a strong international reputation within her field. However, initially she struggled with the cultural differences in supervision between the UK and her home country. She had a closer and more personal relationship with supervisors in the past, whereas in the UK her supervisory relationship was more distant and professional. Antonia found this challenging as she received less support from her supervisor than she had anticipated. Further, she was expected to take on additional responsibilities in the lab, such as supervising undergraduate students, because her supervisor was so busy. Whilst she felt this was good experience, she recognised that this took a lot of time and that this had a negative impact on her own research.

During her PhD, Antonia found it difficult to access support when she experienced difficulties with her PhD. Whilst she had a good working relationship with other doctoral students in her lab, she felt this was superficial as they did not discuss any of the problems they encountered during the PhD. Antonia did not have many friends in the UK, and travelled back to her home country to see her partner, friends and family as often as she could. The impact of living away from her partner, family and friends was significant, and Antonia was keen to return to her home country after finishing her PhD.

Whilst Antonia's academic aspirations remained, she re-prioritised her future goals after her experiences of studying away from home, and by her second year placed more importance on her personal life than her career goals. She perceived that securing an academic role in her home country would be difficult, as there are fewer opportunities there than in the UK. She was concerned about job prospects and the potential of struggling financially; though these concerns about the future and her academic career were secondary to her desire to return to her home country.

## Pepper

Pepper was in her early 20s when she began her doctorate in Engineering at Redbrick University. Before this, she studied for her undergraduate and integrated master's degree at another institution, which had been challenging as she had experienced discriminatory attitudes from her male peers. She had dealt with this by working very hard to prove herself and obtain superior results than them. Pepper was in a relationship, with no caring responsibilities. She had not planned to do a PhD, and had received job offers at the end of her previous degrees, including one from a high-profile international company. However, she was motivated to do a PhD because she enjoyed problem-solving and working independently. When she began her PhD, Pepper was unsure of what she wanted to do in her career, and hoped that doing a PhD which had direct links with partners in the engineering industry would help her to get a job in the future.

Pepper's experience of the PhD was difficult. She found the transition to doctoral study challenging, as many of her peers were much older than her, or had existing industrial experience. She felt that her supervisors and other academics were not sympathetic to her comparative lack of experience, and perceived that they had unrealistic expectations of her abilities given that she had only just finished her master's degree. Pepper experienced significant imposter syndrome, and often questioned her

## 2 Theorising Gender and Belonging in the (Early Career) Academy

abilities. She also struggled with anxiety, which she had experienced during her undergraduate degree, but which was compounded by the stresses of doctoral study. Whilst she had not previously disclosed this to her supervisor, she found it necessary to share this with him when she was unable to prepare the paperwork for her confirmation,[1] a year into her studies.

During her PhD, Pepper struggled to maintain a healthy work-life balance and felt that the culture of her department encouraged doctoral students to work long days and on weekends. The pressures of working in this way were not something that her peers discussed, and she perceived that there was a culture of not acknowledging difficulties and issues amongst the doctoral student community, which made it harder to ask for help. The difficulties Pepper faced in managing her workload were compounded by the expectation that she and other PhD students would supervise other students, but she felt unable to refuse. Pepper struggled with her supervisor's style of supervision, which focused on academic advice rather than pastoral support, as this was very different to the academic support she had previously had. She had also expected more autonomy as a doctoral student, and felt that due to her supervisor's frequent input into her research, she was not able to take ownership of her work. Her supervisor expected her to engage in writing for publication and to present at conferences, which she found stressful. Pepper also experienced conflict between the expectations of her academic and industry supervisors, which was frustrating and had a negative impact on her progress.

Throughout her studies, Pepper had ongoing thoughts about leaving her doctorate, and viewed academia as a stressful and difficult environment. She felt that academics were often more concerned with self-promotion than making a positive impact, which conflicted with her own values. However, Pepper found it difficult to make the decision to leave her doctorate as she had put a considerable amount of time and effort into her research, and her parents wanted her to continue. By her

---

[1] An institutional process which UK doctoral students must undertake, usually within the first year of their full-time degree. Also sometimes referred to as an upgrade, this process requires students to present on the progress of their research, while examiners judge whether or not the candidate's work is of a doctoral level.

second year, Pepper had taken a formal leave of absence, and sought advice which helped her consider her career prospects and she saw the advantages of working in sectors outside of academia. Successfully completing a placement at the company where her industrial supervisor worked enabled her to see the benefits of working in this sector, where she perceived fewer hierarchies, less pressure and better remuneration and working conditions than in academia. Pepper eventually decided to leave her doctorate in November 2016, after the end of her second year.

# 3

# Contesting Power Structures: Encountering Gatekeepers to Belonging in STEM

This chapter draws attention to how participants in STEM disciplines encountered barriers to belonging to their academic communities during the doctorate. These barriers were largely manifested in the context of their relationship with their supervisor. Supervisory relationships in STEM subjects are often characterised by rigid status distinctions, with a clear hierarchical structure between doctoral students and technicians and postdocs and more senior scientists in the research group (Parry, 2007). Doctoral supervisors in STEM disciplines, who are named principal investigators (PIs) of labs or research groups, often have a different supervisory dynamic to the more individualised personal relationships present in the humanities, social sciences and some health and related sciences (Delamont et al., 2000). All supervisors play a crucial role in supporting the professional development of their supervisees, acting as gatekeepers into the disciplinary community (Parry, 2007) and often facilitating post-PhD career opportunities (see Denicolo & Becker, 2008; Dever et al., 2008; Wisker, 2007). Yet in STEM subjects, this dynamic is intensified due to the high level of competition for postdoctoral positions, and the tendency of research group leaders to recruit individuals already known to them to postdoctoral roles (see Coulthard-Graf, 2020; Herschberg et al., 2018). Clearly, being able to maintain a positive relationship with one's PI has significant implications for who is able to succeed in academic STEM.

A wealth of international literature on gender and science has highlighted the differential rates of progression between men and women in these traditionally male-dominated disciplines, often describing the lack of women scientists at senior career stages through the metaphor of the 'leaky pipeline' (see Allen & Castleman, 2001; Baringa, 1993; Blickenstaff, 2005; Hatchell & Aveling, 2008; Soe & Yakura, 2008). Researchers have argued that the masculine traditions of scientific disciplines have produced gendered academic cultures which can marginalise women (Becher & Trowler, 2001; Benschop & Brouns, 2003; Hall & Sandler, 1982; Kulis et al., 2002; Rosser, 2004). In the UK, despite initiatives such as Athena SWAN designed to address issues of gender inequality in STEM and increase the representation of women in these subjects, women continue to leave academic science at a significantly higher rate than men, and particularly after the completion of the doctorate (see Fisher et al., 2019; Royal Society of Chemistry, 2008, 2018; Wellcome Trust, 2013).

Factors contributing to women's ongoing under-representation in STEM fields have been found to be persistent gender discrimination within scientific research cultures, including harassment and bullying (Blair-Loy et al., 2017; De Welde & Laursen, 2011; Howe-Walsh & Turnbull, 2016), unequal access to guidance and support for women doctoral students compared with male peers (Etzkowitz et al., 2000; Etzkowitz & Gupta, 2006; Royal Society of Chemistry, 2018) and with the perceived incompatibility of a career in academic science with family life (Royal Society of Chemistry, 2018; Ward & Wolf-Wendel, 2012). Expectations of geographical mobility, long working hours and lack of part-time and flexible working options (Weisgram & Diekman, 2017; Wellcome Trust, 2013), along with the high level of competition for jobs and external research funding (Royal Society of Chemistry, 2018), a lack of transparency in recruitment and progression processes (Herschberg et al., 2018) and a lack of female role models (Institute of Physics, 2015), have been identified as additional factors which contribute to gendered patterns of progression in academic STEM.

In this chapter, I explore how various experiences during the doctorate impacted womens' sense of belonging to their academic community and their ability to envisage themselves belonging in the future as academic scientists. I highlight how individuals negotiated gendered disciplinary cultures, the competitive culture of academic STEM as well as disparity between their understanding and their PIs' conceptions of the role of PhD students. These experience challenged individuals' sense of belonging and their ability to construct a viable academic identity. Drawing on participants' experiences, I highlight the strategies that some individuals employed to negotiate the power dynamics implicit in their supervisory relationship and develop a sense of belonging to their academic communities. These included establishing strong peer groups, as well as actively resisting neoliberalised cultural expectations, such as the pressure to work outside normal working hours and to publish work during their doctorate. Yet not all were able to demonstrate this same agency, as I will discuss.

## Studying for a Doctorate in STEM

Doctoral research in STEM subjects is often characterised as an individual contribution to a wider, collective research endeavour through a process of scientific experimentation (Delamont et al., 2000; Parry, 2007). Doctoral students in these disciplines often have less autonomy than their counterparts in the humanities and social science. Research topics are largely determined by individual PI's ongoing research, linked to external research grants, thus constituting a singular component of a wider effort undertaken by the research group. Rather than providing regular practical guidance, PIs largely work at a more strategic level, steering the direction of the research group and securing grants. Instead, the role of practical, day-to-day doctoral supervision is largely taken on by postdoctoral scientists, who may prove to be role models for doctoral students aspiring to a career in academic science (Delamont et al., 1997). In this way, each member of the group is expected to contribute to the wider learning of other members of the research group, enabling the collective research efforts to be progressed. This model, which is very different to the more individualistic endeavours of those in the humanities and social sciences, has been described as facilitating 'pedagogic continuity' (Delamont et al., 1997) within the discipline by ensuring that scientific techniques and skills are passed on to the next generation of scientists. However, there is potential for the power dynamics inherent within a scientific research group to result in the manipulation, marginalisation or even exploitation of those at the lower end of the hierarchy (Becher, 1994; Phillips & Pugh, 2015), particularly for individuals who belong to historically under-represented groups.

Researchers have drawn attention to how doctoral students in STEM subjects become integrated, or encultured, into their disciplinary communities through meaningful contributions to and participation within the research group or lab (Becher et al., 1994; Delamont et al., 1997; Etzkowitz et al., 2000). Indeed, the research group acts as a social mechanism for the enculturation of new scientists (Delamont et al., 2000), offering doctoral students the opportunity to contribute to a research team and providing the potential to reduce the isolation often experienced by doctoral students in the humanities and social sciences. However, as Walsh (2010) highlights, individuals working in scientific research groups are not necessarily immune from isolation, particularly if they are doctoral students from non-UK countries. Further, whilst the laboratory may constitute 'an arena for enculturation' (Delamont et al., 2000, p. 12), it is also a distinctive site in which particular hierarchies and power relations must be navigated (Knorr-Cetina, 1995).

For women studying for a doctorate in STEM subjects, attempts to belong within their academic communities could be impeded by the gendered nature of the academic cultures they encountered within their discipline, department and research group. Academic disciplines reflect traditional gender roles in wider society and as such are not 'culturally neutral' (Becher & Trowler, 2001, p. 55). Indeed, feminist researchers have drawn attention to the inherently masculine nature of scientific cultures (see Benschop & Brouns, 2003; Harding, 1986; Knights & Richards, 2003), and 'in these contexts, masculinity and power are intertwined in such a way that men represent the standard: they naturally occupy the norm against which women's performance is measured' (Van Den Brink & Stobbe, 2009, p. 454). Thus, the attitudes, behaviours and values embedded within STEM disciplines pose barriers for women working in traditionally male-dominated subject areas, positioning them as 'other'. This creates a challenging environment within which women doctoral students attempt to establish a sense of belonging. Indeed, studies have highlighted that an inability to meaningfully participate in the disciplinary community can contribute to doctoral student attrition (see

Castelló et al., 2017; Pyhältö & Keskinen, 2012), and research in the US indicates how women in STEM are more likely to leave their PhD programme than men (see Lott et al., 2009).

Even for those who complete the PhD, evidence suggests that there are gendered patterns of progression in academic science, with the doctorate being a crucial stage of attrition. Research commissioned by leading scientific bodies in the UK over the last two decades highlights how women in these disciplines become less likely to intend to pursue academic careers as they progress through the doctorate (Institute of Physics, 2015; Royal Society of Chemistry, 2008, 2018; Wellcome Trust, 2013). Other, qualitative studies have highlighted some of the factors which contribute to this trend. In a study in Australia, Hatchell and Aveling (2008) observed how being subjected to overt gender discrimination and harassment during their PhD led to 'gendered disappearing acts' by women students, who left academic science after their doctorate because of these experiences. Further, in their study of women doctoral students in STEM fields in the US, de Welde and Laursen (2011) showed how women faced sexism and sexual harassment during their studies, contributing to feelings of not belonging and influencing individuals' decisions to leave STEM fields. Gender discrimination has been found to persist within academic research cultures; women are more likely than men to both experience and witness gender-based bullying and harassment (Nature, 2019; Wellcome Trust, 2020). It is evident that studying for a doctorate as a woman in STEM is not a straightforward experience. The impact of studying in this environment on individuals' ability to feel a sense of belonging within academic STEM is explored in this chapter, specifically in relation to participants' experiences during the doctorate.

## Gendered Disciplines: Perceptions of Women Engineers

There are significant variations in women's participation across scientific disciplines, with more women than men in the UK studying for doctorates in biological sciences, but participation remaining low in areas such as computer science and engineering (see Advance HE, 2021). Yet research has highlighted how as more women enter some STEM fields, such as biology, these fields become culturally perceived as lower status (Cheryan et al., 2017; Fox, 2006; McIlwee & Robinson, 1992). Further, the sub-disciplines where women remain under-represented, such as engineering and computer science, are often the more lucrative STEM fields (see Corbett & Hill, 2015) and thus perceived as higher prestige (Stout et al., 2016).

The way in which participants perceived themselves as women in STEM differed from individual to individual. While for Jane and Harriet their awareness of the gendered nature of academic science careers developed during the doctorate, Pepper, an engineering PhD student at Redbrick University, was already accustomed to feeling 'other' within her discipline. This is perhaps due to the more overt under-representation of women in engineering, compared with biological sciences. Whilst women are under-represented in all STEM doctoral programmes, making up around 45% of doctoral students in STEM subjects, just 26% of engineering doctoral students are women (Advance HE, 2021). Pepper continues to experience alienation during her PhD due to gender discrimination and gendered expectations.

Pepper described encountering sexism during her first degree: *"at undergrad, there was always like…oh women in engineering, get back in the kitchen that kind of stuff"* (Interview 1). These experiences are common amongst women who study male-dominated disciplines, with those pursuing doctoral degrees in engineering being likely to have encountered sexism and discrimination throughout their previous studies (Lazarus et al., 2000). Pepper's response to this was to ensure that she performed to a very high academic standard: *"the way that I've always handled it is just prove myself, just to be very good at what I'm doing…my coursework grades are always better than them"*. Pepper's description of her experience of undergraduate study indicates how she has become accustomed to being positioned as an outsider within her discipline, and the way in which she has attempted to establish a sense of belonging. Her experiences speak back to research which highlights how women in scientific disciplines often have to outperform their male counterparts in order to be accepted as competent members of the group (see Hughes et al., 2017; Van Den Brink & Stobbe, 2009).

Pepper's experiences draw attention to the ways in which women in male-dominated disciplines are often highly visible; something which can reinforce their status as outsiders. In their research based at a Dutch university, van den Brink and Stobbe (2009) observed how women students strived to assimilate, aiming to be seen as 'one of the boys' and seeking to avoid any suggestions of gender difference in experiences. Yet they were simultaneously required to make themselves visible in order to prove themselves as valid members of their disciplinary community, achieving superior results and taking less time to complete their degree than the men on the same course. Despite this, they were still viewed by academics as less well-suited to a career in academic science than their male peers. Similarly, Pepper finds that despite having proved herself with excellent results during her undergraduate, she continues to be marked as different, and cannot but be made visible. She described the reaction of others when she discusses her doctoral research: *"when I tell people what I'm doing…the reaction…is always like wow…oh my god, you're doing a PhD in…Engineering and you're a woman"*. These experiences inhibit Pepper's ability to feel a sense of belonging to her academic community; as a woman studying a doctorate in her discipline, she continues to be positioned by others as 'out of place' (May, 2013, p. 93).

This increased visibility as a woman doctoral student in a male-dominated discipline can have a negative impact on individuals' well-being. Research highlights that women in subject areas where the participation of women is particularly low, such as engineering and physics, may experience isolation and marginalisation (De Welde & Laursen, 2011; Nerad & Cerny, 1999; Rosser, 2004). Further, women students in male-dominated disciplines are likely to find it difficult to ask for help due to feelings of inadequacy (see Lazarus et al., 2000), which may manifest themselves in imposter syndrome (see Chakraverty, 2019; Handforth, 2022). This is borne out in Pepper's experiences during her doctorate. She described how she feels unable to admit to struggling during the first year of her PhD, as her peers seem not to be experiencing difficulties:

It just feels like oh god everyone else seems to be doing ok, why am I finding this so hard? This shouldn't be so hard. So even though there are a few first years that I know, it's still difficult to voice my frustration, or that I'm struggling with it. (Interview 1)

Pepper's lack of ease within her immediate social context and her inability to connect with her peers indicate her struggle to feel a sense of belonging. Further, her visibility as a woman within her subject area, combined with her liminal status as a doctoral student, compounds her feelings of self-doubt and prevents her from feeling able to seek help. Her perception that "*everyone else seems to be doing ok*" leads her to view herself as inadequate, and she fears that others will do the same, which, in turn, produces significant anxiety:

I'm always just worried that…I feel so stupid, or that people think I'm not doing enough, or that…people think that it won't be good, it's just always just that very personal worry that, am I actually cut out to do this, or is it a waste of time? (Interview 1)

Similarly, Antonia—an international PhD student in engineering at Modern University—had a distant and superficial relationship with her peers: "*it's a good relation but it's not a close relation. I mean, you can talk about the weather here always*" (Interview 1). She struggled initially with the lack of peer support, and found that there was a culture of silence in her research group which she ascribed to UK culture:

In the first year it was difficult because I always tried to find someone to talk about my problems but I think this is completely different from [home country]…they are very polite but they don't talk about personal issues…they try to look like everything is ok…This is the British way. (Interview 2)

Antonia's experience highlights how even when doctoral students are working as members of established research groups, some may still feel unsupported and marginalised, particularly if they are from other countries (see Walsh, 2010). Both Pepper and Antonia's experiences illuminate how for women doctoral students in strongly male-dominated subjects, disciplinary cultures may inhibit their ability to connect with others and to feel at ease within their immediate community, which has a negative impact on their well-being—and thus their ability to feel a sense of belonging.

Beyond interactions with her peers, Pepper perceived a wider culture of hostility from academics in her discipline, reflecting what has been termed the 'chilly climate' for women in science (see Britton, 2017; Brooks, 2001; Soe & Yakura, 2008). When presenting her work at a conference for doctoral students to showcase their research, she encountered male academics who were highly critical of her work, and whose behaviour she perceived as combative rather than supportive:

> He was quite you know, intense and…at the end as everybody starts leaving he sits there and he says do you know what I'm going to be blunt with you, I just think ok I know exactly what's going to happen, and he just rattles off you know I don't think it's good, I think this, I think that, blah, blah you know and I got quite, actually I dealt with it quite well because I got quite annoyed, I got quite heated with him…I didn't think in any situation like that I would be able to back myself up but I was just like I've already answered all your questions, I've already said this, the whole point of the presentation is to prove its validity, why are you attacking me now? (Interview 2)

Pepper was frustrated that the feedback she received on her work at an event designed for doctoral students was not constructive but rather felt like a personal attack by a male academic. However, in reflecting on the situation, she viewed this type of criticism as common within her experience of the STEM academic environment: *"there are people that just sort of, some will kind of tear you down rather than build you up…I've handled it fairly well I think but it's, it can be quite difficult to deal with sometimes"* (Interview 2). Pepper perceived this attitude as symptomatic of the culture both of her discipline and of academia more generally: *"it seems to be engineering PhD level or academia, that just seems to be the way it is"* (Interview 2). Thus, Pepper's attempts to belong to her disciplinary community are challenged by the response of those who hold powerful positions within her discipline. These experiences lead her to resolve to leave the academic STEM environment after her PhD:

As soon as I'm done with this I'm, I'm out like, definitely…all the pressure and everything that you do…even then to like sometimes still get put down…I really don't want that. I want to be challenged but I don't want to be put down you know. (Interview 2)

Pepper's account of her experiences highlights the long-term impact of experiencing marginalisation, from her undergraduate degree through to her doctorate. It is perhaps not surprising, therefore, that she becomes discouraged from pursuing a career within academic STEM. Whilst research indicates how women in STEM subjects are less likely than their male counterparts to progress into academic careers after the PhD (Institute of Physics, 2015; Nature, 2019; Royal Society, 2014a; Royal Society of Chemistry, 2008, 2018; Wellcome Trust, 2013), in Pepper's case she decided to leave the academic environment during the doctorate due to her negative experiences of the academic culture, leaving her PhD in November 2016 after 2 years of study.

## Being Positioned as 'Other': Gendered Academic Cultures and Belonging

Disciplinary cultures are generated and perpetuated by the actions of those who wield power and influence within them, and the ability of newcomers to feel a sense of belonging is predicated on the willingness of senior academics to recognise them as valid members of the community (Emmioglu et al., 2017; Parry, 2007; Teeuwsen et al., 2014). Yet participants encountered gendered expectations from other academics—including their supervisors—of both their scientific abilities and their career plans, which affected their ability to develop this sense of belonging.

It was evident that these experiences during the doctorate affected how able participants were to imagine themselves as future academics. Gendered academic cultures were encountered both at macro and micro levels; as with Pepper, individuals recognised that they were often in the minority in their discipline, which, in turn, made them highly visible within their department. Participants also experienced lad culture on a day-to-day basis, within their research group and in their labs and immediate workspaces. This had implications for individuals' sense of belonging, in terms of feeling marginalised and feeling able to seek support. Further, witnessing the career experiences of women scientists was often disillusioning, as women doctoral students learned about the gendered barriers that they could face, such as discrimination and difficulties in balancing an academic career with family life. The impact of this on participants' immediate well-being, as well as their ability to develop viable academic identities, is explored here.

For Jane, a PhD student in Conservation at Redbrick University, her awareness of gender as a factor which could affect her future career shifted during the course of her doctorate. Very early on in the first year of her PhD, she attended an event on implicit bias and women in science. Jane asked a question as to what women could do to negotiate implicit bias, but was frustrated at the advice she received, which included attempting to conceal on a CV any career breaks:

> She said…how women are really affected is when it implies that they are a mother on their CV…that really massively affects their career progression so she said if you can…make your CV…look more masculine almost, you know and don't put hobbies down, and things like that then you are kind of hiding away, if you are a mother, you are kind of hiding it away and trying to look more…masculine which is kind of…tough…I could see where she was coming from that it was a pragmatic solution, but also it was a bit like shit…if we're at the stage where we are having to hide the fact that we're women that is not very good. (Interview 1)

The advice Jane received was from the chair of her department's Athena SWAN committee, who had organised the event. This indicates the persistence and pervasiveness of gender discrimination within academic science; despite the purpose of the Athena SWAN scheme being to address structural gender inequalities, the advice given to younger generations of women scientists by a senior woman academic was that they should attempt to conceal their gender on future job applications, and specifically their potential role as mothers. This experience, early on in her doctoral studies, challenges Jane's ability to feel a sense of belonging within her academic community; she learns that if she pursues a career in academic science, she would likely be discriminated against based on her gender and her potential status as a mother. From this encounter Jane comes to understand that successful academic identities are those which are packaged and presented to future employers as male, and which conform to the model of the ideal academic who has no external caring responsibilities (Lynch, 2010).

The language Jane used to describe her feelings about being advised to make her CV appear more "*masculine*"—that it was "*tough*" and "*a bit like shit*"—indicates her frustration at encountering this attitude. Viewing identity as informed by 'the values we share or wish to share with others' (Weeks, 1990, p. 88), and understanding doctoral students' academic identity development as formed in relation to the values of the community to which they are attempting to belong (Henkel, 2004), it appears that Jane is reluctant to embrace this approach to career development, as it is underpinned by values which she finds problematic.

Attending this event was a critical incident within Jane's academic identity construction, bringing the realisation that women in academic science are routinely discriminated against and that, as such, she may be disadvantaged in pursuing this career. It was also an experience which highlighted Jane's other-ness within her academic community, challenging her ability to establish a sense of belonging as a woman in science. She acknowledges that previously she had had little knowledge of the gendered nature of academic careers; "*up until then I had just kind of assumed that if you were good, you were good and it didn't matter what gender you were. So I thought, I am alright, I should do alright*" (Interview 1). This awareness of potential future discrimination can have a considerable impact on individuals' perceptions of their current and future status within the academy. In their research with women and minority ethnic doctoral students in STEM fields in the US, Fisher et al. (2019) highlight how experiences which reinforced their under-representation could challenge individuals' ability to feel accepted and also lead them to expect future discrimination. This had a negative impact on individuals' well-being during their studies, as well as their attainment, retention and career aspirations.

For Jane, the realisation that gender discrimination may be a factor in developing a career in academic science, is frustrating, not least because

### 3 Contesting Power Structures: Encountering Gatekeepers...

she felt that she should have done enough to be successful by this stage. She outlined how she had already overcome significant barriers to academic success, such as failing the 11 plus exam,[1] and attending a challenging local comprehensive secondary school, but managing to secure a place at an elite UK university:

> I feel like I've jumped through quite a lot of…hurdles to get to where I am already, so I was kind of hoping I suppose that by now I'd secured my position if you know what I mean, and proved myself…so it is kind of annoying I suppose. (Interview 1)

These experiences have made Jane determined to succeed. Interestingly, though she recognised that gender discrimination has been a barrier for other women in academia, in our first interview, 6 months into her PhD, Jane questioned whether or not she would struggle in the face of similar obstacles in the future:

> There is a small part of me that also…likes the challenge. I don't know I've always kind of…felt a little bit, I'm quite stubborn, so if somebody says I can't do something then I'm like, damn you, I will. So, that is another argument for being an academic which is what I have always wanted to do and just because…lots of other women have not managed it doesn't mean that I can't. So…I guess it hasn't put me off entirely it just made me kind of go oh…ok. Take a step back and have a think about it. (Interview 1)

This attitude, also expressed by participants in other disciplines (see Chaps. 4 and 5), is significant in that though she recognised the possibility for future discrimination, Jane's response was to play down the potential impact of this on her own future career trajectory. Thus, despite her increased awareness of the gendered barriers to academic career progression, initially this did not necessarily alter Jane's ambition of becoming an academic. Learning about the discrimination that other women have faced does not dissuade Jane from her academic aspirations, although she considers that it does cause her to reflect further upon them. This appears

---

[1] An exam taken in some UK primary schools to assess whether 11-year-old pupils should attend a secondary grammar school or comprehensive secondary school.

a positive finding, especially in the context of research which highlights how women doctoral students, more than their male counterparts, are more likely to shift their aspirations away from academic careers during the doctorate (Institute of Physics, 2015; Royal Society of Chemistry, 2008, 2018; Wellcome Trust, 2013).

Indeed, Jane's assertion that she may be able to succeed where other women have not, due to having overcome previous structural barriers, may be viewed as a strategy for establishing a sense of belonging in both the short and long terms, enabling her to construct a viable academic identity. Yet this assertion also indicates that Jane has at some level already internalised neoliberal values, viewing herself as exceptionally able to successfully play the academic game (Hancock, 2019; Lucas, 2006). This echoes Archer's (2008) finding that early career academics, having been inculcated into the neoliberalised academic environment, drew on discourses of individual productivity, performance and success in relation to their career development, using the language of neoliberalism within their identity construction. However, in doing so, Jane minimises the experiences of other women scientists who have not progressed into academic roles—*"just because…lots of other women have not managed it doesn't mean that I can't"*. This is problematic, in that it presents the issue of women's' under-representation in senior roles as caused by individual women and their inherent ability to succeed, rather than by structural inequalities which make academic career progression more difficult for women scientists (see Allen & Castleman, 2001; Soe & Yakura, 2008). Jane's assertion here also echoes research which highlights how women in STEM may downplay encounters with sexism as an unconscious strategy to enable them to maintain their career goals within a male-dominated environment (see Hughes et al., 2017).

Jane's awareness of the role of gender in academic career progression was further developed through interactions with one of her supervisors, Ian, and his wife Monica, who was beginning her academic career in the same field. Through observing their relationship and comparing their career trajectories, Jane became aware of how gendered expectations may shape individuals' ability to be successful in applying for academic roles:

Ian was saying that on average men will put themselves forward for things that they think maybe they're not entirely qualified for, and then just have the confidence and the…charisma to sell it and make themselves appear better than they perhaps are, and get that job whereas the women can be a little bit more reserved, and maybe wouldn't even apply for things that they weren't 100% sure they could do…I feel like Monica is…the epitome of that, where she is clearly very good…but she's very self-doubting and she doesn't push herself forward. (Interview 1)

Through these encounters with her supervisor and his wife, Jane learns that a successful academic scientist is characterised as confident and charismatic, and that self-belief rather than qualifications is likely to be rewarded. Her reflections echo literature which highlights how male academics expect career success more than women (Baker, 2012; Gasser & Shaffer, 2014), and speak back to literature which argues that a major obstacle to women's career advancement across employment sectors is their lack of confidence and self-promotion (Chesterman et al., 2005; Doherty & Manfredi, 2006; Sandberg, 2013). However, once again this view draws on a deficit model of individuals, citing an inherent lack of confidence as the reason for women scientists being less successful than men, rather than drawing attention to the structural factors within the system which reward certain types of behaviours over others. Researchers have critiqued 'the confidence culture rhetoric that lays the blame for the scarcity of women in the upper hierarchies firmly on the shoulders of the individual' (Crabtree & Shiel, 2019, p. 3), which may further marginalise women, who are already often othered within academic STEM.

Based on this observational learning, Jane perceives that she may need to alter her values and behaviour in order to become a successful academic scientist. Thus, in imagining her future career, she constructs an academic identity on the basis of her understanding that she may be required to behave in what she perceives as a more masculine way, in order to succeed: "*[it] makes me…feel like I have to act more…confidently and sell myself more than I perhaps would…in order to get the…the job that I want because…men do it*" (Interview 1). It is clear that once again, at this early stage in her doctorate, Jane envisages herself engaging in performative, neoliberalised behaviours in order to achieve academic career success and overcome gender discrimination. This understanding reflects literature which highlights that adopting masculine behaviours is a common strategy amongst women in male-dominated environments (De Welde & Laursen, 2011; Van Den Brink & Stobbe, 2009), and one which is often successful in terms of individual career progression (Blackmore, 2002).

Thus, as a strategy to envisage herself belonging within her academic community in the long term, Jane embraces neoliberalised values in the hope that they will help her to succeed:

> I'm going to try and walk the fine line between…being true to myself but perhaps pushing myself a little bit more…to sell myself a little bit more…I suppose in a way act a little bit more like a man, but not too much more. Because I, I do feel like…if I'm good enough I'm good enough, and that should be evident…at the same time I don't want to cut, cut off my nose to spite my face, so I guess I will end up doing it a little bit, but I will try not to do it too much, if you see what I mean. (Interview 1)

Yet, even at this early stage of her doctorate, Jane was only willing to play the academic 'game' to a certain extent. She constructed an academic identity within certain parameters and was not willing to fully embrace an identity which would require her to compromise her values completely (Weeks, 1990), instead elaborating her intention to progress her career whilst maintaining her sense of self. It is clear, though, that envisioning a future in which she is able to belong within her academic community requires a considerable amount of identity work and flexibility in self-presentation (see Archer, 2008; Davies & Petersen, 2005).

A further challenge to women doctoral students' ability to feel a sense of belonging within their academic communities was the discrimination they envisaged facing as women scientists with children. Though she had no immediate plans to start a family, even in the first year of her doctorate Jane expressed concern that taking career breaks to have children would disadvantage her promotion prospects—a fear which has a solid grounding in reality (see Correll et al., 2007; Jackson, 2017; Mason et al., 2013):

> That would be really bad because I would have these big gaps in my CV…and I wouldn't have published as much, and even though I would

have a really good excuse that probably wouldn't...help me very much when I was applying for a lectureship position...if I was up against a man, who hadn't had or another woman who hadn't had that gap. (Interview 1)

Again, witnessing the experiences of women in this position provided valuable learning opportunities for participants, who understood the difficulties that they faced. Harriet, a PhD student in Biology at Redbrick University, echoed Jane's concerns about an academic career being potentially incompatible with having a family. Though Harriet began her PhD with aspirations of pursuing a postdoctoral research role afterwards, working alongside Margaret, the only woman postdoc in her lab who recently returned from maternity leave, gave her insight into how the culture of academic science is discriminatory to women, and particularly mothers. Harriet perceived that the opportunity to work flexibly in labs is rare, viewing Margaret's part-time contract as "*a struggle in itself*" (Interview 1) to obtain, echoing research highlighting how the lack of part-time opportunities acts as a barrier for women in science (Wellcome Trust, 2013). Harriet acknowledged that Margaret's position as part-time postdoc was not a comfortable one, and felt that others in the lab "*took a while to warm up to her*" (Interview 1) due to discriminatory attitudes: "*I think instantly everyone in their mind was just like oh she's been out of the lab for this many years, having her babies...so, she definitely had to work harder, I would say*" (Interview 1). Even in the first year of her PhD, Harriet was aware of how men and women academics are perceived differently as parents: "*I think for a woman...people doubt you a lot more after you've had kids, whereas I think it's the opposite for men*" (Interview 1).

These perceptions echo research which has found that whilst having a family negatively affects women's career progression, constituting what has been termed a 'motherhood penalty' (Correll et al., 2007), it does not inhibit men's careers (Mason et al., 2013). Indeed, there is evidence to suggest that being a parent actually benefits a male academic's career. Research in the US highlights how parenthood can enhance how men are perceived on job applications; whilst fatherhood is seen as indicative of positive interpersonal qualities, the same does not hold true for female applicants with children (Benard & Correll, 2010). Indeed, a White Paper on the position of women in science in Spain found that whilst mothers were perceived as less competent and committed than women without children, employers actually favoured fathers in applications for professorial promotion (Sánchez de Madariaga et al., 2011). It has also been suggested that male academics use 'dad chat' to bond with one another at conferences, constituting a further perpetuation of male networks (Jackson, 2017). This is especially significant given the significant positive impact of informal professional networks for academic career development (see Xu & Martin, 2011), and the persistence of 'boy's clubs' in STEM disciplines which marginalise women academics (see Barnard et al., 2010; De Welde & Laursen, 2011; Hughes et al., 2017).

Harriet's view of academia as discriminatory towards mothers shaped her ability to envisage herself as belonging in academic science in the future. While she was able to imagine encountering the same challenges that Margaret faced, Harriet was not able to imagine resolving them: "*it's like…how do you be a good mum and…do all your research?*" (Interview 1). Harriet's inability to answer the question that she poses reflects the difficulty she has in constructing an identity in which she can successfully reconcile these roles. She acknowledged that "*some days I just get really put off by it, and like, it's not worth doing*" (Interview 1). Harriet's perceptions reflect research which highlights that women are more likely to be discouraged from an academic career than men, because they perceive academia as not family-friendly (Mason et al., 2013; Mason & Goulden, 2004; Royal Society of Chemistry, 2008; Wellcome Trust, 2013). Harriet connects her own concerns about the future with the lack of women who pursue this career, considering that her own worries are likely to be what prevents other women from continuing in academic science:

> I'm not even thinking about having a family now, like, at all, but in the back of your mind you're like oh, what if I get to the stage where I want to and I can't, because my job…I think that's what like, deters women from doing it past the post-doc level. (Interview 1)

Harriet and Jane's concerns about pursuing an academic career due to their perception that it is difficult to balance with motherhood resonates with literature which highlights this as a significant factor in the lack of women progressing in academic science (Institute of Physics, 2015; Royal

Society of Chemistry, 2008, 2018; Wellcome Trust, 2013). If there is a real desire for increased diversity in STEM, there is considerable work to do to enable women doctoral students to envisage these two future identities of academic and mother not as mutually exclusive, but as compatible, and even potentially desirable.

Beyond their struggles to envisage belonging within their academic communities in the future, women doctoral students experienced marginalisation during their studies by encountering gendered expectations of their abilities. Despite research which indicates how women in STEM subjects often try to minimise the impact of gender in reporting their experiences (see Hughes et al., 2017; Van Den Brink & Stobbe, 2009), in this study participants reflected on day-to-day encounters in which they perceived gender to have played a part. These related to how they were treated by colleagues in their research group, and by their supervisors. This is significant, as research highlights how supervisors and other academics may facilitate doctoral students' belonging (Denicolo & Becker, 2008; Vekkaila et al., 2012; Wisker, 2007) and how the student-supervisor relationship can enable students to imagine themselves in similar roles and identify as future members of the academic community (Manathunga, 2014; Rossiter, 2004). Indeed, supervisors act as gatekeepers into the disciplinary community (Parry, 2007), with a key part of their role being to prepare and support their doctoral students to pursue a range of possible careers, including for those who hope to progress into academic careers (Vitae, 2019).

Yet whilst supervisors and other academics can act as role models, their behaviour and actions may also inhibit women doctoral students' ability to feel a sense of belonging within their academic community. Research indicates how women doctoral students are less likely than their male peers to be encouraged to engage in additional academic career-related activities such as publishing and presenting work during their doctorate (see Asmar, 1999; Curtin et al., 2016; Dever et al., 2008; Giles et al., 2009). This has implications for individuals' career trajectories, and also appears to be a trend replicated in later career stages; in the UK, the Equality Challenge Unit's (2017) research with STEM academics showed how women were less likely than men to receive training relating to grant applications skills and financial management—skills necessary for obtaining more senior positions.

For Harriet, there are a number of instances in which she is treated differently to her male peers by her supervisor, which challenge her ability to feel a sense of belonging within her immediate academic community. In her first year, Harriet reported how Sam, a male student a year ahead of her, is actively encouraged by their PI to undertake additional activities in the lab to expand his skills and experience: *"John would come over and be like oh Sam we're having a meeting to talk about what you're doing and stuff…they'd just have a one-on-one sort of thing"* (Interview 1). Yet Harriet felt that she would be unlikely to receive the same individual attention, echoing findings of research conducted by the Institute of Physics (2015) which found that women doctoral students' supervisory relationships tended to be less positive than those of their male peers. However, though Harriet perceived that she was treated differently to Sam, she was initially reluctant to attribute this to gender, considering that it may instead relate to his advanced stage in the PhD:

> It could be nothing to do with like a gender thing, but I do feel like it's a…maybe they don't think that you know, I can handle being pressured to do things…which is probably just because I'm a first year, but they also don't, you know, John probably wouldn't call me over just for a meeting to talk about what I'm doing. (Interview 1)

Despite considering that their different treatment might be a result of Sam being a year ahead of her, Harriet still felt that gender shaped her experience: *"it feels like sometimes that I'm not…being as pushed or being as like…treated you know the same as they would Sam like last year"* (Interview 1). Harriet perceived that the expectations of her and Sam were not equal, and that she was seen as not able to *"handle being pressured"* in the same way as him.

Understanding belonging as affective, involving connections with others and requiring individuals to feel accepted and valued by other, more powerful members of the community, it is clear that Harriet does not feel recognised as a legitimate member of her departmental community. Indeed, her comments indicate that there are a number of instances which reinforce her marginalisation, such as the ad-hoc meetings that her PI has with her male peer to discuss his progress. Whilst researchers have argued that supervisors act as gatekeepers to the disciplinary community and should facilitate doctoral students' participation within these communities (see Manathunga, 2014; Stubb et al., 2011), it is evident that this does not happen equally. The ways in which supervisors interact with doctoral students—and crucially the types of support that they offer their students—are not uniform. This has significant implications for those from marginalised groups, who may find establishing a sense of belonging within academic STEM communities more challenging. Harriet's experience reflects research which shows how, during the PhD, women students receive less support from their supervisor than their male peers, and that this is linked to their decreasing expectations of securing an academic position in the future (see Institute of Physics, 2015). This has clear implications for who is supported to progress into academic STEM after the PhD.

Harriet continued to encounter situations in which she was reminded that she does not fit into the culture of academic science in the way that her male peers do, reflecting the argument that belonging is not a straightforward accomplishment and must be continually renegotiated (May, 2013). Early on in the PhD, she was asked to write a literature review for a project that the lab was working on but was given little support. Harriet felt that this was due to the gendered expectations of the academics she was working with, based on an assumption that women are likely to be stronger at writing rather than at practical work:

> They assume that I'm more confident in the writing side of things…than the practical side of things, which I think is quite a standard gendered stereotype…in the back of probably a lot of people's minds it's kinda like oh you should be doing writing and teaching and that's where you're stronger…rather than…lab stuff. (Interview 1)

Harriet's perception that those in her lab have gendered expectations of her skills echoes literature on the gendered nature of academic career trajectories, which highlights the cultural assumption that women's academic abilities are in teaching or administration, rather than in research (see

Crabtree & Shiel, 2019; Guarino & Borden, 2017; White, 2013). This stereotyping has implications for individuals' ability to progress their academic career, particularly in STEM subjects where career progression is largely determined by individuals' ability to secure external research grants.

Other aspects of Harriet's day-to-day experiences as a doctoral student highlight how aspects of academic STEM culture position women as outsiders, making belonging more problematic (White, 2004). Harriet's experience of academic cultures is largely filtered through the microenvironment of her lab, where she was based for the majority of her doctoral research. In our first interview, she referred to the "*laddy environment*" she encountered there, which she described as "*a bit uncomfortable sometimes*" (Interview 1). The male scientists engage in disruptive behaviours, which are normalised by the participation of the majority of scientists, who are men, in these actions:

> They'll…be throwing stuff at each other and like flicking each other with stuff, or like…in the office they'll like show each other like ridiculous videos, and…someone will try and like benchpress someone else. (Interview 1)

Harriet's experiences indicate the presence of lad culture, which often manifests itself in disruptive behaviour in learning and teaching contexts (Jackson & Sundaram, 2020) to the exclusion of women (see Phipps, 2018; Phipps & Young, 2013). The behaviour of her male peers demonstrates how cultures are formed through 'sets of taken-for-granted…ways of behaving, which are articulated through and reinforced by recurrent practices' (Becher & Trowler, 2001, p. 23), and how some cultures position groups of people on the periphery. Harriet described how she and the only other woman in the lab were marginalised when these behaviours were enacted:

> They all get quite laddy sometimes and Margaret's just like, she gets so angry um, and I just think when that happens, they're just in that mood sometimes and it's all really laddy and you just get completely ignored, so it's quite hard then when the atmosphere's like that…it doesn't get like that too much, it's just like Friday afternoons just stay out of the lab if they're all there! That's another thing that's just like, the atmosphere isn't how you would want it all the time. (Interview 1)

These comments highlight the challenges that Harriet faced to feeling a sense of belonging within her everyday working environment due to these behaviours. She acknowledged that it is "*quite hard*" and she is "*completely ignored…when the atmosphere's like that*", whilst her female colleague gets "*so angry*". Harriet's comments reveal how whereas a sense of belonging 'makes us feel good about our being and our being-in-the-world' (Miller, 2003, p. 219), Harriet's experience (and those of her female colleague) is antithetical to this. They are unable to develop connections with others due to the exclusionary nature of the attitudes being expressed, and the way in which she is ignored by her male colleagues precludes Harriet from being accepted within this community. She acknowledged her reluctance to speak out against this behaviour unless a female colleague intervened first, engaging in a form of self-presentation which is complex and multilayered: "*she will shout at them so it's fine (laughs) I just hide behind Margaret and be like I agree with what she's saying! (laughs)*". The marginalisation of Harriet and Margaret in this situation reflects literature which highlights the outsider status of women in the academy (Morley, 2009; Puwar, 2004; Reay, 2000; White, 2013).

Whilst Harriet perceived that these types of behaviours were more likely to occur on Friday afternoons than at other times, it is clear that these were not isolated incidents, as a subsequent entry in her research diary indicates:

> 27/03/2015
> I'm feeling good about my research today! I think I have a good figure as well for my other experiment, so it feels like I'm progressing a bit. It was very "laddy" in the lab today and I have been singled out a lot as a woman who "would be more offended by swearing" and that certain conversations "aren't good for me". It annoys me but not enough to complain really. If it keeps happening I will say something.

Understanding belonging as informed by the extent to which individuals are able to move from a position of peripherality to a more central, legitimate position within their community (Lave & Wenger, 1991), it is clear that, here, Harriet is deliberately kept on the outside of the academic community of her lab. Significantly, she is excluded but also simultaneously defined by her non-participation by her male colleagues. Harriet's comments here imply that these instances of 'laddy' behaviour are common, reinforcing an understanding of belonging as something which requires continual negotiation (May, 2013). Despite having a positive day with her research and making progress, encountering these kinds of behaviours in the lab affected Harriet's daily sense of belonging within her immediate environment. She described the way in which her male colleagues singled her out, positioning her as an outsider to their conversations and the language they use, indicating that their use of "banter" acts to exclude those deemed as other, such as women in male-dominated environments (Phipps & Young, 2013). These experiences highlight how issues of gender and power can be manifested even on a small scale, in everyday encounters. Harriet's decision to record this incident in her diary indicates the extent to which she is made to feel 'out of place' rather than 'at home' (May, 2013, p. 93), jeopardising her ability to feel a sense of belonging.

Beyond a discussion of 'banter' as a manifestation of lad culture which women doctoral students encountered, sexual harassment constitutes an even more overt example of how women may be marginalised within academic cultures. The persistence of sexual harassment in higher education institutions has been well documented internationally (see Gibbons, 2018; Levin, 2017; Murray, 2021; Weale & Batty, 2017; Zhou, 2017), highlighting how women continue to be othered in the academy. It has been argued that sexual harassment constitutes part of the 'organisational culture' of higher education institutions (Ahmed, 2021), thus undermining women's ability to develop a sense of belonging within these spaces (Leonard, 2001).

For Jane, who described an encounter with a male lecturer whilst on a fieldwork trip abroad during her second year, her experience of sexual harassment was compounded by being the only woman doctoral student within the group. As there were no women staff members present, Jane acknowledged that she *"ended up being the kind of…mother hen"* (Interview 2) and felt responsible for the well-being of women undergraduate students on the fieldwork trip. She described the behaviour of the male staff member towards her and an undergraduate student:

> He was absolutely drunk off his face and he had been drinking for a really long time and he was just saying the most inappropriate things to some of the girls. Like one of them was my assistant and he said to her…is it ok if I am sexually attracted to you…oh no he said that to me he said something else to her, I think he called her sexy or something and I was just like you can't no, you can't say that. It was horrible. (Interview 2)

Jane outlined how she felt responsible for the younger women and attempted to defend them against his behaviour, putting herself in a vulnerable position. However, in terms of her own experience, being objectified by a male member of staff inhibits Jane's ability to feel that she is accepted or valued within her academic community, indicated by her feelings of awkwardness and embarrassment:

> I felt a lot of responsibility and a lot of embarrassment because you know it was directed at me as well as everybody else, and just shock really yes. It makes me feel incredibly awkward, and also very guilty I haven't said anything yet. But he doesn't show the faintest bit of recognition, so I think he doesn't remember it. (Interview 2)

The feeling of belonging requires individuals to negotiate power relations and be recognised by others as legitimate members of a particular community (Emmioglu et al., 2017; Lave & Wenger, 1991; White & Nonnamaker, 2008). For Jane, experiencing sexual harassment negatively affected her ability to develop this feeling. She acknowledged that she felt marginalised by this experience, feeling "*awkward*", "*guilty*" and "*embarrassed*", indicating how she feels 'out of place' rather than 'at home' (May, 2013, p. 93). These feelings of other-ness are relived on returning to her institution and seeing the perpetrator in her department. She had concerns for the welfare of the undergraduate students who also were subjected to sexual harassment by the staff member, as she was aware that they would continue to encounter this lecturer in their studies. Jane described feeling "*very guilty I haven't said anything yet*" as she felt that she had a responsibility to report him, but perceived that her position as a PhD student made this difficult, as she did not hold the power to ensure that his behaviour is addressed:

Since I've got back he is in the department that is like a really awful position because a lot of the undergraduates will see him again, and yes I feel perhaps this is why I was a bit concerned there being no female staff member as well because, I feel like she would have been in a better position to do something about that, whereas me being a PhD student, like, I don't know what to do about it really, I mean, I don't know who to go to, she at least could have spoken to him directly or spoken to his senior. (Interview 2)

Jane's experiences draw attention to the structurally powerful position that male academics have over students, which makes the power dynamics of reporting sexual harassment difficult for victims (Lee, 1998). Further, there seems little incentive to report incidents when high-profile cases of sexual abuse and violence—for example at the University of Sussex (see Turner, 2017)—indicate that institutions prioritise their reputations over the safety and well-being of victims (Ahmed, 2021). An investigation by *The Guardian* resulted in over 100 cases of women reporting sexual harassment and violence from university staff (Weale & Bannock, 2016). Though there has been some recognition of the issue, a recent report by Universities UK (2016) was criticised for its lack of focus on sexual harassment perpetrated by staff against students (Weale & Batty, 2016). Addressing sexual harassment as part of the organisational culture of universities (Ahmed, 2021; Eyre, 2000) is crucial if higher education institutions are to challenge perpetrators and adequately support victims, and if women are to feel safe to study and work within academic spaces.

## Power in Supervisory Relationships: Negotiating and Resisting Expectations

Positive relationships with supervisors are critical to doctoral students' success (Churchill & Sanders, 2007; Matthiesen & Binder, 2009; Parry, 2007; Phillips & Pugh, 2015). Yet the power dynamics of participants' supervisory relationships were often complex, and many experienced difficulties because of their conflicting conceptions of the role of doctoral students. Supervisors often expected doctoral students to undertake activities such as supervising more junior members of the lab, publishing papers or contributing to funding applications.

Despite this being usual within the context of supervision in STEM disciplines (see Cumming, 2009; Delamont et al., 2000), participants often had not expected that these demands would be made of them, and viewed them as additional forms of labour which distracted from their overall aim of completing the PhD. Further, whilst engaging doctoral students in this type of academic work may be viewed as providing valuable academic experience, it was apparent that in some cases individuals viewed these expectations as overly burdensome and distracting. Supervisors' expectations of doctoral students in relation to the supervision of other lab members and publishing work could, in fact, negatively impact individuals' ability to feel a sense of belonging during their doctorate.

This mismatch between students' and supervisors' understandings of doctoral work in STEM cultures draws attention to how the experience of doctoral study often runs counter to students' expectations (Wisker, 2010). This disparity generated conflict in relation to working practices, with participants reporting expectations of long working hours, presenteeism in the lab during holiday periods and publishing papers alongside doing their doctoral research. These aspects of the academic culture in STEM, which have been described as neoliberalised working practices (Meschitti, 2020; O'Hagan et al., 2019) in the way in which they demand productivity and total dedication to work from individuals, were off-putting to those considering a career in academic STEM. For those considering how they might balance a family with this career in future, the perception of working in this way was largely negative, reflecting broader concerns that women are less likely to pursue these careers than men (see Institute of Physics, 2015; Nature, 2019; Royal Society, 2014a; Royal Society of Chemistry, 2008, 2018; Wellcome Trust, 2013).

For Jane and Harriet in particular, the expectation that they would undertake work which they viewed as additional to their PhD, including writing publications, created considerable tension within their supervisory relationships. They had not anticipated this, and felt pressure to acquiesce to their supervisors' demands, challenging their ability to feel a sense of belonging within their academic communities. Their experiences reflect the inherent power dynamics within supervisory relationships in STEM, where doctoral students in STEM subjects are often treated as junior research assistants, with supervisors exerting a strong influence over the activities undertaken by them (Parry, 2007; Phillips & Pugh, 2015). Researchers observe that this relationship has the potential to become exploitative, as supervisors' priorities are publishing research papers which can be used to attract further funding, and thus they need to draw on the labour of all lab members to produce the results needed for these publications (Becher, 1994; Herschberg et al., 2018; Phillips & Pugh, 2015). Thus, whilst inculcating doctoral students into these ways of working may be viewed as strategies to facilitate individuals' belonging within academic STEM, it is evident—especially given the few jobs available post-PhD—that the motivation is more likely to be the furthering of the PI's research priorities.

During the early stages of her PhD, Harriet became increasingly aware that her supervisor's priority and the focus of her lab was on producing publications. She was reluctant to engage with this process, but felt she had little choice but to comply with these cultural expectations:

> It's that kind of environment when…they suddenly need to publish something but they need to do the groundwork, then suddenly everyone's involved because…I guess you get your name on the paper, then that's good but I just feel like I shouldn't have to be thinking about that at this point, but, apparently I do. (Interview 1)

In Harriet's lab she feels that "*they see you as workers*" (Interview 2), and in her first year she reported being allocated a master's student to supervise because there were not enough senior scientists to do so. Harriet was under pressure to help the student succeed, as his work was important for a paper that her lab was keen to publish. However, she had doubts about her capability to supervise this student, and struggled to do so. She described that she was criticised for the lack of his progress:

> What he's doing is quite important to the paper but obviously he is learning how to do everything so he's doing everything a bit slower and I'm being attacked quite a lot for like him messing up is suddenly my fault…they want me to literally stand over his shoulder and tell him how

to do it, show him what to do you know absolutely everything but…I've only got one year's more experience than him…so I don't, you know I'm not going to stand there and say I know everything because I don't…I've been a bit attacked just for how slow it's progressing and stuff and then now Peter is taking over a bit of looking after him I think just because he doesn't think obviously I've done a good enough job. (Interview 2)

This was a disempowering experience for Harriet, who resented the imposed responsibility and was frustrated that it led to her being criticised by her supervisor and other senior colleagues, and eventually being deemed unfit to take on this supervisory role. Indeed, the way in which Harriet describes "*being a bit attacked*" indicates how her perceived failure to support the master's student results in her feeling marginalised and inadequate. This experience therefore has a significant impact on her ability to feel a sense of belonging; she is made to feel 'out of place' (May, 2013) and is not able to make positive connections with others within her academic community. Crucially, she is not recognised as a legitimate member of her lab group, and her labour is rejected as being of insufficient quality. Further, from Harriet's description of the dynamics of her lab, it appears that the PI often exerted his authority in a way which undermined other members of the lab group, indicating that experiences of marginalisation are not uncommon within her immediate academic community: "*he just has days where suddenly everyone gets shouted at for no reason and we just sort of sit there, and you just accept it because it's what happens*" (Interview 2).

Further, through her experience of supervising this master's student, Harriet became concerned about the negative impact of spending time on publishing work rather than on her thesis. She perceived that her supervisor's expectation that she would focus on producing academic papers may have negative implications for her progress towards the doctorate, as well as for her personal development, as she indicates in a research diary entry made during her second year:

09/10/15
I had a meeting with John and Peter this evening about the work I will need to do in the future. It seems that I will be doing anything left over that Peter hasn't finished when he leaves in a couple of weeks. John tried to make it seem better by saying he will give me joint first authorship on the

paper which is great, but I can't help feeling this is detracting from my PhD thesis which is the main reason I'm here. At this rate, my thesis is going to be really "bitty" and not a good story if I keep just doing little things here and there. I suppose John doesn't really care about my thesis and just thinks about papers. I can almost see why so few people have left this lab and gone on to non-scientific careers as your personal and project development is so hindered by John's outlook on what work you should be doing.

Harriet's awareness of her supervisor's differing priorities compared with her own speaks back to literature, highlighting how academic STEM places critical importance on publications (Royal Society, 2010; UK Council for Science and Technology, 2007). Her perception that she would have to do "*anything left over*" when one of the postdocs leaves, despite feeling it would detract from her thesis, indicates the power dynamics at play in her supervisory relationship. Though he "*tried to make it seem better by saying he will give me joint first authorship*", it appears that Harriet does not feel that this opportunity warrants her spending so much time away from her thesis. Further, the way Harriet views her PI as attempting to "*make it seem better*" by allocating her as joint first author, indicates that she feels she is being manipulated into undertaking this work. Despite their opposing views on the types of work they feel are important, it is clear that Harriet did not feel she had a choice but to do the additional work that was expected. This perceived lack of autonomy indicates her marginalised position and highlights the challenge she faces in attempting to belong within her academic community. Whilst belonging involves being recognised as a legitimate member of the disciplinary community, which arguably her PI does by treating Harriet as a valuable contributor to a scientific publication, it also requires a sense of positive affect, which Harriet does not experience.

Harriet's perception of her supervisor's interests as very different from her own illuminates how there may be significant disparity in how doctoral students and supervisors in STEM prioritise students' career development. Research highlights how this is often of considerable importance to students, but of low importance to their supervisors (see Pearson et al., 2009). Harriet's comment that "*your personal and project development is so hindered by John's outlook on what work you should be doing*" highlights how the 'output orientation' (Herschberg et al., 2018, p. 309) of supervisors in STEM may narrow the opportunities available to doctoral students after the PhD. Whilst there has been a considerable shift towards the development of doctoral students' generic and research skills during the PhD, partly due to the introduction of structured doctoral training in the UK and throughout Europe (see Borrell-Damian et al., 2010), there remains some resistance from supervisors to PhD students undertaking activities which are perceived as unnecessary for pursuing an academic career (see Royal Society, 2014b; Vitae, 2017).

Despite struggling with her supervisor's expectations in relation to the type of work that she should focus on, Harriet determined to resist his expectations concerning her career options. She acknowledged her lack of knowledge of the full range of careers open to her outside of the academic career path and considered the possibility of doing a placement at a different organisation during her PhD, though she envisaged that her supervisor would oppose this:

> When you don't really know what is out there it's kind of hard to say…I think I'll have to experience some of the things hopefully might try and get a placement, because I'm allowed to take a couple of months out to do that so that would be a good thing to do I don't know how John would feel about it but…if I get the money and if I work it out myself there is nothing he can do really, I would just have to pick a good enough, like a good time of the year I suppose probably the summer, to go and do it. (Interview 2)

Even this small instance of planning to undertake a placement during her PhD signifies Harriet's ability to demonstrate agency in resisting the expectations of her supervisor, though it is clear that this may not be straightforward. In this way, Harriet envisages being able to successfully negotiate the power differentials of her supervisory relationship in order to secure the experience that she wants, and to construct a postdoctoral identity which she feels more positive about.

Further, Harriet draws on peer support in order to develop a sense of belonging within her academic community. In her second year, she becomes more involved with her wider disciplinary postgraduate community through her departmental postgraduate society. She demonstrates agency in joining the organising committee and forging closer connections with her peers, including those outside of her lab:

> I'm now on the…PhD society committee which has been brilliant because I've got to know a lot more people in the department, organise socials and stuff which has been really fun, so I think that has made us like a big closer group. There is 30 odd of us in, just in my year…so that's been really nice because obviously everyone goes through a lot of similar things and it's a bit more of an outlet sometimes like we'll go out for a drink and it will just, everyone will just rant for ages ((laughs)) but it's probably a good thing that we do it, to each other, and not to like you know your supervisor necessarily…that's been really, really helpful. (Interview 2)

Literature highlights how the development of strong peer support networks can ameliorate some of the difficulties of doctoral study and positively contribute to students' ability to feel belonging to their academic communities (see Morris & Wisker, 2011). This was apparent in the way Harriet describes having more connections amongst her peers as having helped create "*a big closer group*". Her ability to discuss her experiences with peers in this way is also seen as beneficial for her supervisory relationship, as she is able to use her connections with others as an "*outlet*" for any frustrations that she feels. Thus, Harriet's agency in establishing a strong peer group helps her to develop a sense of belonging within her wider disciplinary community, as well as navigate the sometimes problematic power dynamics she experiences with her supervisor.

For Jane as well as Harriet, it is the conflict in her attitude towards publishing during her PhD, compared with that of her supervisors, which caused most tension and challenged her ability to feel a sense of belonging within her academic community. It also had a negative impact on her ability to envisage herself in academic STEM after the PhD. Though in her first year, when she had initially been determined to become an academic, Jane recognised that publishing was a necessary achievement in order to pursue this career, she also acknowledged that it should not be the sole focus of her efforts:

> I'm conscious that I don't want to get bogged down too much with this pressure to publish, because I think especially in conservation, being such an applied subject, papers do not equal success necessarily…but in terms of getting me where I need to be, papers are obviously important. (Interview 1)

Thus, whilst recognising the significance of publications for career success in academic STEM, Jane was also resistant to the idea of embodying the type of academic who prioritises publishing over real-world impact: "*it is very easy to go into academia and lose sight of the actual…point of being a conservationist, and just publishing papers willy-nilly and that's not what I want to do*" (Interview 1). Yet there is an implicit expectation that doctoral students in STEM will contribute to their field by publishing their results (Delamont et al., 2000), indicating a clash between what is expected of students in these disciplines and what they expect when embarking upon a doctorate.

The way in which Jane viewed academics and publishing echoes literature about the increasing neoliberalisation of academic work, especially in relation to research performativity in academia (see Gill, 2009; Hey, 2004). Yet, Jane's desire to avoid getting "*bogged down*" in publishing is compromised during her PhD by the attitude of her supervisors, who expect her to make progress with a publication before collecting further data:

> I think they won't let me go to the field again until I have a manuscript ready if not in review then at least ready to be submitted. So, there is definite pressure to get on that at the moment. Yes. Which is quite terrifying really because I know that I have got a lot to do before I'm ready to submit anything. They know that to go on in academia having papers is really important…they are sort of saying well it takes so long to get things through the publication process, you want to start as early as you possibly can, so I know they have good reasons for pressuring me to get things written up and submitted. [It's] still quite scary though. (Interview 2)

Jane's comments indicate how her supervisors wield an enormous amount of power as gatekeepers, overruling her own views on the relative importance of publishing. The effect of their insistence that she not return to her fieldwork before producing a publication on Jane is significant. She uses the words "*terrifying*" and "*scary*" to describe the pressure that she feels, indicating a lack of belonging in her inability to feel 'at home' in this environment (May, 2013).

Further, despite her supervisors' encouragement to her to submit scientific work which would arguably facilitate her recognition by the scientific community, Jane's lack of enthusiasm for publishing implies that as with Harriet's experience, her supervisors' approach may be more likely to be self-motivated. Indeed, her supervisors' exercise of power led to Jane being concerned that not fulfilling their expectations during the doctorate could have negative long-term implications for her career:

> You worry as well that these are the people that are going to be doing your references and what not, and if you don't work as they want you to work, maybe they'll give you a rubbish reference. And who is going to stand up for you? (Interview 2)

The fears that Jane expresses about a future where she lacks the support of her supervisors indicate the significant amount of power that supervisors wield as disciplinary gatekeepers, whose actions may either facilitate or preclude doctoral students' belonging to their academic community, both in the short and long terms (Lee, 2008; Parry, 2007). Further, the concerns that Jane expresses about her future career illuminate the key role of supervisors in facilitating post-PhD career opportunities (see Bryan & Guccione, 2018; Denicolo & Becker, 2008; Wisker, 2007).

Jane's acquiescence to her supervisors' expectations in relation to publishing speaks back to the argument that undertaking doctoral study means engaging in 'performative academic labour' (Bansel, 2011, p. 543), and that the 'performative force' of undertaking such activities supports doctoral students' academic identity development. Yet for Jane, the issue of publishing is a large part of what makes her question whether she wants to engage in this process of academic identity development; her views on the value of publication run counter to how publications are perceived within scientific and academic cultures. Thus, this experience both compromises Jane's ability to feel a sense of belonging within academia as a doctoral student, and also on how able she is to imagine herself belonging as a future academic.

The encouragement that Jane's supervisors give her to publish and thus engage in playing the 'research game' of academia (Lucas, 2006) is interesting in the context of research which has highlighted that women doctoral students are less likely than men to be encouraged to undertake activities related to pursuing an academic career, such as publishing and presenting work (see Dever et al., 2008). This evidently does not reflect Jane's experience, and her supervisors' efforts could be viewed as attempting to facilitate her belonging by encouraging her to contribute to her disciplinary community. However, given Jane's reluctance and concerns around publishing, this interpretation seems less plausible. There are other interpretations of their encouragement; there is a tradition of supervisors claiming credit for their doctoral students' work (Macfarlane, 2017; Oberlander & Spencer, 2006), something which continues to be written about in higher education blogs and in newspaper articles (see Cundy, 2019; Martin, 2014). Thus, Jane's perception that her supervisor views her simply as "*a means to an answer of a question and lots of papers*" (Interview 2) raises questions about who benefits from doctoral students being pressured to publish work.

## Navigating Academic STEM Culture: Imagining Non-academic Futures

During their doctorate, individuals learned about what would be required of them as future academics by participating in the academic STEM environment and through a process of observational learning (Rossiter, 2004). In this chapter I have shown the ways in which individuals came to understand that as women, they could often be positioned as 'other' within academic STEM. This was experienced through encountering gendered expectations of their (and other women's) abilities and needing to navigate various power dynamics within their departments, disciplines and everyday workspaces. The extent to which participants felt a sense of belonging to their academic community as doctoral students shaped their ability to envisage belonging in the future as academics. Thus, experiences of the culture of academic STEM, such as encountering expectations around publishing work and of total dedication to their research, shaped participants' perceptions of academia and their desire to become an academic in the future (see McAlpine et al., 2010; Stoilescu & McDougall, 2010). Whilst there were some examples of individuals devising strategies which enabled them to feel a sense of belonging during the doctorate, imagining non-academic future was a common feature of individuals' response to the culture of academic STEM.

Through witnessing academics' working practices during their PhD, participants came to perceive the model of a successful academic as based on the requirement to totally dedicate themselves to their research, and work long days, evenings and weekends. This perception reflects the intensification of academic work in the neoliberal academy (Gill, 2009) and the expectations of individuals to model themselves on the 'ideal academic' (Lynch, 2010). Jane, despite having initial strong academic aspirations, struggled to feel a sense of belonging within her academic community and to construct a viable academic identity because she came to view her values as in direct conflict with the culture of overwork she perceived in academia. Sustaining what she viewed as a healthy work-life balance was important to Jane, and at the start of her doctorate she was determined to prioritise her well-being: *"I am trying to constantly keep checking…while I am doing my PhD…that I am happy…working hard but not killing myself"* (Interview 1). Yet, as Jane progressed through her studies, she witnessed academics in her department work very long hours, and observed how these behaviours encouraged others to behave similarly:

> It just makes me really angry…the expectation to work…the idea that the more you work, the more productive you are is just silly because there is so much evidence that killing yourself and working too many hours and not having enough breaks is counterproductive…but still I find I look around me and everybody, the first years who have only just arrived sometimes are there way after I've left, one of the Master's students slept here the other day. I was like what are you doing? This is really unhealthy…I think, a lot of it is seeing other people doing that and, and just thinking well they are doing it, I must have to do it, it's kind of I don't know it's so deeply ingrained…lecturers work like that as well half the time so that doesn't help. (Interview 2)

Jane's desire to avoid working in a way which she perceived as detrimental to her health was therefore in direct conflict with the academic identities she saw performed by lecturers in her department. This has implications for her ability to feel a sense of belonging to her academic community; Jane described being "*really angry*" about the implicit expectation of long working hours, and was unable to feel a positive sense of connection with others due to her own values running counter to these expectations. It is clear that these behaviours, enacted by senior members of the academic community, have a significant impact on those in more junior positions. Despite being frustrated by this cultural expectation of long working hours, Jane acknowledged that her own behaviour was also influenced by this working culture: "*it's really difficult to get up and go I'm leaving now…I don't always manage it, sometimes I'm like oh but nobody else has left yet, it's really difficult*" (Interview 2). This clash between her own values and those that she sees performed within her academic community makes Jane feel marginalised, and she recognises that she is not always able to resist conforming to the working practices she considers to be unhealthy. Her repetition of the phrase "*really difficult*" indicates the extent to which this struggle positions her as 'other' within her academic community.

Beyond her own experience in her department, Jane recognised that these working practices are indicative of the culture of academia more widely: "*I read a horrible statistic the other day that said…they reckoned 53% of academics in the UK had some mental health issues, and somehow that it's just kind of brushed under the carpet*" (Interview 2). These concerns reflect research into well-being amongst UK academics, which highlights reported high levels of psychological distress amongst academics due to a poor work-life balance (see Kinman & Jones, 2008). Further, concerns about academics' mental health have been linked to increasing pressures on individuals in the context of the performance-driven culture in the UK higher education (see Davies & Bansel, 2005; Gill, 2014; Morrish, 2019; Read & Leathwood, 2018). It is clear that the disparity between her own values and intentions, and those she sees performed by others in her academic community, had a negative impact on Jane's ability to feel a sense of belonging.

These experiences also affect Jane's ability to construct a positive academic identity. Whilst initially Jane hoped to pursue a postdoc position after the PhD, she expressed fears about the implications of the competition for these positions, in terms of her own well-being:

Only like 5% of people end up doing post-docs after PhD…obviously the competition's really high…if it's like high to the extent that they require millions of publications and stuff that I…would not be able to achieve without making myself…stressed and miserable…that would be a barrier. (Interview 1)

Significantly, Jane is not concerned that the competition for these positions may mean that she is unable to be successful, but that she would have to compromise her happiness and her mental health in order to succeed. She equates a future in which she would have to have "*millions of publications*" with one where she would be "*stressed and miserable*" as a result. Thus, in order to continue to belong and be recognised as a legitimate and valuable contributor to her academic community, Jane perceives that she would need to make herself unhappy. This perception makes her question the desirability of taking on this postdoc identity, echoing the argument that increasing demands of research productivity have influenced not only 'what educators, scholars and researchers do' but also 'who they are' (Ball, 2003, p. 215).

Understanding identity as 'what you have in common with some people and what differentiates you from others' (Weeks, 1990, p. 88), it is clear that Jane is not willing to embody the model of the 'ideal academic' (Lynch, 2010) who is prepared to dedicate themselves totally to academic work. It is therefore perhaps unsurprising that Jane has considerable doubts about taking on an academic identity, and reflects that: "*I have often thought that my life would be easier outside of academia, because those other jobs are a lot more 9 to 5*" (Interview 1). Therefore, despite initially aspiring to an academic career, by her second year Jane planned instead to pursue a career in policy, illuminating how identities shift during the doctorate (Baker & Lattuca, 2010; Jazvac-Martek, 2009; Wisker, 2010). Jane's experiences are not uncommon, echoing international research which has found that 'not all individuals doing doctorates continue to desire academic careers when they see close at hand the actual work expectations' (McAlpine & Akerlind, 2010, p. 11, see also Mason et al., 2009). Jane's aspirations follow the same trajectory, and she comes to reject the possibility of developing an academic identity due to her perception that this would mean embodying behaviours which conflict with her values of self-care and require her to work in a way which she feels is "*unhealthy*".

Similarly, though Harriet originally intended to try and secure a post-doctoral research position, her experiences of the culture of academic STEM during her PhD lead her to become disillusioned with this career. She recognised at an early stage the difficulties inherent within academic careers, not least the pressure to produce publications: "*The whole…like career structure and everything is literally just based on how many papers you get, as opposed to like, necessarily on lab experience, which is really unfair I think*" (Interview 1). This, along with an expectation of total dedication to work, is something that Harriet struggles with during her studies. Her PI has expectations of all lab members being present in the lab between certain hours, including doctoral students, and there is little flexibility in relation to taking time off over holidays:

> [John] got annoyed because obviously a lot of us are leaving not on Christmas Eve we are leaving a couple of days earlier…our families don't live [here]…and obviously it was like oh…you know you think you can just leave and all this sort of stuff. (Interview 2)

Beyond Harriet's supervisor, other senior scientists in her lab also perpetuated a culture of presenteeism and long working hours, and unlike in Jane's experience, this is made explicit rather than being implied by the working practices of more senior academics. Indeed, the senior scientists in Harriet's lab instruct doctoral students to work very long days and make clear that this way of working is expected:

> They'll just say oh we expect you to do that…you need to put in all these hours, blah, blah, blah, but that's not something I'm prepared to do I'm not prepared to give up my evenings and I know that's what they'll say I have to do…They say…back in my day I had to work all these hours and they all just go on about their past and how they did it and it's just like well it doesn't…you know just because you did it that way doesn't mean I have to do it that way. (Interview 2)

Understanding belonging as shaped by power dynamics, it is clear that for Harriet, whose ways of working are called into question by the actions and instructions of both her supervisor and other senior scientists, developing a sense of belonging to her academic community is not straightforward. However, Harriet becomes determined to resist what she perceives as unreasonable expectations, and instead work in a way which she felt would result in a healthier work-life balance. Thus, whilst not engaging in a direct counterargument, Harriet resisted these expectations in a more subtle way, instead developing her own ways of working. She recognised that earlier on in her PhD she had put herself under a lot of pressure and developed working habits which she perceived as unhealthy, as well as counterproductive. Since making efforts to put less pressure on herself, she found that she was better able to progress with her work, without having to work very long hours or on weekends:

> It's all doable and you don't have to give up too much of your…evenings and weekends…I think all that comes down to is just timing and like if you organise it so you don't have to come in on a Saturday to finish a certain thing then you don't have to and it's fine…as long as you just I think stay a bit relaxed about it it's ok…when I put too much of myself, I think the beginning of this year I would say I was just doing too much in a day for a couple of weeks and I was just messing things up…I think I learnt from that quite a lot just to calm down and just give that extra day like it might take you but it will be worth it because you won't mess it all up and it should hopefully be more likely to work. (Interview 2)

Thus, Harriet is able to find her own ways to belong within her academic community, developing an approach whereby she is able to successfully conduct her research without conforming to cultural expectations of total dedication to work. Yet despite this, witnessing the experiences of more senior scientists in her lab has a significant impact on Harriet's ability to envisage herself belonging in academic STEM after the PhD. Working with postdocs who struggled to balance family life alongside their academic career shaped how she viewed the possibility of pursuing the same path. Indeed, Harriet reflected on how the experience of doing a PhD can dissuade individuals, including herself, from pursuing this career, due to the expectations of long working hours and the perceived negative impact on family life:

> Going through this has…shown people the bad side in a way…of academia, everyone is getting a bit more stressed, so you kind of just want to get out of it, I think a lot of people feel like that anyway, and they want to find a more stable job where they don't have to come in at weekends and things necessarily…I don't know if it's changed my opinion really like I've always felt like that is what it is going to be like…I think seeing Peter and like his family like having all these issues that he has had with his job and having to work so late and not see them and stuff, I think that puts people off quite a lot because I'm sure a lot of people are like that throughout the year probably…yes I think seeing that put me off a bit. (Interview 2)

Yet, despite the culture of academic STEM being unappealing to Harriet in some ways, she acknowledges that she is not immune to the competitive nature of this environment and may be inculcated into playing the academic game. Even at an early stage of her studies, Harriet recognised that her attitudes may well be influenced as a result of participating in this environment as a doctoral student:

> I think the atmosphere does put me off…quite a lot, but then I guess if suddenly I'm the one with the first authored paper, I'd be like this is great… I can do this now! I just have no idea…until that happens, hopefully…(laughs) I'm not really sure, but yeah I think it's quite, it's quite a toxic environment I would say. (Interview 1)

Harriet's candid comments, expressed at a very early stage in her PhD, indicate an ambivalence towards an academic career which is demonstrated by participants in other subject areas (see Chap. 4). Whilst Harriet recognises the academic STEM environment as "*toxic*", with its competitive culture and high expectations of productivity, she does not rule out the possibility of her becoming inculcated into these ways of working and learning to belong within this environment. This indicates how doctoral students can become encultured into the academic sphere during the PhD (see Delamont et al., 2000; Parry, 2007), and how they may internalise neoliberalised criteria for academic success (see Archer, 2008), especially in relation to accruing research publications (see Rolf, 2021).

## Summary

This chapter has shown how women doctoral students in STEM subjects encountered a number of barriers to belonging within their academic communities, largely in relation to the power structures inherent in their disciplines and within their supervisory relationships. PIs and senior colleagues acted as powerful gatekeepers, whose expectations and perceptions of women doctoral students shaped individuals' experiences during the doctorate, but also the extent to which they were able to feel a sense of belonging within their academic communities. This had significant implications for their ability to imagine themselves as future academics. By participating in the academic STEM environment during their studies, individuals learned that they would need to conform to neoliberal ideals of performativity and productivity in order to embody the 'ideal academic' (Lynch, 2010), and present themselves as confident, 'care-free' and willing to completely dedicate themselves to research, particularly in relation to publishing work.

Thus, participating in the competitive environment of academic STEM during their doctorate had a considerable impact on individuals' potential approach to developing an academic career. Whilst participants largely became disillusioned with the prospect of this career, most did not dismiss it entirely, and individuals considered the ways in which they could envisage themselves continuing to belong within the highly competitive research culture. This involved significant personal compromise and a willingness to embrace the aspects of contemporary academic work which individuals had been so critical of. Jane's assertion that she may be able to succeed where other women have not by *"selling herself"*, and Harriet's reflection that if she had a first-authored paper she would be able to view herself as potentially succeeding at the academic 'game', reinforce findings from other research which highlight how early career academics may internalise neoliberal values (see Archer, 2008). Whilst understandable, this approach is problematic in its conception of academic careers as inherently meritocratic and its focus on individual ability, rather than illuminating the structural inequalities which make it harder for women and other marginalised individuals to become successful academic scientists.

Attending to participants' experiences also revealed how women doctoral students were often positioned as 'other' in a number of ways during their studies, experiencing hostile disciplinary cultures, gendered expectations of their abilities, lad culture and sexual harassment. These barriers to belonging contributed to feelings of marginalisation during the doctorate, and led one individual to choose to leave her PhD before completing her studies. Witnessing women academics encounter gender discrimination during their careers, and the perception of an academic career as not family-friendly, led participants to question their desire to take on this identity and instead consider alternative, non-academic futures. These findings echo other research which has highlighted the barriers that women face in pursuing a career in academic STEM (see Royal Society of Chemistry, 2008; Wellcome Trust, 2013), with clear consequences for the future diversity of academic science. Despite the wealth of research around these issues, there is evidently considerable progress still to be made to enable women doctoral students to envisage the identities of academic and mother not as mutually exclusive, but as compatible, and even potentially desirable.

Despite encountering structural, cultural and gendered barriers to belonging as women in academic STEM, participants demonstrated considerable agency in trying to find their own ways to belong to their academic community during the PhD. Strategies included developing strong peer communities and attempting to resist what they perceived as unreasonable expectations of their supervisors in relation to working practices and publishing work, despite the significant power differentials involved in these relationships. These small acts of resistance open up the possibility for others to push back against the neoliberalisation of academic labour, and perhaps shift the culture of academic STEM towards a more inclusive environment, within which a sense of belonging may be easier to develop for those from marginalised groups.

# References

Advance HE. (2021). *Equality in higher education: Student statistical report 2021*.

Ahmed, S. (2021). *Complaint!* Duke University Press.

Allen, M., & Castleman, T. (2001). Fighting the pipeline fallacy. In A. Brooks & A. Mackinnon (Eds.), *Gender and the restructured university* (pp. 151–165). Open University Press.

Archer, L. (2008). The new neoliberal subjects? Young/er academics' constructions of professional identity. *Journal of Education Policy, 23*(3), 265–285. https://doi.org/10.1080/02680930701754047

Asmar, C. (1999). Is there a gendered agenda in academia? The research experience of female and male PhD graduates in Australian universities. *Higher Education, 38*(3), 255–273.

Baker, M. (2012). *Academic careers and the gender gap*. UBC Press.

Baker, V. L., & Lattuca, L. R. (2010). Developmental networks and learning: Toward an interdisciplinary perspective on identity development during doctoral study. *Studies in Higher Education, 35*(7), 807–827. https://doi.org/10.1080/03075070903501887

Ball, S. J. (2003). The teacher's soul and the terrors of performativity. *Journal of Education Policy, 18*(2), 215–228. https://doi.org/10.1080/0268093022000043065

Bansel, P. (2011). Becoming academic: A reflection on doctoral candidacy. *Studies in Higher Education, 36*(5), 543–556. https://doi.org/10.1080/03075079.2011.594592

Barinaga, M. (1993). Science education: The pipeline is leaking women all the way along. *Science, 260*(5106), 409–411. https://doi.org/10.1126/science.260.5106.409

Barnard, S., Powell, A., Bagilhole, B., & Dainty, A. (2010). Researching UK women professionals in SET: A critical review of current approaches. *International Journal of Gender, Science and Technology, 2*(3).

Becher, T. (1994). The significance of disciplinary differences. *Studies in Higher education, 19*(2), 151–161.

Becher, T., Henkel, M., & Kogan, M. (1994). *Graduate education in Britain* (vol. 108). Higher Education Policy Series 17.

Becher, T., & Trowler, P. (2001). *Academic tribes and territories: Intellectual enquiry and the culture of disciplines*. McGraw-Hill.

Benard, S., & Correll, S. J. (2010). Normative discrimination and the motherhood penalty. *Gender & Society, 24*(5), 616–646.

Benschop, Y., & Brouns, M. (2003). Crumbling ivory towers: Academic organizing and its gender effects. *Gender, Work & Organization, 10*(2), 194–212.

Blackmore, J. (2002). Globalisation and the restructuring of higher education for new knowledge economies: New dangers or old habits troubling gender equity work in universities? *Higher Education Quarterly, 56*(4), 419–441. https://doi.org/10.1111/1468-2273.00228

Blair-Loy, M., Rogers, L. E., Glaser, D., Wong, Y. L., Abraham, D., & Cosman, P. C. (2017). Gender in engineering departments: Are there gender differences in interruptions of academic job talks? *Social Sciences, 6*(1), 29. https://doi.org/10.3390/socsci6010029

Blickenstaff, J. C. (2005). Women and science careers: Leaky pipeline or gender filter? *Gender and Education, 17*(4), 369–386. https://doi.org/10.1080/09540250500145072

Borrell-Damian, L., Brown, T., Dearing, A., Font, J., Hagen, S., Metcalfe, J., & Smith, J. (2010). Collaborative doctoral education: University-industry partnerships for enhancing knowledge exchange. *Higher Education Policy, 23*(4), 493–514.

Britton, D. M. (2017). Beyond the chilly climate: The salience of gender in women's academic careers. *Gender & Society, 31*(1), 5–27.

Brooks, A. I. (2001). Restructuring bodies of knowledge. In A. Brooks & A. Mackinnon (Eds.), *Gender and the restructured university* (pp. 15–45). SRHE/Open University Press.

Bryan, B., & Guccione, K. (2018). Was it worth it? A qualitative exploration into graduate perceptions of doctoral value. *Higher Education Research & Development, 37*(6), 1124–1140.

Castelló, M., Pardo, M., Sala-Bubaré, A., & Suñé-Soler, N. (2017). Why do students consider dropping out of doctoral degrees? Institutional and personal factors. *Higher Education, 74*(6), 1053–1068.

Chakraverty, D. (2019). Impostor phenomenon in STEM: Occurrence, attribution, and identity. *Studies in Graduate and Postdoctoral Education, 10*(1), 2–20.

Cheryan, S., Ziegler, S. A., Montoya, A. K., & Jiang, L. (2017). Why are some STEM fields more gender balanced than others? *Psychological Bulletin, 143*(1), 1.

Chesterman, C., Ross-Smith, A., & Peters, M. (2005, May). "Not doable jobs!" Exploring senior women's attitudes to academic leadership roles. *Women's Studies International Forum, 28*, 2–3, 163–180. https://doi.org/10.1016/j.wsif.2005.04.005

Churchill, H., & Sanders, T. (2007). *Getting your PhD: A practical insider's guide*. Sage.

Corbett, C., & Hill, C. H. (2015). *Solving the equation: The variables for women's success in engineering and computing*. American Association of University Women.

Correll, S. J., Benard, S., & Paik, I. (2007). Getting a job: Is there a motherhood penalty? *American Journal of Sociology, 112*(5), 1297–1338. https://doi.org/10.1086/511799

Coulthard-Graf, R. (2020, April 24). How do group leaders recruit postdocs? EMBL Careers [Web log post]. Retrieved from https://blogs.embl.org/careers/how-do-group-leaders-recruit-postdocs/

Crabtree, S., & Shiel, C. (2019). "Playing mother": Channeled careers and the construction of gender in academia. *SAGE Open, 9*(3), 2158244019876285.

Cumming, J. (2009). The doctoral experience in science: Challenging the current orthodoxy. *British Educational Research Journal, 35*(6), 877–890.

Cundy, A. (2019, September 8). Taking the credit: Can universities tackle academic fraud? *Financial Times*. Retrieved from https://www.ft.com/content/054c9dce-afc5-11e9-8030-530adfa879c2

Curtin, N., Malley, J., & Stewart, A. J. (2016). Mentoring the next generation of faculty: Supporting academic career aspirations among doctoral students. *Research in Higher Education, 57*(6), 714–738.

Davies, B., & Bansel, P. (2005). The time of their lives? Academic workers in neoliberal time (s). *Health Sociology Review, 14*(1), 47–58.

Davies, B., & Petersen, E. B. (2005). Neo-liberal discourse in the Academy: The forestalling of (collective) resistance. *Learning & Teaching in the Social Sciences, 2*(2).

Delamont, S., Atkinson, P., & Parry, O. (2000). *The doctoral experience: Success and failure in graduate school*. Routledge.

Delamont, S., Parry, O., & Atkinson, P. (1997). Critical mass and pedagogic continuity: Studies in academic habitus. *British Journal of Sociology of Education, 18*(4), 533–549.

Denicolo, P., & Becker, L. (2008). The supervision process and the nature of the research degree. In G. Hall & J. Longman (Eds.), *The postgraduate's companion* (pp. 123–143). Sage.

Dever, M., Laffan, W., Boreham, P., Behrens, K., Haynes, M., Western, M., & Kubler, M. (2008). *Gender differences in early post-PhD employment in Australian universities: The influence of PhD experience on women's academic careers*. Final report.

De Welde, K., & Laursen, S. (2011). The glass obstacle course: Informal and formal barriers for women PhD students in STEM fields. *International Journal of Gender, Science and Technology, 3*(3), 571–595.

Doherty, L., & Manfredi, S. (2006). Women's progression to senior positions in English universities. *Employee Relations, 28*(6), 553–572. https://doi.org/10.1108/01425450610704498

Emmioglu, E., McAlpine, L., & Amundsen, C. (2017). Doctoral students' experiences of feeling (or not) like an academic. *International Journal of Doctoral Studies, 12,* 73–91.

Equality Challenge Unit. (2017). *ASSET 2016: Experiences of gender equality in STEMM academia and their intersections with ethnicity, sexual orientation, disability and age.* Equality Challenge Unit.

Etzkowitz, H., & Gupta, N. (2006). Women in science: A fair shake? *Minerva, 44*(2), 185–199.

Etzkowitz, H., Kemelgor, C., & Uzzi, B. (2000). *Athena unbound: The advancement of women in science and technology.* Cambridge University Press.

Eyre, L. (2000). The discursive framing of sexual harassment in a university community. *Gender and Education, 12*(3), 293–307. https://doi.org/10.1080/713668301

Fisher, A. J., Mendoza-Denton, R., Patt, C., Young, I., Eppig, A., Garrell, R. L., Nelson, T. W., Rees, D., & Richards, M. A. (2019). Structure and belonging: Pathways to success for underrepresented minority and women PhD students in STEM fields. *PLoS One, 14*(1), e0209279.

Fox, M. F. (2006). Gender, hierarchy, and science. In *Handbook of the sociology of gender* (pp. 441–457). Springer.

Gasser, C. E., & Shaffer, K. S. (2014). Career development of women in academia: Traversing the leaky pipeline. *Professional Counselor, 4*(4), 332–352. https://doi.org/10.15241/ceg.4.4.332

Gibbons, K. (2018, July 28). Sex harassment victims force University College London to end gagging orders. *The Times.* Retrieved from https://www.thetimes.co.uk/article/sex-harassment-victims-forceuniversity-college-london-to-end-gagging-orders-h9v9v279f

Giles, M., Ski, C., & Vrdoljak, D. (2009). Career pathways of science, engineering and technology research postgraduates. *Australian Journal of Education, 53*(1), 69–86. https://doi.org/10.1177/000494410905300106

Gill, R. (2009). Breaking the silence: The hidden injuries of neo-liberal academia. In R. Ryan-Flood & R. Gill (Eds.), *Secrecy and silence in the research process: Feminist reflections* (pp. 228–244). Routledge.

Gill, R. (2014). Academics, cultural workers and critical labour studies. *Journal of Cultural Economy, 7*(1), 12–30. https://doi.org/10.1080/17530350.2013.861763

Guarino, C. M., & Borden, V. M. (2017). Faculty service loads and gender: Are women taking care of the academic family? *Research in Higher Education, 58*(6), 672–694.

Hall, R. M., & Sandler, B. R. (1982). *The classroom climate: A chilly one for women*. Association of American Colleges.

Hancock, S. (2019). A future in the knowledge economy? Analysing the career strategies of doctoral scientists through the principles of game theory. *Higher Education, 78*(1), 33–49.

Handforth, R. (2022). Feeling "stupid": Considering the affective in women doctoral students' experiences of imposter 'syndrome'. In *The Palgrave handbook of imposter syndrome in higher education* (pp. 293–309). Palgrave Macmillan.

Harding, S. G. (1986). *The science question in feminism*. Cornell University Press.

Hatchell, H., & Aveling, N. (2008). Gendered disappearing acts: Women's doctoral experiences in the science workplace. In *Australian Association for Research in Education conference, Brisbane* (vol. 30).

Henkel, M. (2004). Current science policies and their implications for the formation and maintenance of academic identity. *Higher Education Policy, 17*(2), 167–182.

Herschberg, C., Benschop, Y., & Van den Brink, M. (2018). Precarious postdocs: A comparative study on recruitment and selection of early-career researchers. *Scandinavian Journal of Management, 34*(4), 303–310.

Hey, V. (2004). Perverse Pleasures—Identity work and the paradoxes of greedy institutions. *Journal of International Women's Studies, 5*(3), 33–43.

Howe-Walsh, L., & Turnbull, S. (2016). Barriers to women leaders in academia: Tales from science and technology. *Studies in Higher Education, 41*(3), 415–428.

Hughes, C. C., Schilt, K., Gorman, B. K., & Bratter, J. L. (2017). Framing the faculty gender gap: A view from STEM doctoral students. *Gender, Work & Organization, 24*(4), 398–416.

Institute of Physics (IOP). (2015). Gazing at the future: The experiences of male and female physics and astronomy doctoral students in the UK.

Jackson, E. (2017, July 26). Damned if you do… banal gendered exclusions in academia, babies and 'dinner with other candidates'. [Web log post]. Retrieved from https://www.thesociologicalreview.com/blog/damned-if-you-do-banal-gendered-exclusions-in-academia-babies-and-the-dinner-with-the-other-candidates.html?utm_content=buffer953fc&utm_medium=social&utm_source=facebook.com&utm_campaign=buffer%20(Jackson,%202017)

Jackson, C., & Sundaram, V. (2020). *Lad culture in higher education: Sexism, sexual harassment and violence*. Routledge.
Jazvac-Martek, M. (2009). Oscillating role identities: The academic experiences of education doctoral students. *Innovations in Education and Teaching International, 46*(3), 253–264. https://doi.org/10.1080/14703290903068862
Kinman, G., & Jones, F. (2008). A life beyond work? job demands, work-life balance, and wellbeing in UK academics. *Journal of Human Behavior in the Social Environment, 17*(1-2), 41–60. https://doi.org/10.1080/10911350802165478
Knights, D., & Richards, W. (2003). Sex discrimination in UK academia. *Gender, Work & Organization, 10*(2), 213–238. https://doi.org/10.1111/1468-0432.t01-1-00012
Knorr-Cetina, K. (1995). Laboratory studies: The cultural approach to the study of science. *Handbook of Science and Technology Studies, 140*–167.
Kulis, S., Sicotte, D., & Collins, S. (2002). More than a pipeline problem: Labor supply constraints and gender stratification across academic science disciplines. *Research in Higher Education, 43*(6), 657–691.
Lave, J., & Wenger, E. (1991). *Situated learning: Legitimate peripheral participation*. Cambridge University Press.
Lazarus, B. B., Ritter, L. M., & Ambrose, S. A. (2000). *The woman's guide to navigating the Ph. D. in engineering & science*. Wiley.
Lee, A. (2008). How are doctoral students supervised? Concepts of doctoral research supervision. *Studies in Higher Education, 33*(3), 267–281. https://doi.org/10.1080/03075070802049202
Lee, D. (1998). Sexual harassment in PhD supervision. *Gender and Education, 10*(3), 299–312. https://doi.org/10.1080/09540259820916
Leonard, D. (2001). *A woman's guide to doctoral studies*. Open University Press.
Levin, S. (2017, March 8). Sexual harassment: Records show how University of California faculty target students. *The Guardian*. Retrieved from https://www.theguardian.com/australia-news/2017/aug/01/sexual-assault-report-universities-called-on-to-act-on-damning-figures
Lott, J. L., Gardner, S., & Powers, D. A. (2009). Doctoral student attrition in the STEM fields: An exploratory event history analysis. *Journal of College Student Retention: Research, Theory & Practice, 11*(2), 247–266.
Lucas, L. (2006). *The Research game in academic life*. SRHE/Open University Press.
Lynch, K. (2010). Carelessness: A hidden doxa of higher education. *Arts and Humanities in Higher Education, 9*(1), 54–67. https://doi.org/10.1177/1474022209350104

Macfarlane, B. (2017). The ethics of multiple authorship: Power, performativity and the gift economy. *Studies in Higher Education, 42*(7), 1194–1210.

Manathunga, C. (2014). *Intercultural postgraduate supervision: Reimagining time, place and knowledge*. Routledge.

Martin, B. (2014, January 2). Exploitation by supervisors must stop. *Times Higher Education*. Retrieved from https://www.timeshighereducation.com/comment/opinion/exploitation-by-supervisors-must-stop/2010096.article

Mason, M. A., & Goulden, M. (2004). Marriage and baby blues: Redefining gender equity in the academy. *The Annals of the American Academy of Political and Social Science, 596*(1), 86–103. https://doi.org/10.1177/0002716204596001104

Mason, M. A., Goulden, M., & Frasch, K. (2009). Why graduate students reject the fast track. *Academe, 95*(1), 11–16.

Mason, M. A., Wolfinger, N. H., & Goulden, M. (2013). *Do babies matter? Gender and family in the ivory tower*. Rutgers University Press.

Matthiesen, J. K., & Binder, M. (2009). *How to survive your doctorate: What others don't tell you*. Open University Press.

May, V. (2013). *Connecting self to society: Belonging in a changing world*. Macmillan International Higher Education.

McAlpine, L., & Akerlind, G. (2010). *Becoming an academic*. Macmillan International Higher Education.

McAlpine, L., Amundsen, C., & Jazvac-Martek, M. (2010). Living and imagining academic identities. In L. McAlpine & G. Akerlind (Eds.), *Becoming an academic: International perspectives* (pp. 129–149). Palgrave Macmillan.

McIlwee, J. S., & Robinson, J. G. (1992). *Women in engineering: Gender, power, and workplace culture*. SUNY Press.

Meschitti, V. (2020). Being an early career academic: Is there space for gender equality in the neoliberal university?. In *Gender, science and innovation: New perspectives* (pp. 16–34). Edward Elgar.

Miller, L. (2003). Belonging to country—a philosophical anthropology. *Journal of Australian Studies, 27*(76), 215–223.

Morley, L. (2009). Momentum and melancholia: Women in higher education internationally. In *The Routledge international handbook of the sociology of education* (pp. 402–413). Routledge.

Morris, C., & Wisker, G. (2011). *Troublesome encounters: Strategies for managing the wellbeing of master's and doctoral education students during their learning processes*. HEA ESCalate Subject Centre Report.

Morrish, L. (2019). *Pressure vessels: The epidemic of poor mental health among higher education staff*. Higher Education Policy Institute.

Murray, J. (2021, May 16). Universities are failing to tackle rape culture on campus. Retrieved from https://www.theguardian.com/world/2021/may/16/universities-rape-culture-on-campus-students-protest

Nature. (2019). Nature PhD survey 2019: Report by Shift Learning. Retrieved from https://figshare.com/s/74a5ea79d76ad66a8af8

Nerad, M., & Cerny, J. (1999). Postdoctoral patterns, career advancement, and problems. *Science (New York, N.Y.), 285*(5433), 1533–1535. https://doi.org/10.1126/science.285.5433.1533

Oberlander, S. E., & Spencer, R. J. (2006). Graduate students and the culture of authorship. *Ethics & Behavior, 16*(3), 217–232. https://doi.org/10.1207/s15327019eb1603_3

O'Hagan, C., O'Connor, P., Myers, E. S., Baisner, L., Apostolov, G., Topuzova, I., Saglamer, G., Mine, T., & Çağlayan, H. (2019). Perpetuating academic capitalism and maintaining gender orders through career practices in STEM in universities. *Critical Studies in Education, 60*(2), 205–225.

Parry, S. (2007). *Disciplines and doctorates.* Springer.

Pearson, M., Cowan, A., Liston, A., Boud, D., & Lee, A. (2009). PhD education in science. In D. Boud & A. Lee (Eds.), *Changing practices of doctoral education* (pp. 100–112). Routledge.

Phillips, E., & Pugh, D. (2015). *How to get a PhD: A handbook for students and their supervisors* (6th ed.). Open University Press.

Phipps, A. (2018). 'Lad culture' and sexual violence against students. In *The Routledge handbook of gender and violence* (pp. 171–182). Routledge.

Phipps, A., & Young, I. (2013). *That's what she said: Women students' experiences of 'lad culture' in higher education.* Project Report. National Union of Students.

Puwar, N. (2004). Thinking about making a difference. *The British Journal of Politics & International Relations, 6*(1), 65–80. https://doi.org/10.1111/j.1467-856x.2004.00127.x

Pyhältö, K., & Keskinen, J. (2012). Doctoral students' sense of relational agency in their scholarly communities. *International Journal of Higher Education, 1*(2), 136–149.

Read, B., & Leathwood, C. (2018). Tomorrow's a mystery: Constructions of the future and 'un/becoming' amongst 'early' and 'late' career academics. *International Studies in Sociology of Education, 27*(4), 333–351.

Reay, D. (2000). "Dim dross": Marginalised women both inside and outside the academy. *Women's Studies International Forum, 23*(1), 13–21. https://doi.org/10.1016/S0277-5395(99)00092-8

Rolf, H. G. (2021). Navigating power in doctoral publishing: A data feminist approach. *Teaching in Higher Education, 26*(3), 488–507.

Rosser, S. V. (2004). *The science glass ceiling: Academic women scientists and the struggle to succeed.* Psychology Press.

Rossiter, M. (2004). Educational relationships and possible selves in the adult undergraduate experience. *The Cyril O'Houle Scholars in Adult and Continuing Education Program Global Research Perspectives, 4*, 138–155. https://doi.org/10.1002/ace.259

Royal Society. (2010). The Scientific Century: Securing our future prosperity. Retrieved from https://royalsociety.org/-/media/Royal_Society_Content/policy/publications/2010/4294970126.pdf

Royal Society. (2014a). A picture of the UK scientific workforce.

Royal Society. (2014b, June 4). Managing the careers expectations of STEMM PhD students roundtable. University of Edinburgh. Retrieved from https://royalsociety.org/-/media/policy/projects/doctoral-students/managing-career-expectations-roundtable-phd-supervisors.pdf?la=en-GB

Royal Society of Chemistry. (2008). *The chemistry PhD: The impact on women's retention.* A report for the UK Resource Centre for Women in SET and the Royal Society of Chemistry, 1–38.

Royal Society of Chemistry. (2018). Breaking the barriers: Women's retention and progression in the chemical sciences. Retrieved from http://www.rsc.org/campaigning-outreach/campaigning/incldiv/inclusion%2D%2Ddiversity-resources/womens-progression/s.

Sánchez de Madariaga, I., de la Rica, S., & Dolado, J. J. (2011). White paper on the position of women in science in Spain.. Ministry of Science and Innovation.

Sandberg, S. (2013). *Lean in: Women, work, and the will to lead.* Random House.

Soe, L., & Yakura, E. K. (2008). What's wrong with the pipeline? Assumptions about gender and culture in IT work. *Women's Studies, 37*(3), 176–201. https://doi.org/10.1080/00497870801917028

Stoilescu, D., & McDougall, D. (2010). Starting to publish academic research as a doctoral student. *International Journal of Doctoral Studies, 5*(7), 79–92. Retrieved from http://ambounds.org/docs/716/Stoilescu,%20Dorian%20and%20Douglas%20McDougall.%202012.pdf

Stout, J. G., Grunberg, V. A., & Ito, T. A. (2016). Gender roles and stereotypes about science careers help explain women and men's science pursuits. *Sex Roles, 75*(9), 490–499.

Stubb, J., Pyhältö, K., & Lonka, K. (2011). Balancing between inspiration and exhaustion: PhD students' experienced socio-psychological well-being. *Studies in Continuing Education, 33*(1), 33–50.

Teeuwsen, P., Ratković, S., & Tilley, S. A. (2014). Becoming academics: Experiencing legitimate peripheral participation in part-time doctoral studies. *Studies in Higher Education, 39*(4), 680–694.

Turner, C. (2017, January 18). Investigation into University of Sussex lecturer unearths further reports of alleged harassment and sexual abuse. *The Telegraph*. Retrieved from http://www.telegraph.co.uk/education/2017/01/18/investigation-university-sussexlecturer-finds-history-harassment/

UK Council for Science and Technology. (2007). *Pathways to the future: The early careers of researchers in the UK*. Council for Science and Technology.

Universities UK. (2016). *Changing the culture: Report of the Universities UK Taskforce examining violence against women, harassment and hate crime affecting university students*. Universities UK.

Van Den Brink, M., & Stobbe, L. (2009). Doing gender in academic education: The paradox of visibility. *Gender, Work & Organization, 16*(4), 451–470. https://doi.org/10.1111/j.1468-0432.2008.00428.x

Vekkaila, J., Pyhältö, K., Hakkarainen, K., Keskinen, J., & Lonka, K. (2012). Doctoral students' key learning experiences in the natural sciences. *International Journal for Researcher Development, 3*(2), 154–183.

Vitae. (2017). *One size does not fit all: Arts and humanities doctoral and early career researchers' professional development survey*. The Careers Research and Advisory Centre (CRAC) Limited.

Vitae. (2019). Do researchers' careers have to be precarious? Retrieved from https://www.vitae.ac.uk/impact-and-evaluation/what-do-researchers-do/do-researchers-careers-have-to-be-precarious-research-article.pdf/view

Walsh, E. (2010). A model of research group microclimate: Environmental and cultural factors affecting the experiences of overseas research students in the UK. *Studies in Higher Education, 35*(5), 545–560.

Ward, K., & Wolf-Wendel, L. (2012). *Academic motherhood: How faculty manage work and family*. Rutgers University Press.

Weale, C., & Bannock, S. (2016, October 7). 'I was so traumatised': accounts of sexual harassment in UK universities. *The Guardian*: https://www.theguardian.com/education/2016/oct/07/i-was-so-traumatised-accounts-ofsexual-harassment-in-uk-universities

Weale, S., & Batty, D. (2016, October 21). University sex abuse report fails to tackle staff attacks on UK students. *The Guardian*. Retrieved from https://

www.theguardian.com/society/2016/oct/21/university-sex-abuse-report-fails-staff-attacks-students

Weale, S., & Batty, D. (2017, March 6). Calls for action by universities on 'epidemic' of harassment on campus. *The Guardian*. Retrieved from https://www.theguardian.com/education/2017/mar/06/calls-for-review-into-how-universities-handle-sexual-harassment-allegations

Weeks, J. (1990). The values of difference in identity. In J. Rutherford (Ed.), *Identity: Community, culture, difference* (pp. 88–100). Lawrence and Wishart.

Weisgram, E. S., & Diekman, A. B. (2017). Making STEM "family friendly": The impact of perceiving science careers as family-compatible. *Social Sciences, 6*(2), 61.

Wellcome Trust. (2013). *Risks and rewards: How PhD students choose their careers*. Ipsos MORI.

Wellcome Trust. (2020). What researchers think about the culture they work in. Retrieved from https://cms.wellcome.org/sites/default/files/what-researchers-think-about-the-culture-they-work-in.pdf

White, J., & Nonnamaker, J. (2008). Belonging and mattering: How doctoral students experience community. *NASPA Journal, 45*(3), 350–372.

White, K. (2004). The leaking pipeline: Women postgraduate and early career researchers in Australia. *Tertiary Education & Management, 10*(3), 227–241. https://doi.org/10.1023/b:team.0000044828.44536.67

White, K. (2013). An outsider in academia. In B. Bagilhole & K. White (Eds.), *Generation and gender in academia* (pp. 103–126). Palgrave Macmillan.

Wisker, G. (2007). *The postgraduate research handbook: Succeed with your MA, MPhil, EdD and PhD*. Palgrave Macmillan.

Wisker, G. (2010). The 'good enough' doctorate: Doctoral learning journeys. *Acta Academica: Critical Views on Society, Culture and Politics, 1*, 223–242.

Xu, Y. J., & Martin, C. L. (2011). Gender differences in STEM disciplines: From the aspects of informal professional networking and faculty career development. *Gender Issues, 28*(3), 134.

Zhou, N. (2017, August 1). Sexual assault report: Universities called on to act on 'damning' figures. *The Guardian*. Retrieved from https://www.theguardian.com/australia-news/2017/aug/01/sexual-assault-report-universities-called-on-to-act-on-damning-figures

## Women in Health and Related Sciences: Restoryings of Participants' Doctoral Journeys

### Jessie

Jessie was in her mid-30s when she started her PhD in Public Health at Modern University. She was married, and had two children under five when she began her studies. Before this, she had worked in market research in a role which had required a significant commute. She had initially planned to do a master's degree in Public Health in order to pursue a career in this sector, but was advised by an academic to apply for a PhD instead because of her previous research experience. She decided to apply to her local institution as it fit well with family life. Jessie hoped to develop a local network of contacts which could lead to future career opportunities, and considered an academic career as a possible career option. She perceived her motivations for doing a PhD as very different to those of her peers, as hers were largely career-oriented. She also recognised that the pressures on her to find a suitable role after the PhD were increased due to her family responsibilities, as her husband supported her and their family financially during the PhD.

Jessie appreciated the opportunity to do a PhD in that it allowed her academic freedom and independence in her work. Initially, she considered the PhD as a route to securing a new career and allowing her a better work-life balance. However, the opportunity to do in-depth research appealed for social justice reasons as well as for her own career development. She perceived that in her previous job, she had often felt as though the work had not made good use of public money, but Jessie felt her doctoral research would make a positive difference. Studying for a doctorate also had a significant impact on Jessie's values and politics. She became more politically aware, and her views changed as a result of what she read and encountered during her studies.

During the PhD, Jessie generally found it more straightforward to balance her work with her caring responsibilities, due to the increased flexibility of doctoral study in comparison to her previous role. She appreciated that whilst her hours were limited, she was able to fit her research around childcare, making up time on evenings and weekends. However, this became more challenging in her second year of the PhD when her eldest child started school. Jessie recognised that the impact of this was gendered, and whilst her husband continued working, her progress with her research was compromised by the need to take on these additional responsibilities and ensure that her child was prepared to start school.

Though Jessie's motivations to do a PhD were strongly career-oriented, she did not start her doctorate with a fixed idea of her post-PhD career options. Whilst she considered various potential career paths, including consultancy, academic work and returning to freelance consultancy, she became aware of some barriers which may prevent her from pursuing an academic role. Jessie was frustrated by the demands of an academic career such as the need to demonstrate a strong publication record, and often the ability of individuals to be mobile, requiring either relocation or a long commute, neither of which she was prepared to do. She also became discouraged from pursuing an academic role as she perceived she would need to work in a more junior role such as a research assistant, which she was not prepared to do given her previous research experience. Further, Jessie became increasingly sceptical about the ability of academic research to effect social change as she progressed with her PhD, and expressed concerns about what impact she would be able to make as an academic.

Despite her criticisms of academia, Jessie did not dismiss the prospect of pursuing an academic career after the PhD. She considered various possible options for developing this type of career, including a postdoctoral role which would allow her to extend her doctoral research. However, she recognised that despite having relevant skills and experience she would likely not be taken seriously without the academic credibility represented by a strong publication record. Jessie was therefore pragmatic about the types of opportunities which may be open to her after the PhD, and considered that she may have to return to freelance consultancy work.

## Sally

Sally was in her mid-30s when she began her PhD in Sports Psychology at Modern University. She was in a relationship, with no caring responsibilities. Prior to her PhD, she had a career in the charity sector before returning to university to qualify as a psychologist. She committed a significant amount of time, effort and money to her decision, returning to university part-time for 2 years to get the academic credit required for a master's, whilst working in two part-time jobs and living off savings. Sally applied for a PhD because she had enjoyed studying and was unsatisfied in her career. She was concerned that a PhD might lead her away from doing applied work in her field, but designed a proposal which she hoped would enable her to make a positive impact. Sally viewed the PhD as an opportunity to develop specialist skills, but was keen to ensure that it was not just a theoretical piece of work. She was unsure of what career she wanted to pursue after the PhD and but considered a range of options, including academia, though she was sceptical about the potential for traditional academic research to have a social impact, and consultancy work.

Adjusting from studying for a master's to doctoral study was initially difficult, and though Sally had a good relationship with her peers, she found studying for a PhD more emotionally challenging than she had expected. Initially Sally struggled with her supervisors' style of supervision, which she perceived as distant and pragmatic rather than emotionally supportive. As she progressed with her studies, however, she saw their approach as helpful in enabling her to become more self-sufficient, though she felt that more positive reinforcement from her supervisors would have been helpful.

During her PhD, Sally's personal circumstances had a considerable impact on her wellbeing and experience of doctoral study. She was in a long-term, long-distance relationship and found it increasingly difficult not being able to plan a future with her partner. This made focusing on her PhD challenging, and caused her to question her commitment to her studies. Sally found that her gender and age meant that others perceived her decision to do a PhD as unconventional, and was frustrated that family and friends would often ask about her plans after the PhD, rather than expressing interest in her research itself. Sally considered leaving her PhD at several points due to these personal pressures, but decided to persist with the doctorate as she was motivated by her topic and the potential to make a positive difference through her research. Though she acknowledged that the easier option would be to return to her previous career, she recognised that she would soon be bored.

Sally considered a range of career options after the PhD. Her supervisors encouraged her to consider a post-doctoral role, but she was uncertain about this due to concerns about the impact on her mental health of progressing straight from a PhD into this type of role, which she viewed as of high pressure. Sally's view of academia as a potential career path was shaped by how she and her peers were treated by her institution during her doctorate. She felt that PhD students were not respected by academics, and became increasingly frustrated that PhD students were often not included in departmental activities. Sally perceived that she and her peers were treated as lower status members of their academic community and not valued for their contributions. However, she was keen to pursue a career which enabled her to use her research skills, and considered potential options such as consultancy and starting her own business.

## Liz

Liz was in her mid-50s when she began her doctorate in Health Sciences at Modern University. Prior to the PhD, she studied for her undergraduate and master's degrees at a different university. Before this, she had previously worked in a clinical role in the NHS. She was married, with no caring responsibilities. Liz was motivated to do a PhD because she enjoyed studying and doing research. She was encouraged to pursue further study by her master's supervisors, and secured a fully funded PhD at Modern University. She did not have a fixed career aspiration when she started the doctorate, but considered applying for an academic job after completing the PhD.

Doing a PhD had not been Liz's original intention when she first returned to education after a career in the NHS. She had left school at a young age and initially worked in an administrative role before training as a clinician. After retiring from the NHS due to ill health, Liz began a part-time course in counselling alongside voluntary work, which led her to an access course in health sciences. She had enjoyed this, and decided to apply to university to do an undergraduate degree in a related discipline. Being offered a place at university was a momentous and emotional experience, as Liz had assumed that higher education would not necessarily be accessible to her as a working-class woman. She enjoyed her undergraduate degree, particularly writing her dissertation, and was awarded funding to do a master's. She was encouraged to apply for PhD funding and became keen to pursue a doctorate as it would enable her to further pursue her research interests. Liz felt that others might perceive her as odd for doing a PhD later in life, but was appreciative of the freedom and independence it represented. Despite her educational success, Liz lacked confidence in her academic abilities and struggled with imposter syndrome during the PhD.

The experience of the PhD in her first year was not what Liz had anticipated; though she had expected it to be academically challenging, she had not considered that she would struggle emotionally with the challenges of doctoral study. She acknowledged that due to her age she had felt entitled to enjoy the experience, whereas in reality she had a difficult relationship with her supervisors, who put her under considerable pressure to publish work from an early stage. The difficulties Liz faced with her supervisors and the pressure she was working under resulted in her developing anxiety, to the point where she considered getting medical help and eventually sought support from a staff member with pastoral responsibilities for doctoral students. She debated whether to leave her PhD on multiple occasions during her first year, due to her concerns about her wellbeing and the impact on her home life. However, her relationship with her supervisors improved over time and she managed to establish a healthier work-life balance in her second year with the support of her husband and peer community, which made a positive difference.

Liz had no fixed plan after the PhD when she began her studies. She considered that she was not on the same trajectory as her younger peers, and was not intending to pursue a particular career path. However, she had various possible options in mind after her doctorate, including academic research, teaching and consultancy work. Liz recognised, though, that there were considerable differences in the way that she viewed her own post-PhD career in comparison to her husband's career, and perceived that his work would need priority.

# 4

# Negotiating Legitimacy: Struggles and Strategies for Feeling Belonging in Health and Related Sciences

This chapter attends to the ways in which participants in health and related sciences—subjects often described as 'practice professions' because of their clinical focus (Boore, 1996)—attempted to develop a sense of belonging within their academic communities. It explores the challenges that participants encountered to belonging and the strategies they developed in trying to overcome these barriers. Drawing on literature which highlights the uncertain status of doctoral students within academic hierarchies (Morris & Wisker, 2011; Wisker et al., 2010), this chapter explores how participants understood their position within their academic communities and how this awareness shaped their sense of belonging. Further, attention is paid to how different aspects of academic cultures influenced individuals' ability to feel a sense of belonging within their departmental community. In particular, this chapter explores the impact of neoliberalised academic working practices, such as expectations of research productivity, on women doctoral students and how they viewed an academic career. This chapter also examines how gendered academic cultures shaped the lived experiences of women doctoral students in health sciences, attending to the ways in which gendered dynamics such as 'lad culture' and 'banter' influenced participants' experiences of doctoral study and contributed to feelings of marginalisation (Jackson & Sundaram, 2020; Phipps & Young, 2013). Using concepts of legitimate peripheral participation (Lave & Wenger, 1991; Teeuwsen et al., 2014), I explore some of the challenges to legitimacy that participants experienced, but also the strategies they devised in order to develop feelings of legitimacy, validity and, ultimately, belonging.

## Studying for a Doctorate in Health and Related Sciences

Whilst more is known about the experiences of doctoral students in the humanities, social sciences and pure sciences, the perspectives of those in health-related disciplines, such as public health and health sciences, are less well documented in the literature. A key characteristic of research in health-related disciplines is the focus on the application of research in relation to practice for the benefit of patients or service users (Boore, 1996). Research (and thus doctoral thesis) topics in these subjects are likely to be influenced or directed by existing work undertaken by relevant professional bodies, or the NHS (Becher, 1994; Boore, 1996; Holloway & Walker, 1999). The applied nature of research in these subjects means that doctoral study in health and related sciences may take the form of a professional doctorate, rather than a PhD, especially for those working in a distinct area of healthcare such as nursing or midwifery (McVicar et al., 2006). However, the experiences discussed in this chapter pertain to those studying for a PhD rather than for another type of doctorate.

As with other disciplinary groups (notably pure sciences), subjects within the broad grouping of health and related sciences are highly gendered in terms of participation and career progression. There is considerable overlap between these subjects (which can range from nursing and physiotherapy to sports and exercise psychology) with the caring professions, which remain overwhelmingly dominated by women (ILO, 2018). This is particularly evident in the proportions of women working in the UK's National Health Service, where women constitute 82% of the workforce (Public Health England, 2017). In the UK, women make up around 80% of those studying subjects allied to medicine, such as physiotherapy, at undergraduate and postgraduate taught levels (Advance HE,

2021a). However, whilst around three quarters of academics in nursing and allied health professions are women (Advance HE, 2021a, 2021b), the majority of professors in these disciplines are men (Santos & Dang Van Phu, 2019). This highly gendered pattern of progression in the health and related sciences constitutes the disciplinary context in which participants studied for their doctorate, and informs the wider culture within which they worked and studied.

In relation to doctoral research, whilst some students may have previous professional experience in the health sector, others may have academic backgrounds in disciplines outside of health (van Schalkwyk et al., 2016). Indeed, research in health and related sciences often spans disciplinary boundaries (Curry et al., 2012), resulting in a wide range of approaches to research in these subjects. Doctoral students in these disciplines are often mature students returning to study, many of whom undertake research part-time whilst continuing their professional practice, though some may undertake doctoral study to pursue an academic research career (Holloway & Walker, 1999). For doctoral students in these subjects, their research is likely to involve working with participants who are past or current patients, carers or other service users, increasing the likelihood that they will be working with vulnerable individuals (*ibid*, 1999).

These particular characteristics of doctoral study in health and related sciences produce a number of challenges for doctoral students attempting to establish academic legitimacy in these fields. Individuals in these subjects are likely to encounter issues not necessarily faced by those working in other disciplines, such as potentially working in challenging settings with vulnerable groups, and negotiating clinical as well as academic gatekeepers (Holloway & Walker, 1999). Further, supervisors may be professional practitioners as well as academics, creating additional power dynamics to be negotiated within supervisory relationships. In addition, the applied nature of research in health and related sciences means that doctoral students need to familiarise themselves not only with their particular departmental culture but also with the clinical or professional setting in which they conduct their research. There is also the need to establish a balance between the academic side of their work and the applied nature of the research. Thus, issues of power and status have a significant impact on doctoral students' ability to develop a sense of belonging.

## Struggling to Belong: The Liminal Status of Doctoral Students

Literature highlights how initiatives which clarify the status of research students and recognise them as valuable contributors to their academic community are key methods by which institutions can facilitate doctoral students' belonging (Deem & Brehony, 2000; Morris & Wisker, 2011). Yet the position of doctoral students within academic hierarchies is often ambiguous, with tension over whether 'the graduate student is, or should be, treated as an independent, autonomous member of the community, or…placed within a subordinate position' (Delamont et al., 2000, p.176). This tension is particularly clear in the experiences of Jessie, who began her doctorate in public health at Modern University in her mid-30s after a successful career. She began the PhD hoping to establish a new career trajectory, and viewed an academic career as a possible option on completing her doctorate. However, she perceived early on in her studies that she and her peers were not viewed as valuable members of the departmental community. This is not uncommon; doctoral students often report a sense of low status within their institutions, which can create feelings of isolation and challenge individuals' ability to develop a sense of belonging (see Kurtz-Costes et al., 2006; Morris & Wisker, 2011). Yet Jessie felt that beyond simply being perceived as low status, academics in her department saw PhD students as an additional burden, whose value would not materialise until they potentially become academics themselves:

> I don't think they see there's any value in PhD students. PhD students are there to kind of…get a job done and to a certain extent they're a bit annoying for the academics, they, you know, they just take up a lot of their time, they don't see the value…until you become sort of part of the…academic staff. (Interview 1)

Jessie's perception that departmental staff feel doctoral students are only valuable once they become academics indicates an ongoing assumption of the PhD simply as preparation for an academic career (Neumann & Tan, 2011). This understanding of the doctorate is problematic, especially as this has led to a lack of adequate advice for doctoral students on how to build a career outside academia (see Vitae, 2017; Wellcome Trust, 2013).

The perception of doctoral students as burdensome to academics is particularly difficult for individuals like Jessie, who started their PhD later in life and have considerable career experience: *"there just seems to be this perception amongst the academic staff that students are all like kind of inexperienced, young…there to be patronised…and not worth my attention"* (Interview 2). Jessie's understanding of how PhD students are viewed by academics reflects the persistent stereotype within institutional and sector policy of doctoral students as young, inexperienced and purely motivated by an academic career (McCulloch & Stokes, 2008; Morris, 2021; Pearson et al., 2011). Despite having considerable previous research experience, her enquiries about contributing to wider research activities taking place in her department were rebuffed, which she interpreted as wilful exclusion:

> I have got a lot of experience at bidding for work, writing proposals, winning work from open tenders, and they all know that, they all know that but not once has anybody come to me and said do you want to have a look over this. (Interview 1)

Jessie's experience of being perceived simply as a student by academics in her department is frustrating, particularly given the sacrifices she made to undertake the doctorate. This included becoming more financially dependent on her husband, due to the transition from her previous salary to a doctoral scholarship, but also the significant compromise she made to her work-life balance. Though Jessie studied full-time for her doctorate, she had childcare commitments 2 days a week, meaning that the majority of weekends and evenings were spent on her doctoral research. Beyond being unable to contribute to wider departmental activities, Jessie also perceived that doctoral students' contributions to the research community were not valued. After volunteering to become a student rep, she helped to organise a doctoral research symposium at the end of her first year but was frustrated that senior academics did not attend, and she viewed this as indicative of their disinterest in doctoral students' research:

> They have said at the away day that they see the PhD students as being really central to everything that they do…but then like none of the senior members of staff from my centre were actually at the symposium…I have found it quite frustrating. (Interview 2)

Understanding belonging as affective, involving connections with others and contingent on the recognition of individuals by others within the community, it is clear that Jessie's attempts to effectively negotiate the power relations within her department and establish a sense of belonging are unsuccessful. Her efforts to support the symposium and participate in her departmental community as a student rep demonstrates her agency in attempting to belong and be recognised as a valuable member of her departmental community (Emmioglu et al., 2017; May, 2013; White & Nonnamaker, 2008). However, her perception of senior academics as disinterested in her and her peers' work indicates how doctoral students may feel marginalised within academic communities if they are unable to participate meaningfully in departmental activities (Deem & Brehony, 2000). In contrast, Jessie compared the culture of her department with that of another department at her institution, where doctoral students are included in wider activities and treated as members of staff:

> They're given an academic staff email, they're invited to the staff do's…it's just the approach, it's like your part of our team, and we want to nurture you and grow you into part of our like staff team, in the long term, if you want that. Whereas this doesn't feel like that at all in ours. (Interview 1)

For doctoral students, belonging is often predicated on being acknowledged by others as valid and valuable members of their academic community (Morris & Wisker, 2011; White & Nonnamaker, 2008). This is particularly important for those who hope to develop academic careers, who must successfully negotiate acceptance into their disciplinary community by gaining the recognition of existing members (Delamont et al., 2000; Parry, 2007). Thus, whilst Jessie exerted agency in attempting to participate as a valid member of her academic community, organising a research symposium and trying to become involved in wider research activities, her failure to secure recognition from academics in her department that she is *"part of the team"* indicates that academic hierarchies pose a significant barrier to her ability to belong. Thus, Jessie's attempts to belong and move from a position of peripheral participation (Lave & Wenger, 1991) to a more central role in her departmental community are blocked by the behaviour of academics in her department. Academics act as gatekeepers into the disciplinary community (Parry, 2007), and in Jessie's experience, their attitude prevented her from being able to participate more fully in her departmental community. This keeps doctoral students on the periphery, contributing to a disempowering experience (Lave & Wenger, 1991) and sustaining the liminal status of doctoral students within the academic hierarchy.

Yet Jessie contrived to develop a proactive approach to developing a sense of disciplinary belonging, taking actions to connect with other scholars in her field in order to establish disciplinary connections outside of her institution. She felt that her own supervisors were not experts in her chosen methodology and therefore established contact with another academic who was an expert in this area:

> I met a woman last week who is basically the supervisor I should have, she's at [institution]. She's doing work which is very practically applied…she's doing a fellowship which is about basically turning academic work into…what it means on the ground, which is exactly where I want to be… I'd written a research question which I sent to her by e-mail, and she said it's actually very similar to one I'd identified, but I haven't got capacity to do it…so she gets the methodology, and she gets the subject area, she's got all the links and the contacts and everything that I might need to help facilitate my project. (Interview 1)

In this way, Jessie demonstrated agency in attempting to secure the academic support that she needs from an individual outside the rigid academic hierarchy she perceived in her own department. She felt that this academic "*gets*" her methodology and subject area, and this provides a source of external validation for Jessie's research. Developing this relationship allowed Jessie to forge a key connection with a gatekeeper in her field who may facilitate her progress as well as her future career; she has "*all the links and the contacts that I might need*". Thus, Jessie was able to establish some sense of disciplinary belonging through this process of networking and receiving recognition from a scholar in her field.

For Jessie, these barriers to belonging within her departmental academic community led her to question the viability of an academic career. She perceived academia as very hierarchical, and she felt that until she obtained her PhD she would not be valued or recognised as a valid member of her academic community. She viewed the doctorate as an "*initiation rite*" (Interview 2) which must be passed before she would be able to gain acceptance and progress her career. Her comments resonate with literature which highlights how the identity shift from professional to student is particularly challenging for doctoral students returning to study after successful careers (see Morris & Wisker, 2011). Beyond the PhD qualification itself, Jessie perceived that there were other various signifiers of prestige which must also be acquired during the academic career journey, such as publications, which she found frustrating, and which made her feel that "*the hierarchy is to a degree intractable*" (Interview 2).

Beyond issues of perceived status, other structural aspects of academic life could also reinforce individuals' sense of liminality, and therefore compromise their ability to feel a sense of belonging to their academic community. Sally—a PhD student in sports psychology at Modern University—encountered numerous administrative hurdles in attempting to start her data collection, which caused significant frustration:

> 13/10/2015
> 
> I'm having one of those days when I am beyond frustrated. I am actually genuinely angry at this point and having to stop myself send a strongly worded email to my supervisors. Before I can submit to NHS ethics I need to get [university] agreement that they will support the project indemnity-wise… Now this should not be an arduous process given that I am only conducting non-invasive qualitative research. I have been waiting over two

months now for a decision which is beyond ridiculous—the NHS process itself is only 14 days and that's much more in-depth. Coupled with this, I have a bunch of clearance checks and governance issues to complete before I can get my NHS research passport to start the project. This must surely have been done by lots of people who have gone before me, yet not one person in any department will take responsibility for signing this off. I am going around and around in circles and have so far been directed to no less than 10 different people.

I just completed my [university form] and answered a whole bunch of questions about whether I have got time to complete my research within the three year time period—well, not if the University continues to hold me up like this. It is difficult enough to get through the ridiculous red tape of the NHS without your own institution preventing you from moving forward. What's most heart-breaking is that a few months ago I was in a good position having built really good solid stakeholder engagement and buy-in. Every day that this ludicrous situation drags on I feel like I am losing that engagement.

The difficulties Sally experienced in navigating university procedures, and the lack of support she received from her department, prevented her from starting fieldwork as planned. She feared that this delay would affect her ability to capitalise on the relationships she had cultivated with stakeholders, and thus the level of engagement from potential participants. Sally's experience of needing to undertake both university and NHS processes in order to start her research highlights how doctoral students doing research in health and related sciences are often required to negotiate gatekeepers within multiple spheres, in clinical as well as academic settings (see Holloway & Walker, 1999). Further, research indicates how the experience of conducting fieldwork during the doctorate can facilitate academic identity development (see Emmioglu et al., 2017; Mantai, 2017), meaning that the delay Sally encountered to engaging in collection of her data also had an impact on her ability to feel like a legitimate member of her academic community.

In the above diary entry, Sally indicates that navigating these various administrative processes has not only delayed the start of her data collection, but may also have consequences for her ability to complete her doctorate on time. The pressure of the thesis submission deadline can negatively affect doctoral students' well-being (see Grover, 2007; Levecque et al., 2017), particularly when this is connected to the end of individuals' funding period—something which has been termed the 'pinch point' of doctoral study (Wellcome Trust, 2013, p.19). Experiencing this delay to her fieldwork therefore has a range of impacts on Sally, both in terms of compromising her progress and in relation to her well-being. Viewing belonging as affective, it is clear from Sally's admission that she was "*beyond frustrated*" and "*genuinely angry*", that encountering university bureaucracy had a negative impact on her ability to feel a sense of belonging to her academic community.

In addition to structural aspects of academic culture which could reinforce the liminal status of doctoral students, the actions of existing members of the academic community had a significant effect on individuals' sense of belonging. This was particularly felt in relation to how individuals were treated as doctoral students by their supervisors as well as by other senior academics. Some supervisors behaved in a way which participants felt reinforced academic hierarchies and was experienced as disempowering. For example, in her second year, Sally was encouraged to work on a publication with her supervisors, alongside academics from other institutions. On accidentally walking into a meeting of her supervisors with the other co-authors, she was frustrated at not having been either invited or introduced:

> I was well aware that there were people in that room who were my co-authors, and they are important people…very senior…and I wasn't introduced to any of them and I felt at that moment I felt extremely invisible…and afterwards I thought, well why wasn't I introduced you know why wasn't I important enough for…my supervisors…to say oh everyone this is our PhD student…she is the one that's writing the article. (Interview 2)

Sally viewed her supervisors' failure to introduce her to their co-authors as an important element in the power dynamics of this situation, ascribing this to her low status as a PhD student. Research indicates how supervisors act as gatekeepers for doctoral students' enculturation into the academic community, often enabling access to key networks and post-PhD career opportunities (see Denicolo & Becker, 2008; Dever et al., 2008; Wisker, 2007). Yet in this case, Sally is not invited to the meeting, and thus is unable to make connections with other academics. Understanding belonging as predicated on making positive connections with others and being recognised as a legitimate member of the community, Sally's admission that she felt *"extremely invisible"* indicates that her attempt to negotiate the power relations of her disciplinary community has been unsuccessful. Her perception that she wasn't *"important enough"* to be introduced to senior academics reflects literature which argues that doctoral students may be treated as subordinates rather than equal members of the academic community (Delamont et al., 2000; Morris & Wisker, 2011), with negative implications for individuals' confidence and academic identity development (see Jazvac-Martek, 2009). A subsequent entry in Sally's research diary highlights how incidents such as this can contribute to ongoing feelings of marginalisation:

19/5/2015
I've been noticing a lot lately about this whole idea of PhD students being "low down on the food chain". We joke about it sometimes in our office, in terms of how important (or rather, unimportant!) we are to our supervisors. But it's not just our supervisors, it seems to be a cultural attitude that permeates throughout the University. It seems that when it suits the University we are treated as staff members and a bunch of responsibilities and expectations go with that, but then in other circumstances we are mere students with arguably lesser rights or voice…I actually think in some ways it can serve to make you feel devalued and undermine your confidence and/or enthusiasm.

Here, Sally links her supervisor's failure to treat her as an equal member of the research team and to a wider institutional culture of being dismissive of doctoral students. She notes that *"when it suits"*, she and her peers are treated like academics with equivalent responsibilities, but at other times are seen as *"lesser"*. Sally's experience shows how doctoral students are 'not always seen as equal to academic staff, although they may simultaneously be working in academic roles and contributing to their academic communities' (Morris & Wisker, 2011, p.8). The encounter that she describes draws attention to issues of power within the academy, and how academic contributions may be valued differentially according to the perceived status of individuals. Sally's attempt to belong to her disciplinary community by engaging in wider research activities with existing scholars was undermined by more powerful members of the community. Their actions—both excluding her from the meeting and failing to recognise her as a legitimate contributor to their research—maintain her peripheral status and contribute to her feelings of marginalisation, meaning she does not feel a sense of belonging to her academic community.

Encounters such as the one that Sally describes are indicative of what have been referred to as the micro-politics of the academy—the 'increasingly subtle and sophisticated ways in which dominance is achieved in academic organisations' (Morley, 1999, p.5). These small, informal encounters are significant in shaping how individuals understand their place within academia, and how able they are to envisage themselves continuing to participate in this environment. By virtue of their position in the academy, doctoral students are assigned a 'role identity…which implies certain hierarchies', but they are also often simultaneously 'endeavouring to develop another identity (that of scholar)' (McAlpine & Amundsen, 2009, p.112). In this instance, Sally's ability to develop a long-term, viable academic identity is impeded by the lack of recognition of her as a scholar by other academics in her field, meaning she cannot easily envisage herself in academia after the PhD:

> My supervisor is always going on about post doc stuff…I don't know that I can see myself doing that…maybe I will as time goes on, and I become more and more known in the university and could see myself being their colleague and working with them, so maybe that will change. (Interview 2)

Drawing on Jessie and Sally's experiences, it is clear that issues of power and status within academic hierarchies contributed to their sense of being in a liminal position as doctoral students. Despite their attempts to belong to their departmental and disciplinary communities, the actions of more senior academics and supervisors often kept them from participating more fully and being recognised as legitimate and valuable members of their academic community. This contributed to feelings of marginalisation and influenced how able they were to envisage themselves taking on academic identities in the future.

Yet one way that women doctoral students could address their liminal status was by seeking institutional support, which could help to facilitate a sense of belonging. For Liz, a mature student studying for a PhD in health sciences at Modern University, the transition to doctoral study had been challenging. Starting a doctorate was a significant milestone, representing a new stage in her life after previously retiring from the NHS due to ill health. Coming from a working-class background and having pursued an access course, followed by undergraduate and master's degrees, Liz acknowledged that she felt a little out of place as a doctoral student: "*I'm still a bit dazed and bemused by it all…I would love to be able to say well you know I planned this all years ago but I didn't at all, I kind of stumbled my way in here*" (Interview 1). Literature indicates how mature learners, especially women, often struggle with confidence and imposter syndrome (Morris, 2021) and may find it difficult to understand and adjust to academic culture as doctoral students (Morris & Wisker, 2011). Further, those from working-class backgrounds are more likely to experience imposter syndrome (Addison et al., 2022; Loveday, 2016), and thus feel marginalised within the academic environment. Whilst in her previous career Liz had worked very close to the university, she recognised that her life had changed dramatically when she started the PhD: "*in some ways I have come less than half a mile, but I feel like I have gone round the whole world in order to get here*" (Interview 1).

Thus, particular aspects of Liz's circumstances reinforced her marginal status, with implications for her ability to feel a sense of belonging. Her age, social class and previous educational experiences position her outside of the traditional conception of a PhD student, usually assumed to be young, ambitious men (see McCulloch & Stokes, 2008; Pearson et al., 2011). In addition, living at a distance from the institution where she studied for her PhD had made adjusting to doctoral study more difficult and reinforced her liminal status within her academic community. In a diary entry from her second year, Liz outlined how she had felt somewhat isolated by living elsewhere, as it meant missing out on social occasions and networking opportunities. However, accessing support from a departmental administrator enabled Liz to make arrangements which helped her to feel more connected to her academic community:

> 29.12.15
> It's a reflective time of year so I'm moved to reflect on my experience of the PhD process so far. It has taken me a while to feel a 'part of' and I think there have been a number of reasons for that…one fact that has impacted on my ability (as well as my desire) to fit in with the other PhD cohort is that it is quite a journey to uni for me. It has been made easier by the PhD administrator who acquires a parking permit for me to park on campus whenever she can and that helps tremendously especially as its quite a scary journey to where I park when its dark…The other is knowing that I won't be engaging in many of the locally held bonding sessions that have been organised, I guess I accept that there are certain times when I will stand alone and I'm used to that. This is especially true of the lunchtime/evening impromptu drinking sessions… That said, this is does seem to have changed lately and I've taken on a couple of roles that mean I will be networking more with others next year. I don't know when or why it changed but it just began to feel more comfortable to engage a bit more and even though I'm nervous about the time management element, I'm looking forward to being (or feeling) more 'part of'…I also went to my first 4 day conference alone with other academics and I think I 'held my own'. Who knows—I spent a lot of energy just trying not to look 'too weird and out of place' but nobody asked me to leave so that has to be a good sign?

Accessing support from her departmental administrator contributes to Liz's ability to feel a sense of belonging. She recognised that it had taken time for her to feel "*part of*" her community, and acknowledged that particularly within her first year she had not felt "*comfortable*", illuminating how belonging is a highly affective experience requiring positive connections with others. Research indicates that mature doctoral students are at increased risk of becoming isolated (Vitae, 2018), and that university campuses are not always perceived as safe spaces for women students (NUS, 2010). Thus, Liz being enabled to park on campus is crucial in allowing her to access institutional workspaces and participate fully in her departmental community, which she recognised as key in helping her to "*fit in*".

Whilst participating more in departmental activities and networking with her peers help Liz to feel more part of her academic community, she recognised that she will still "*stand alone*" at times, particularly when social events for PhD students are centred around drinking alcohol. This recognition of herself as remaining on the periphery of her departmental community highlights how belonging is an ongoing accomplishment (May, 2013). Further, participating in her wider disciplinary community through attending a conference was a positive experience wherein Liz was able to feel that she "*held her own*". This reflects research which highlights academic conferences as events which can facilitate doctoral students' academic identity development (Emmioglu et al., 2017; Mantai, 2017; McAlpine et al., 2009), as they offer the opportunity to be recognised publicly as valuable contributors to their academic community. However, Liz's acknowledgement that she expended a lot of energy attempting to appear as though she belonged, and that despite this she still feared being "*asked to leave*", indicates that this experience was not a total success in facilitating her sense of belonging.

Liz's experiences illustrate how securing institutional support can be critical in facilitating doctoral students' belonging. Even apparently small details, such as access to parking spaces on campus, can have a significant impact on individuals' experiences, enabling them to participate in their departmental communities in a way which would have otherwise not been possible. This, combined with positive experiences of participating in academic conferences, can facilitate women doctoral students' sense of belonging and address feelings of marginalisation and liminality.

## Gendered Experiences of Supervision

Whilst individuals did not often directly refer to gender discrimination, interviews highlighted day-to-day encounters in which gender was perceived to have played a part, particularly in relation to supervision. Literature highlights that the uncertain status of doctoral students can be problematic for students' academic identity development, and the implicit and inscribed power of supervisors within supervisory relationships has been well documented (Bartlett & Mercer, 2000; Hemer, 2012;

Manathunga, 2007). Despite the considerable attention paid to the subject of supervision within international literature of doctoral education, little has been written on supervisory dynamics within the context of health-related subjects (van Schalkwyk et al., 2016).

Sally perceived gender to have been an issue which affected her relationships with her supervisors, and her interactions with them illuminate how this affected her ability to feel a sense of belonging within her academic community. For the majority of her studies Sally had a partner who lived overseas, a situation which she found difficult. She felt that she would have been more able to be open with a female supervisor about the challenges that her personal circumstances caused:

> I have actually come out of the supervisor meeting and thought, would I feel better if I had a female supervisor because I have got three men, sometimes I just feel like…they don't know anything about my personal life, they don't know about my relationship situation, which is obviously, can be stressful like it is difficult to live in a long distance relationship and I don't feel like I could ever bring that up with them. (Interview 1)

Sally's admission reflects the argument that gender may be more significant in some supervisory relationships than in others (Deem & Brehony, 2000). Though her supervisors were academically supportive, Sally found it frustrating that they were unaware of her personal life, expressing a desire for her supervisors to have some understanding of her situation. This reflects literature which highlights how women doctoral students may prefer women supervisors to men, as they can act as positive role models (see Gaule & Piacentini, 2018; Smeby, 2000). However, Sally's implicit assumption that having a woman as a supervisor would enable her to be more open about her personal life speaks back to gendered expectations of caring, in which the provision of pastoral support is viewed as women's work (Clegg, 2013). Further, research on gender and supervision in the US suggested that for women doctoral students, the general supportiveness of supervisors was more important than their gender (Kurtz-Costes et al., 2006). Yet Sally also perceived other gendered dynamics in her supervisory relationships, compared to that of one of her male peers who had the same supervisory team. She recognised that the nature of the interactions between her and her supervisory team was very different to that of her male peer, and that she was unable to replicate the same type of relationship:

> He like has like a laugh with them about different things, and like going on a stag do and that kind of stuff…I kind of felt like I don't really have that kind of chat with them, I don't really have that banter. I think probably individually with them I would but sat in a room with 3 of them I don't think I would feel comfortable to be like oh, I am doing this at the weekend, or, and I kind of do feel as well like sometimes they just, they wouldn't be interested in they are so busy, that I don't think that they would ever be interested to sit and listen to what I have got going on in my life. (Interview 1)

Sally's experience echoes research which understands "*banter*" as an exclusionary, gendered discourse which negatively impacts women's experiences of higher education (Phipps & Young, 2013). Indeed, Sally's inability to "*feel comfortable*" in discussing her personal life with her supervisors speaks back to research which highlights how women doctoral students may purposefully avoid any personal or social interactions with their male supervisors, for fear of accusations of impropriety (see Hughes et al., 2017). Further, the difference between Sally's conversations with her male supervisors and the "*banter*" that her male peer is able to have with them—about "*going on a stag do and that kind of stuff*"—are indicative of how academics may play a role in perpetuating lad culture (Jackson & Sundaram, 2020). It appears that Sally does not feel a sense of ease within her immediate social context (Miller, 2003); even in simply making small talk with her supervisors, she is uncomfortable in relating to them more personally and is not able to make this connection with them, thus compromising her ability to feel a sense of belonging.

The way in which Sally perceives gendered barriers to engaging in light-hearted, non-academic conversations with her supervisors also has an impact on her ability to discuss her concerns about her work and seek the support she needs with her studies. The power dynamics implicit in all supervisory relationships (see Bartlett & Mercer, 2000; Hemer, 2012; Manathunga, 2007) are compounded by Sally's view of her male supervisors as "*such experts*" and her perception that if she admitted to struggling they would think less of her:

> I don't ever want to say to them I am struggling I feel like I always need to go in there and pretend that I am dealing with it…I dread the day when one day I just go in there and just break down to be honest I think I will feel mortified…I think I just, I just want them to like believe in me and I think I want to impress them, they are such experts in their areas…and I want them to feel like I am worthy of sitting around the table with them all and I don't want them to feel like I am like this student that they have got that is like struggling and needs all of this help, and…I feel like I want them to, I just want their respect I suppose and I feel like, and it is really bad like I feel like if I admit that I am struggling then I feel like I am going to lose their respect. (Interview 1)

The language Sally uses to describe her inability to be open with her supervisors is highly affective; she perceives the possibility of becoming emotional in a supervision meeting is something she "*dreads*", and she acknowledges that she would be "*mortified*" if this happened. Her use of language highlights how belonging is something which is innately felt (or not), and how not belonging is directly connected with feelings of otherness (May, 2013).

Sally's experience of supervision reflects an understanding of belonging as a negotiated accomplishment involving others (May, 2013), and requiring the validation of the individual by more powerful members of a community. She expressed fears that admitting to personal problems during her doctorate could negate her supervisors' potential validation of her as a legitimate member of her academic community (Lave & Wenger, 1991). Her response—to conceal her struggles from her supervisors—means not only that she is not able to access support, but that she is not able to feel that she fully belongs in academia more generally. Further, Sally's concern that she may not be seen as "*worthy of sitting around the table with them all*" speaks back to discourses of imposterism, showing how this may contribute to feelings of isolation and marginalisation, as well as indicating the gendered nature of the power dynamics of her supervisory relationship.

## Conflicting Personal and Academic Values

Participants' ability to belong within their academic community was also shaped by the extent to which they were able to align their personal values to those they felt they would need to take on as academics. Values are central to identity (Weeks, 1990), and therefore perceptions of academic values had significant implications for how the possibility of becoming an academic was viewed. Interestingly, the prospect of taking on a long-term academic identity by pursuing an academic career was not a core aspiration for any participants in health and related sciences. For those returning to academia after pursuing other careers, the doctorate was simply an opportunity to build credibility and to develop specialist research skills. There was a general perception that academic work lacked the ability to make an impact on people's lives; for example, Sally implied that she does not view academia as a sector in which she would be able to make a difference:

> After the MSc I could have gone forward and…train and do my chartered training as a psychologist, and work in the field with clients, so doing the PhD…I had to decide is this going to compromise that too much is it going to take me too far away from applied work. I didn't ever want to just be, I don't want to just be an academic, I kind of want to do something applied and that is my reasoning, my motivation to be a psychologist is to make a difference to people's lives and you know help people out and I don't want to just be doing something that is just theoretical and it never gets, never gets taken into practice in any way. (Interview 1)

Like Sally, Jessie describes her motivation for the PhD, but also for her post-PhD career, as "*improving people's health and wellbeing*" (Interview 1), thus connecting her values with the vocational side of her discipline, as a public health advocate. She left a successful career in market research to study for her doctorate, and had high expectations of how academia could help her to achieve this goal: "*one of the reasons I came back to academia was because I was, I felt like I was lacking people to learn from…people to inspire me*" (Interview 2). However, as she becomes immersed in different academic communities over the course of her PhD, she becomes increasingly disenchanted with academia and less convinced about its ability to help her improve the health and well-being of others. Attending conferences and meeting experts in her field was particularly disappointing in terms of both the attitudes Jessie witnessed being expounded and in relation to the level of debate she had expected:

> 06/12/2015
> I am feeling a little disillusioned with academia…In November I had, on two separate occasions the opportunity to meet with leading academics in both my fields. With the exception of three individuals, I found people to be uninspiring and, worse, lacking in common sense.

Whilst academic conferences provide the potential for facilitating doctoral students' belonging within their academic community (see Emmioglu et al., 2017; Mantai, 2017), this was not the case for Jessie. In fact, her interactions with academics at events undermined her sense of belonging. She describes this process of disillusionment as akin to balloons being burst:

> His final keynote was good but in the conference dinner he was the speaker and he made a misogynistic and unfunny joke, and I know it's not really necessarily related to his intellectual abilities but I just thought, you total loser, you know it kind of popped another balloon so I had a conference of balloon popping where these people that I had aspired to, or been inspired by just sort of…showed themselves to be human I suppose, idiots, and actually not that clever. (Interview 2)

Whilst Jessie "*had aspired*" to be like the academic experts she met, the reality of these encounters was that she perceived these individuals as either misogynistic or uninspiring, and thus was unable to make a positive connection with them. These events therefore led Jessie to become disillusioned with an academic career, as her ability to feel a sense of belonging to her academic community was compromised by the values she encountered. Her experience speaks back to literature which highlights how the process of undertaking doctoral study may discourage women from pursuing an academic career (see Guest et al., 2013; Hatchell & Aveling, 2008).

Thus, Jessie's perceptions of academia by her second year were largely negative, and she found it more difficult to imagine herself belonging within academia in the long term. The combination of these experiences, along with a significant change in her home life when her eldest child began school, meant that in the second year of her PhD Jessie felt under significant pressure. Though she had felt prepared for the emotional upheaval of her child starting school, Jessie had not expected the additional administrative burden and recognised that this had fallen to her: "*it was stark that…getting [child] ready to start school and sorting everything out like ironing name labels into, into you know that was my job… it would never have happened if…I didn't do it*" (Interview 2). Jessie felt that whilst she was able to manage her work-life balance effectively much of the time, her capacity to do so was exceeded during this period, due to having to provide this additional emotional labour: "*it's one last thing and suddenly everything starts to fall. I mean it's very typical you know, you're juggling, and I do think that that's fallen to me…that juggling role has fallen to me because I'm the mother*" (Interview 2). Jessie acknowledged that gendered assumptions about who would undertake this labour had a negative impact on her progress with her research, as her priority was her child's well-being: "*I felt unsupported generally and so the PhD suffered, because my immediate priority was [child] had to have a good start at school… even if I copped it, at uni*" (Interview 2). Whilst the situation improved over time, Jessie recognised that this period of upheaval had taken a toll: "*it's possible that I'm still recovering from that now that you know, just the sort of emotional and cognitive demands*" (Interview 2).

At this stage in her studies, Jessie became increasingly frustrated with the academic cultures she encountered, and began to view an academic career both as potentially not possible and also as undesirable. This was largely due to the values she perceived as being espoused within academia:

06/12/2015

> It is frustrating that people can become so engrossed in their avenues of inquiry that they seem to forget what, I believe to be critical, the 'point of it all'. Progress towards actually influencing decision making, or even making decisions seems painfully slow…I came back to academia to be inspired and whilst I have learnt a lot, I can clearly see that academic pursuits alone will not actually have any impact. I have also learnt that despite

having some good ideas and a practical outlook I probably won't be taken seriously in academia because I do not have the pedigree of publications behind me. The hierarchy is intractable. Measures of success are extremely limited…It is very self-serving, it is painfully slow. By the time you get a publication the results are a minimum of six months out of date by which stage the world has moved on…There needs to be some way of working more closely with policy makers, or even commercial researchers who are the ones delivering research that actually influences policy or practice, adding the academic basis or theories that can then be taken forward by the more responsive, less bureaucratic teams.

In considering her own priorities for the impact of her research, Jessie was particularly critical of institutional focus on the Research Excellence Framework, perceiving it as a self-interested exercise which universities use to enhance their reputation: *"it's about what can we demonstrate to show how good we are as opposed to what are we doing that makes a difference to people"* (Interview 2). This view reflects wider criticisms of the REF as overly focused on metrics and research performativity (see Lucas, 2006; Martin, 2011; Scott, 2013). Jessie's perception of academia as *"self-serving"*, *"bureaucratic"* and not focused on the needs of the wider community is anathema to her own values, and she therefore recognised that she may be both unable and unwilling to belong to this community in the long term.

Yet despite her criticisms of academics as losing sight of *"the point of it all"*, Jessie expressed concerns that even as a doctoral student, she was becoming more detached from others as a result of working in this environment. Since progressing with her research, she found it increasingly difficult to communicate her research to those outside of academia: *"I have to make sure I retract myself from this…academic kind of wormhole to be able to then speak to a real person again"* (Interview 2). Understanding identity as both 'a product of personal desire and activity, but also of interactions with members of local academic communities' (Baker & Lattuca, 2010, p.813), the mismatch between Jessie's values and those she perceived as embedded in academia meant that she struggled to envisage herself taking on this identity and belonging to this community. Jessie's relationship with academia was complex; whilst she was sceptical about the impact of academic work on people's lives, she simultaneously hoped that she may be wrong:

> I actually feel like I would really have failed if I left academia…I would be really disappointed if it wasn't possible to do that sort of thing through academic [work] because that would just confirm my suspicions that there's…a lot of money being wasted, a lot of resources being wasted, in both people's intellect, and the actual physical money it takes to do it, that's not making a difference to real people's lives. (Interview 1)

Jessie's admission that she would feel like a failure if she did not become an academic resonates with literature which highlights that this is common amongst doctoral students, who often enter doctoral study with the assumption that this is the usual post-PhD career trajectory (UK Council for Science and Technology, 2007) and have the perception that leaving academia is a failure (Royal Society, 2014). Though Jessie did not dismiss the possibility of an academic career after the PhD, she questioned the appropriateness of this career for achieving her goals: "*I'm not sure that it is the route that will help me to achieve what I want to achieve*" (Interview 1).

During her PhD, Jessie became sceptical about the impact that academic work can have on people's lives and was "*increasingly frustrated with the sort of ivory tower…lack of genuine…connection and effort to making a real difference to people*" (Interview 2). Yet despite this, she does not completely reject the possibility of developing an academic identity. Instead, in response to the conflict she perceived in relation to her own values and those she perceives as embedded within academia, Jessie takes up an ambivalent position towards the possibility of pursuing an academic career. This strategy enables her to still perceive this career as possible, but without it being constructed as a necessarily strong aspiration. Taking up this ambivalent position also insulates her, to some extent, from the feelings of failure that she previously acknowledges. During her studies, Jessie therefore moves from a position where she sees a career outside academia as a failure, to a more empowered position of equivocality. Jessie's strategy of ambivalence highlights her agency in trying to find ways to belong in academia:

> Does that mean that I don't want to sort of pursue a career in academia not necessarily, I just feel like I have to work bloody hard to make a career do the things that I also want it to do…and the effort that it requires to make, do something differently, is quite a lot of effort…I believe that it's possible and I believe that you can take people with you and you can say there is a different way of doing things, but it's a massive effort. (Interview 2)

Jessie's experience highlights how perceived conflict between academic and personal values can challenge doctoral students' ability to feel a sense of belonging in academia, and how the pressures of balancing work alongside childcare responsibilities may make the work involved in developing an academic identity more challenging. This sense of belonging within the academic community is often harder for women to achieve, especially for those such as Jessie, who study for a PhD later in life, having changed career and trying to balance doctoral study with family commitments (Brown & Watson, 2010). Viewing belonging as shaped by feelings of legitimacy and forging connections with others within a particular community, Jessie felt that she would not be able to belong within academia, as she would not be recognised as a valid member of her disciplinary community without a strong publication record. However, significantly, her experiences also reflect her reticence to belong to a community in which she perceived she would need to compromise her personal values in order to succeed.

## Resisting the Pressure to Publish: Implications for Well-Being

Participants' views of academic working practices also shaped how they viewed the possibility of pursuing an academic career, particularly in relation to the pressure to publish work. The competitive culture of the contemporary academy (Gill, 2009), influenced by neoliberal expectations of productivity and an increased focus on individual performativity (Ball, 2003, 2012; Collini, 2012), constituted the environment wherein women doctoral students learned what would be expected of them as academics. Research highlights how managerialist initiatives across higher education sectors—such as the Research Excellence Framework in the UK—have intensified the pressures on academics who are increasingly expected to "produce more, better, and faster" (do Mar Pereira, 2016, p.100). This intensification of expectations around research productivity has been found to have a detrimental impact on individuals' well-being (see Kinman, 2014; Loveday, 2018; Morrish, 2019). As with participants in STEM disciplines, women doctoral students in health and related sciences also experienced the 'publish or perish' culture. Even at an early stage in their potential academic careers, it was clear that individuals encountered significant pressure to publish, often as a result of direct pressure from supervisors, which contributed to poor mental health and well-being.

For Liz, the expectations of research productivity in the first year of her doctorate took her by surprise. She felt that she had not had time to understand her topic properly because her supervisors expected her to be writing at a publishable standard straight away; "*I need to be able to read to understand the subject matter, but because they want me to just write, write, write*" (Interview 1). She struggled with supervision due to a strained relationship with her main supervisor and having had a difficult first supervision, where she was told that her work was inadequate:

> I had submitted some work, and his words were, we have a certain level expected of [a] PhD and this isn't it…That was very, very scary. That was really scary. Because that was the one where I thought, I can't do it, from an academic position you know the words were, this isn't it. (Interview 1)

Despite this criticism of her writing, her supervisors were keen for Liz to write for publication and made this clear from an early stage. However, Liz had not anticipated this and was unsure of her ability to fulfil their expectations:

> I was told that I should be, it is all about publication, so they wanted to see by the end of March, by the end of April sorry…a draft of a published literature review…they said well what we want you to do is to do a literature review chapter and then an article will fall out of that, so I was like ok I don't know how that is going to happen but I will just do what you want

me to do…I feel like I am working to their agenda but I am not even sure I know what their agenda is. Actually, I know what their agenda is, it is to publish, publish, publish. (Interview 1)

The power dynamics of Liz's relationship with her supervisory team was something which she struggled with throughout the doctorate. Liz found it difficult to adjust to her supervisors' style of supervision, which was less collaborative than she had expected. She felt unable to take ownership of her research and found supervision increasingly challenging:

I find that the supervision I just dread it, I just you know it feels like…you know I don't sit there crying or anything, inside I am, but I kind of I feel like I have got no teeth in there and people, my friends have said to me you need to take charge of these supervision sessions that is what you need to do. You need to set an agenda, and you need to you know take charge of it, here is what I want to discuss, and I have tried that, I have tried doing that but then what happens is, I don't really get, I feel like I haven't got a voice. (Interview 1)

Feeling a sense of belonging is linked to mattering, where individuals feel accepted and valued by others (May, 2013; White & Nonnamaker, 2008), which generates 'a sense of accord with the various physical and social contexts in which our lives are lived out' (Miller, 2003, p.220). Further, literature highlights how supportive academic cultures can contribute to well-being and individual belonging through 'collegiality and a valuing of research students' (Morris & Wisker, 2011, p.5). Yet it is clear that Liz did not feel valued by her supervisors and struggled with a sense of disempowerment; she has "*got no teeth*" and felt unable to "*take charge*". Her inability to establish a positive relationship with her supervisors and to effectively negotiate their expectations meant that Liz did not feel a sense of belonging within her academic community. These difficulties led to Liz considering quitting her PhD during her first year:

I am counting the number of supervision sessions I have got to tolerate, I have had 5 supervisions now and in the three years I am going to have 36 so that is another 31, can I put myself through this another 31 times, I don't really think I want to. (Interview 1)

Her meetings with supervisors had a negative impact on Liz's well-being; they were something which she felt she had to endure, which echoes literature which positions the doctorate as something to be 'survived' (see Karp, 2009; Matthiesen & Binder, 2009; Phillips & Pugh, 2015). This is particularly significant in the context of reported poor levels of well-being and mental health of doctoral students (see Havergal, 2017; Levecque et al., 2017), and research which indicates that well-being amongst women doctoral students is lower than their male counterparts (Hargreaves et al., 2017).

Liz's experiences echo literature which highlights how neoliberal expectations of research productivity, embedded within the contemporary academy, have percolated through to PhD students, who may encounter significant pressure to publish during their doctorate (see Badenhorst & Xu, 2016; Bansel, 2011; Rolf, 2021). It is clear that experiencing this pressure from her supervisors had a negative impact on Liz's experiences of doctoral study, as this was not what she had expected the PhD to involve:

> I thought have I just been brought here to churn out articles…and I felt very demoralised by that and thought you know I don't…I can do that for 3 years, well I don't know if I can I've never had to, I've never been under that kind of pressure. (Interview 1)

The mismatch between what she felt was expected and what Liz felt willing and able to produce had a negative impact on her well-being. She acknowledged that she felt disempowered; rather than learning to become an autonomous scholar, she felt she was simply working to fulfil her supervisors' agenda—"*to churn out articles*". Understanding belonging as innately affective and necessitating the negotiation of power relations to secure recognition from existing community members, it appears that Liz struggled to establish this sense of belonging because of her reluctance to engage in the process of publishing work. Whilst she indicated that she would fulfil their expectations, "*I will just do what you want me to do*", it is clear that this had negative implications for her well-being; she was "*demoralised*" by the thought of having to subscribe to these expectations for the duration of her doctorate, and questioned whether she would be able to withstand *"that kind of pressure"* for 3 years. Though it has been argued that the PhD is the period in which individuals learn the rules of the academic game (Parry, 2007), it is clear that Liz was uncomfortable with the prospect of playing the game and doubted whether she could align herself with these values; all of this had a negative impact on her ability to feel a sense of belonging within her academic community.

Liz's interactions with her supervisors were a key way in which she learned about the kinds of working practices which are expected of the contemporary academic. Through her encounters with them, she perceived the culture of academia as target-driven and directive; *"it feels like I have just got to, you know hit whatever target they come up with next. But then you know that is maybe that is academia"* (Interview 1). These perceptions reflect literature which highlights how the neoliberalisation of higher education generates an understanding of individuals' abilities as measured by their performance against a series of stringent targets and metrics. This is most visibly understood through the requirements of the Research Excellence Framework (REF) and the Teaching Excellence Framework (TEF). In this way, academics are recast by the neoliberal academy as 'productive individuals, new kinds of subjects…[who] are the central resource in a reformed, entrepreneurial public sector' (Ball, 2012, p.20). Liz's experiences highlight how doctoral students may become inculcated into this performative culture as a result of pressure from supervisors to publish during the PhD, with a significant detrimental on both her well-being and potentially on her ability to complete the doctorate.

The attitude that Liz's supervisors hold towards research productivity relates to the pressures they themselves faced to publish work. Indeed, they acknowledged that their expectations of her were therefore simply a matter of *"business":*

> I think because it is a university and it is a business…and I hear the pressures they are under you know I hear them saying, they have said to me you know, we are under pressure, so we are putting you under pressure, this isn't personal, this is business. One of them actually used those words, this is not personal, this is business, you know we are under pressure from above so, if it feels like we are putting pressure on you, we are putting pres-

sure on you because we are under pressure so I suppose it hasn't quite been what I, I think it is fair to say it hasn't quite been what I thought it might be…I just don't know if it is right, I just don't know if I can be this publishing machine for them really. (Interview 1)

Liz's supervisors' description of their treatment of her as being "*business*" rather than "*personal*" speaks back to literature illuminating how changes to UK higher education over the last two decades have placed neoliberal values at the centre of the sector, leading to the development of the 'entrepreneurial university' (Clark, 1998; Slaughter & Leslie, 1997; Slaughter & Rhoades, 2004) and the commodification of academic practices relating to teaching and research (Ball, 2012; Collini, 2012). Indeed, neoliberal values have become central to institutional and individual attitudes to research (Ball, 2012; Hey, 2004) where academics become subjects who prove their individual worth and value through their research productivity (see Loveday, 2018). Liz's experiences also draw attention to the ways in which supervisory relationships may exploit doctoral students, often with supervisors using students' publications to boost their own publishing record (see Löfström & Pyhältö, 2014; Manathunga, 2014; Nelson & Friedlander, 2001).

For Liz, her comparatively late arrival into higher education and struggles with imposter syndrome (Breeze, 2018; Handforth, 2022) contributed to her feelings of marginalisation and disempowerment within her supervisory relationship and meant that she struggled to resist her supervisors' expectations in relation to publishing. Research indicates that new students are often not aware of what to expect from doctoral study, particularly in relation to supervisory relationships (see Grevholm et al., 2005; Wisker, 2012). Yet there is often an assumption within guidance literature for doctoral students that all are able to fulfil the agentic, assertive model of a doctoral student who can 'manage' their supervisors. However, only those who feel they are legitimately participating as members of their academic community (Lave & Wenger, 1991) are able to overcome the inherent power imbalance within their supervisory relationships and assert themselves in this way. For Liz, whose confidence in her abilities was undermined at an early stage, it was difficult for her to engage in these assertive behaviours and resist her supervisors' expectations in relation to publishing work.

Liz's experiences prior to the doctorate thus led her to position herself as 'other' in relation to the traditional, ideal model of a PhD student who has had a straightforward, linear academic journey, which has implications for her ability to feel a sense of belonging within academia. She acknowledged that she struggled with feelings of self-doubt and perceived a gendered sense of entitlement to education in others that she has never felt, contrasting her own attitude with that of some of her male peers:

> I know a lot of men that lack confidence, but it is a bullishness, there is a bullishness there and I think maybe if I had some of that bullishness I wouldn't get quite so upset about things and I wouldn't question myself as much. (Interview 1)

Understanding identity as 'who we are and what we want to be and become' (Weeks, 1990, p.89), it is clear that Liz is reluctant to embody an identity which involves constant pressure to produce work. She was doubtful about whether she can fulfil her supervisor's expectations, which she views as burdensome; "*I just don't know if I can be this publishing machine for them*". Whilst the pressure to produce publications has been argued to have a greater impact on early career academics (The Res-Sisters, 2016), the impact on doctoral students as a distinct group has not been fully considered. This pressure has damaging consequences for doctoral students like Liz, who are discouraged from taking on an identity which means working under significant pressure, and who may leave academia after their doctorate as a result (see Grant & Sherrington, 2006). This has clear implications for academic institutions and the higher education sector as a whole in terms of the future recruitment and retention of academics.

Witnessing academics under pressure to publish work thus influenced understandings of what becoming an academic would require, and Liz struggled to imagine taking on an identity which involves continuously working under pressure to produce publications. Neoliberal understandings of academic labour therefore pervaded understandings of what it might mean to belong as an academic, beyond the PhD. Liz rejected the possibility of subscribing to these neoliberal values, reflecting that being subjected to this pressure as a doctoral student and witnessing her supervisors' experiences have led her to conclude that "*the world of academia is not for me*" (Interview 1). This echoes literature which highlights how doctoral students may reject academic careers on the basis of not wanting to lead lives like their supervisors, who they perceived to be under significant pressure and lack a healthy work-life balance (see Mason et al., 2009).

Yet as she progressed through the doctorate, Liz developed strategies which help her to exert agency within her supervisory relationship. Though she continued to experience difficulties with her main supervisor, by her second year she was better able to deal with this because she felt more secure in her position as a doctoral student, having developed a sense of belonging to her academic community by interacting more with her peers. Initially, living at a distance from her university and being unable to regularly work alongside peers in a shared office meant that Liz felt "*a bit like a spare part*" (Interview 1). Other than enabling on-campus parking, little effort was made by her institution to facilitate the belonging of doctoral students who do not live nearby. This speaks back to literature which highlights how certain groups of doctoral students need support in developing a sense of belonging within academic spaces (see White & Nonnamaker, 2008). Liz acknowledged that "*it feels like two different experiences almost the first year and the second year…possibly because it's taken me a while to settle*" (Interview 2). Towards the end of her first year, Liz was encouraged by one of her peers to help organise a departmental student symposium, which helped as it allowed her to connect with other students and members of staff:

> It's great because…other people have to e-mail me with any topics they want to discuss…so there is lots of communication going on, perhaps [before] anyone in that room I would have no reason really to e-mail them or they me. (Interview 2)

Belonging involves 'mattering, whereby students believe the community has accepted them and values their contributions' (White & Nonnamaker, 2008, p.354), and despite the distance from her institution, Liz tried to work in the shared office in her department as often as possible—"*there is always someone that I can identify with which is why I do make the effort to be in*" (Interview 2). This comment illuminates the significance that peer groups have for individual doctoral students' belonging (Morris & Wisker, 2011), and draws attention to how belonging is not something which can be completely accomplished but which must be continually achieved through individual agency (May, 2013). Liz therefore began to feel more at ease within her peer group: "*they make me feel normal because there is nothing I've gone through, that one of them hasn't*" (Interview 2). For Liz, actively engaging with her peer community helped her to establish a sense of belonging, reflecting literature which highlights how peer support can be invaluable for doctoral students in helping combat isolation (Ali et al., 2007; Lovitts, 2001; Morris & Wisker, 2011; Phillips & Pugh, 2015).

By her second year, therefore, Liz had grown in confidence and was able to employ a number of strategies in order to manage her relationships with her supervisors and negotiate an increased sense of belonging. Participating more in her departmental community and accessing support from peers helped her to become more self-sufficient and "*find my own stability*" (Interview 2), rather than relying on her supervisors for support or reassurance. Further, in order to push back against her supervisors' expectations of her research productivity, she sought help from another (woman) academic with pastoral responsibility for doctoral students:

> I didn't raise it with them but I did raise it with…the PhD tutor, I did raise it with her. She was very good… she took on board what I'd said and…said I'm sorry you feel like that and what do you want to do, do you want me to monitor how the situation goes and have a word with them, she was very good…and I don't know whether she did or she didn't, I have no idea but I know [the pressure] stopped. (Interview 2)

Seeking this external support from both her peers and another academic helped Liz to distance herself from her struggles with her supervisors and develop a more pragmatic view of her supervisory relationship. She was able to take comments made by her main supervisor less personally as a result: "*there are going to be times when I'm going to be completely flavour of the month and…times when I'm not and that's ok*" (Interview 2). Further, Liz developed a more sympathetic view of her supervisor: "*I know she's had her struggles…I am dealing with human beings here…I mustn't think of them as these big authoritarian…professors that never have…any kind of issues*" (Interview 2). Finally, Liz altered her conception of her supervisory relationship to one which reflected an employment situation, which helped her to consider how she could work most effectively with her supervisors:

> It'd be ideal if we all got on, but the truth is this is a job…we are a team, sometimes teams work together sometimes teams don't work so well what I need to do is to take the best out of that team. (Interview 2)

Liz's experiences show how developing meaningful relationships with her peers and seeking additional support from her institution improve her well-being, with a positive impact on her experience of doctoral study. The stark contrast between her first year in which she considered leaving the PhD, and her second year when she was able to develop connections with her peers and participate meaningfully as a member of her departmental community, shows how belonging is not a fixed state but rather a negotiated accomplishment which requires constant maintenance (May, 2013). Her ability to feel a sense of belonging to her academic community is facilitated not only by her positive interactions with peers but also by the interventions of another academic, who took actions to ensure that Liz's supervisors removed the pressure to publish, which had such a negative impact on her well-being during the first year of her studies.

## Summary

This chapter has shown how women doctoral students in health and related sciences negotiated various challenges to belonging within their academic communities. The main barrier to belonging was the perception of doctoral students as being low status within the academic hierarchy—something reinforced through the behaviour of academics and supervisors. For participants—all mature students returning to academia after professional careers—the lack of recognition of the value of their contributions was difficult and led them to become frustrated at the hierarchical nature of the academy. This was particularly challenging for Jessie, whose caring responsibilities put her under additional pressure. Perceived disinterest in their research, as well as the failure of academic colleagues and supervisors to give credit or recognise the contributions of doctoral students, reinforced academic hierarchies and challenged individuals' ability to feel a sense of belonging. Whilst supervisors may act as gatekeepers into the disciplinary community (Parry, 2007), gendered experiences of supervision and neoliberal expectations of research productivity contributed to feelings of marginalisation and imposterism, especially for those from working-class backgrounds. Thus, this chapter demonstrates the significant role of academics and supervisors in maintaining women doctoral students' peripheral status within their academic community.

Despite this, it was evident that individuals demonstrated considerable agency in trying to develop strategies for belonging. These included seeking institutional support, making connections with academics and clinicians beyond those in their department and developing stronger relationships with their peers. These strategies were successful to a point, enabling individuals to make connections with others and to feel more 'at home' in their academic community. Yet these feelings of belonging were often short term. Negotiating burdensome academic administrative procedures and bureaucracy, combined with perceptions of academia as self-serving rather than focused on positive community impact, meant that individuals struggled to envisage themselves belonging in academia in the longer term. Experiencing the academic environment during their studies led individuals to perceive the kinds of working practices and values to which they would need to embody as academics, and as they progressed with their studies, women doctoral students largely became disillusioned with the prospect of pursuing an academic career, or developed an ambivalent stance towards this career. Crucially, the perceived clash between personal values and those embedded in academic work meant that individuals understood that significant compromise would be needed if they were to pursue an academic career. Thus, whilst these strategies made it possible for some to develop a sense of belonging in the short term, they did not enable individuals to envisage belonging in academia in the longer term.

## References

Addison, M., Breeze, M., & Taylor, Y. (2022). *The Palgrave handbook of imposter syndrome in higher education*. Palgrave Macmillan.

Advance HE. (2021a). Equality in higher education: Staff statistical report 2021.

Advance HE. (2021b). Equality in higher education: Student statistical report 2021.

Ali, A., Kohun, F., & Levy, Y. (2007). Dealing with social isolation to minimize doctoral attrition—A four stage framework. *International Journal of Doctoral Studies, 2*(1), 33–49. https://doi.org/10.28945/3082

Badenhorst, C., & Xu, X. (2016). Academic publishing: Making the implicit explicit. *Publications, 4*(3), 24. https://doi.org/10.3390/publications4030024

Baker, V. L., & Lattuca, L. R. (2010). Developmental networks and learning: Toward an interdisciplinary perspective on identity development during doctoral study. *Studies in Higher Education, 35*(7), 807–827. https://doi.org/10.1080/03075070903501887

Ball, S. J. (2003). The teacher's soul and the terrors of performativity. *Journal of Education Policy, 18*(2), 215–228. https://doi.org/10.1080/0268093022000043065

Ball, S. J. (2012). Performativity, commodification and commitment: An I-spy guide to the neoliberal university. *British Journal of Educational Studies, 60*(1), 17–28.

Bansel, P. (2011). Becoming academic: A reflection on doctoral candidacy. *Studies in Higher Education, 36*(5), 543–556. https://doi.org/10.1080/03075079.2011.594592

Bartlett, A., & Mercer, G. (2000). Reconceptualising discourses of power in postgraduate pedagogies. *Teaching in Higher Education, 5*(2), 195–204.

Becher, T. (1994). The significance of disciplinary differences. *Studies in Higher education, 19*(2), 151–161.

Boore, J. R. (1996). Doctoral level education in the health professions. *Teaching in Higher Education, 1*(1), 29–48.

Breeze, M. (2018). Imposter syndrome as a public feeling. In Y. Taylor & L. Kinneret (Eds.), *Feeling academic in the neoliberal university*. Palgrave Macmillan.

Brown, L., & Watson, P. (2010). Understanding the experiences of female doctoral students. *Journal of Further and Higher Education, 34*(3), 385–404. https://doi.org/10.1080/0309877X.2010.484056

Clark, B. (1998). *Creating entrepreneurial universities.* Pergamon.

Clegg, S. (2013). The space of academia: Privilege, agency and the erasure of affect. *Privilege, Agency and Affect: Understanding the Production and Effects of Action,* 71–87. https://doi.org/10.1057/9781137292636_5

Collini, S. (2012). *What are universities for?* Penguin UK.

Curry, L. A., O'Cathain, A., Clark, V. L. P., Aroni, R., Fetters, M., & Berg, D. (2012). The role of group dynamics in mixed methods health sciences research teams. *Journal of Mixed Methods Research, 6*(1), 5–20.

Deem, R., & Brehony, K. J. (2000). Doctoral students' access to research cultures-are some more unequal than others? *Studies in Higher Education, 25*(2), 149–165. https://doi.org/10.1080/713696138

Delamont, S., Atkinson, P., & Parry, O. (2000). *The doctoral experience: Success and failure in graduate school.* Routledge.

Denicolo, P., & Becker, L. (2008). The supervision process and the nature of the research degree. In G. Hall & J. Longman (Eds.), *The postgraduate's companion* (pp. 123–143). Sage.

Dever, M., Laffan, W., Boreham, P., Behrens, K., Haynes, M., Western, M., & Kubler, M. (2008). *Gender differences in early post-PhD employment in Australian universities: The influence of PhD experience on women's academic careers.* Final report.

do Mar Pereira, M. (2016). Struggling within and beyond the performative university: Articulating activism and work in an "academia without walls". *Women's Studies International Forum, 54,* 100–110. https://doi.org/10.1016/j.wsif.2015.06.008

Emmioglu, E., McAlpine, L., & Amundsen, C. (2017). Doctoral students' experiences of feeling (or not) like an academic. *International Journal of Doctoral Studies, 12,* 73–91.

Gaule, P., & Piacentini, M. (2018). An advisor like me? Advisor gender and post-graduate careers in science. *Research Policy, 47*(4), 805–813.

Gill, R. (2009). Breaking the silence: The hidden injuries of neo-liberal academia. In R. Ryan-Flood & R. Gill (Eds.), *Secrecy and silence in the research process: Feminist reflections* (pp. 228–244). Routledge.

Grant, W., & Sherrington, P. (2006). *Managing your academic career.* Palgrave Macmillan.

Grevholm, B., Persson, L., & Wall, P. (2005). A dynamic model for education of doctoral students and guidance of supervisors in research groups.

*Educational Studies in Mathematics, 60*(2), 173–197. https://doi.org/10.1007/s10649-005-4497-2

Grover, V. (2007). Successfully navigating the stages of doctoral study. *International Journal of Doctoral Studies, 2*(1), 9–21.

Guest, M., Sharma, S., & Song, R. (2013). *Gender and career progression in theology and religious studies*. Durham University.

Handforth, R. (2022). Feeling "stupid": Considering the affective in women doctoral students' experiences of imposter 'syndrome'. In *The Palgrave handbook of imposter syndrome in higher education* (pp. 293–309). Palgrave Macmillan.

Hargreaves, C., De Wilde, J., Juniper, B., & Walsh, E. (2017). Re-evaluating doctoral researchers' well-being: What has changed in five years? Retrieved from https://www.imperial.ac.uk/media/imperial-college/study/graduate-school/public/well-being/Wellbeing-for-GS.pdf

Hatchell, H., & Aveling, N. (2008). Gendered disappearing acts: Women's doctoral experiences in the science workplace. In *Australian Association for Research in Education conference, Brisbane* (Vol. 30).

Havergal, C. (2017, April 13). Universities can do more to support PhD students' mental health. *Times Higher Education*. Retrieved from https://www.timeshighereducation.com/opinion/universities-can-do-more-support-phd-students-mental-health

Hemer, S. R. (2012). Informality, power and relationships in postgraduate supervision: Supervising PhD candidates over coffee. *Higher Education Research & Development, 31*(6), 827–839. https://doi.org/10.1080/07294360.2012.674011

Hey, V. (2004). Perverse pleasures—Identity work and the paradoxes of greedy institutions. *Journal of International Women's Studies, 5*(3), 33–43.

Holloway, I., & Walker, J. (1999). *Getting a PhD in health and social care*. Wiley-Blackwell.

Hughes, C. C., Schilt, K., Gorman, B. K., & Bratter, J. L. (2017). Framing the faculty gender gap: A view from STEM doctoral students. *Gender, Work & Organization, 24*(4), 398–416.

Jackson, C., & Sundaram, V. (2020). *Lad culture in higher education: Sexism, sexual harassment and violence*. Routledge.

Jazvac-Martek, M. (2009). Oscillating role identities: The academic experiences of education doctoral students. *Innovations in Education and Teaching International, 46*(3), 253–264. https://doi.org/10.1080/14703290903068862

Karp, J. R. (2009). *How to survive your PhD: The insider's guide to avoiding mistakes, choosing the right program, working with professors, and just how a person actually writes a 200-page paper*. Sourcebooks.

Kinman, G. (2014). Doing more with less? work and wellbeing in academics. *Somatechnics, 4*(2), 219–235.

Kurtz-Costes, B., Andrews Helmke, L., & Ülkü-Steiner, B. (2006). Gender and doctoral studies: The perceptions of Ph. D. students in an American university. *Gender and Education, 18*(2), 137–155.

Lave, J., & Wenger, E. (1991). *Situated learning: Legitimate peripheral participation*. Cambridge University Press.

Levecque, K., Anseel, F., De Beuckelaer, A., Van der Heyden, J., & Gisle, L. (2017). Work organization and mental health problems in PhD students. *Research Policy, 46*(4), 868–879. https://doi.org/10.1016/j.respol.2017.02.008

Löfström, E., & Pyhältö, K. (2014). Ethical issues in doctoral supervision: The perspectives of PhD students in the natural and behavioral sciences. *Ethics & Behavior, 24*(3), 195–214.

Loveday, V. (2016). Embodying deficiency through 'affective practice': Shame, relationality, and the lived experience of social class and gender in higher education. *Sociology, 50*(6), 1140–1155.

Loveday, V. (2018). The neurotic academic: Anxiety, casualisation, and governance in the neoliberalising university. *Journal of Cultural Economy, 11*(2), 154–166.

Lovitts, B. E. (2001). *Leaving the ivory tower: The causes and consequences of departure from doctoral study*. Rowman & Littlefield.

Lucas, L. (2006). *The Research game in academic life*. SRHE/Open University Press.

Manathunga, C. (2007). Supervision as mentoring: The role of power and boundary crossing. *Studies in Continuing Education, 29*(2), 207–221. https://doi.org/10.1080/01580370701424650

Manathunga, C. (2014). *Intercultural postgraduate supervision: Reimagining time, place and knowledge*. Routledge.

Mantai, L. (2017). Feeling like a researcher: Experiences of early doctoral students in Australia. *Studies in Higher Education, 42*(4), 636–650.

Martin, B. R. (2011). The research excellence framework and the 'impact agenda': Are we creating a frankenstein monster? *Research Evaluation, 20*(3), 247–254. https://doi.org/10.3152/095820211x13118583635693

Mason, M. A., Goulden, M., & Frasch, K. (2009). Why graduate students reject the fast track. *Academe, 95*(1), 11–16.

Matthiesen, J. K., & Binder, M. (2009). *How to survive your doctorate: What others don't tell you*. Open University Press.

May, V. (2013). *Connecting self to society: Belonging in a changing world*. Macmillan International Higher Education.

McAlpine, L., & Amundsen, C. (2009). Identity and agency: Pleasures and collegiality among the challenges of the doctoral journey. *Studies in Continuing Education, 31*(2), 109–125. https://doi.org/10.1080/01580370902927378

McAlpine, L., Paré, A., & Starke-Meyerring, D. (2009). Disciplinary voices: A shifting landscape for English doctoral education in the twenty-first century. In L. McAlpine & C. Amundsen (Eds.), *Doctoral education: Research-based strategies for doctoral students, supervisors and administrators* (pp. 157–169). Springer.

McCulloch, A., & Stokes, P. (2008). The silent majority: Meeting the needs of part-time research students. In A. Martin (Ed.), *Issues in postgraduate education: Management, teaching and supervision, series 2 no.5*. Society for Research into Higher Education.

McVicar, A., Caan, W., Hillier, D., Munn-Giddings, C., Ramon, S., & Winter, R. (2006). A shared experience: An interdisciplinary professional doctorate in health and social care. *Innovations in Education and Teaching International, 43*(3), 211–222.

Miller, L. (2003). Belonging to country—A philosophical anthropology. *Journal of Australian Studies, 27*(76), 215–223.

Morley, L. (1999). *Organising feminisms: The micropolitics of the academy*. Palgrave Macmillan.

Morris, C. (2021). "Peering through the window looking in": Postgraduate experiences of non-belonging and belonging in relation to mental health and wellbeing. *Studies in Graduate and Postdoctoral Education*. https://doi.org/10.1108/SGPE-07-2020-0055

Morris, C., & Wisker, G. (2011). *Troublesome encounters: Strategies for managing the wellbeing of master's and doctoral education students during their learning processes*. HEA ESCalate Subject Centre Report.

Morrish, L. (2019). *Pressure vessels: The epidemic of poor mental health among higher education staff*. Higher Education Policy Institute.

National Union of Students (NUS). (2010). *Hidden marks: A study of women students' experiences of harassment, stalking, violence and sexual assault*. NUS.

Nelson, M. L., & Friedlander, M. L. (2001). A close look at conflictual supervisory relationships: The trainee's perspective. *Journal of Counseling Psychology, 48*(4), 384.

Neumann, R., & Tan, K. K. (2011). From PhD to initial employment: The doctorate in a knowledge economy. *Studies in Higher Education, 36*(5), 601–614. https://doi.org/10.1080/03075079.2011.594596

Parry, S. (2007). *Disciplines and doctorates*. Springer.

Pearson, M., Cumming, J., Evans, T., Macauley, P., & Ryland, K. (2011). How shall we know them? Capturing the diversity of difference in Australian doctoral candidates and their experiences. *Studies in Higher Education, 36*(5), 527–542. https://doi.org/10.1080/03075079.2011.594591

Phillips, E., & Pugh, D. (2015). *How to get a PhD: A handbook for students and their supervisors* (6th ed.). Open University Press.

Phipps, A., & Young, I. (2013). *That's what she said: Women students' experiences of 'lad culture' in higher education*. Project Report. National Union of Students.

Public Health England. (2017). Facing the facts, shaping the future: A draft health and care workforce strategy for England to 2027.

Rolf, H. G. (2021). Navigating power in doctoral publishing: A data feminist approach. *Teaching in Higher Education, 26*(3), 488–507.

Royal Society. (2014). A picture of the UK scientific workforce.

Santos, G., & Dang Van Phu, S. (2019). Gender and academic rank in the UK. *Sustainability, 11*(11), 3171.

Scott, P. (2013, November 4). Why research assessment is out of control. *The Guardian*. Retrieved from https://www.theguardian.com/education/2013/nov/04/peter-scott-research-excellence-framework

Slaughter, S., & Leslie, L. L. (1997). *Academic capitalism: Politics, policies, and the entrepreneurial university*. John Hopkins University Press.

Slaughter, S., & Rhoades, G. (2004). *Academic capitalism and the new economy*. John Hopkins University Press.

Smeby, J. C. (2000). Same-gender relationships in graduate supervision. *Higher Education, 40*(1), 53–67.

Teeuwsen, P., Ratković, S., & Tilley, S. A. (2014). Becoming academics: Experiencing legitimate peripheral participation in part-time doctoral studies. *Studies in Higher Education, 39*(4), 680–694.

The International Labour Organisation (ILO). (2018). Care work and care jobs for the future of decent work.

The Res-Sisters. (2016). I'm an early career feminist academic: Get me out of here?': Encountering and resisting the neoliberal academy. In R. Thwaites & A. Pressland (Eds.), *Being an early career feminist academic* (pp. 267–284). Palgrave Macmillan.

UK Council for Science and Technology. (2007). *Pathways to the future: The early careers of researchers in the UK*. Council for Science and Technology.

van Schalkwyk, S. C., Murdoch-Eaton, D., Tekian, A., Van der Vleuten, C., & Cilliers, F. (2016). The supervisor's toolkit: A framework for doctoral supervision in health professions education: AMEE guide no. 104. *Medical Teacher, 38*(5), 429–442.

Vitae. (2017). *One size does not fit all: Arts and humanities doctoral and early career researchers' professional development survey*. The Careers Research and Advisory Centre (CRAC) Limited.

Vitae. (2018). Exploring wellbeing and mental health and associated support services for postgraduate researchers. Retrieved from https://www.vitae.ac.uk/doing-research/wellbeing-and-mental-health/HEFCE-Report_Exploring-PGR-Mental-health-support/view

Weeks, J. (1990). The values of difference in identity. In J. Rutherford (Ed.), *Identity: Community, culture, difference* (pp. 88–100). Lawrence and Wishart.

Wellcome Trust. (2013). *Risks and rewards: How PhD students choose their careers*. Ipsos MORI.

White, J., & Nonnamaker, J. (2008). Belonging and mattering: How doctoral students experience community. *NASPA Journal, 45*(3), 350–372.

Wisker, G. (2007). *The postgraduate research handbook: Succeed with your MA, MPhil, EdD and PhD*. Palgrave Macmillan.

Wisker, G. (2012). *The good supervisor: Supervising postgraduate and undergraduate research for doctoral theses and dissertations*. Palgrave Macmillan.

Wisker, G., Morris, C., Cheng, M., Masika, R., Warnes, M., Trafford, V., & Lilly, J. (2010). *Doctoral learning journeys: Final report*. Higher Education Academy. Retrieved https://www.heacademy.ac.uk/system/files/doctoral_learning_journeys_final_report_0.pdf

# Women in the Humanities and Social Sciences: Restoryings of Participants' Doctoral Journeys

## Martina

Martina, an international student from Europe, was in her mid-20s when she started her doctorate in Politics at Redbrick University. Prior to the PhD, she worked as an administrative assistant for an EU wide NGO after having completed a master's degree. She was in a relationship, with no caring responsibilities. The PhD was something she always wanted to do, but she wanted to take a break after her masters to get some professional experience.

After working in an administrative role for an NGO for a couple of years, she developed a sense of the topic that she wanted to research. She also planned the timing of her PhD around her desire to have children after she turned 30. However, she only managed to secure partial funding for the PhD, and had to get financial support from her parents in order to move to the UK and start her doctorate. Martina's decision to return to studying without full funding was not easy, and throughout the PhD she questioned her choice. She felt considerable guilt for not having a job and for being financially reliant on her parents, comparing herself with friends who were progressing in their careers. However, her parents were very supportive and encouraging of her doing the PhD, as was her partner, who moved to the UK with her.

Martina found the PhD harder than she had initially expected due to the uncertainty she experienced in terms of her research topic, combined with changes in her personal life. Martina struggled to adjust to the independent nature of doctoral research and experienced imposter syndrome during her PhD. She was highly mobile during her studies, moving back to her home country during the second year of her PhD as her partner secured a job there. Whilst she enjoyed being closer to her family, this move made her feel isolated and Martina made the decision to return to the UK for the final year of her PhD.

After the PhD Martina hoped to either work in an academic role which fitted with her interests, or work for an NGO, though she expressed concerns about the security of such positions, as they are often reliant on short-term funding. An academic career appealed to her to some extent, but she recognised that this would depend on the type of role, and the location, given that her partner was based in her home country.

## Chloe

Chloe was in her late 20s when she began her doctorate in social policy at Modern University. Prior to this, she studied full-time for her master's degree. She previously worked in marketing whilst studying part-time for an undergraduate degree. She was in a relationship with an academic, and had some caring responsibilities for her older parents. Chloe applied for a PhD because she had enjoyed returning to study and came across the opportunity to apply for funding to do a PhD which suited her research interests. She was unsure about what career she would pursue after the PhD, but considered a career in academia or policy.

Having originally begun an undergraduate degree at 18, Chloe had struggled with her choice of degree, and was told by her personal tutor that university was not for her. She left without finishing this degree, which negatively affected her confidence and her relationships with friends and family. Chloe took a low-paid job afterwards, but was motivated to develop her skills and was quickly promoted. However, she found herself unable to progress further without a degree. Chloe studied part-time for an undergraduate degree which fitted around her full-time job, which she enjoyed, and was encouraged to do a masters by one of her lecturers. Chloe decided to study full-time, in the hope that this would enable her to change careers and work in the public sector afterwards. She then saw a funded PhD opportunity at a university near her which fitted with her research interests. The PhD appealed as it offered the opportunity for her to work independently, and develop her confidence in her academic abilities.

Chloe perceived her route to doctoral study as unconventional in comparison to her peers. Whilst her friends and family were largely supportive of her decision to do a PhD, she felt that some of them viewed it as strange due to her age and gender. For Chloe, being accepted onto a PhD was a validating experience after leaving university during her first degree. Chloe had a long-term partner when she began her PhD, who worked as an academic in a similar discipline. She had been conscious of the fact that she did not have an undergraduate degree when their relationship started, and felt that she was unable to participate in certain conversations with her friends. After the breakdown of this relationship at the end of her first year, Chloe had concerns about her ability to complete the PhD, both in relation to the emotional upheaval she experienced and also due to the financial implications of the relationship breakdown, which meant a significant change to her living situation.

Initially, Chloe struggled with imposter syndrome, and struggled to adjust to the demands of doctoral study, compounded by living at a distance from her institution during her first year. Yet after the breakdown of her relationship in her second year, Chloe became more ambitious and career-motivated. Part of this was due to financial concerns; her funding was for 3 years and she recognised that she would not have the financial support she had anticipated at the end of her funding period. She recognised that though she had supported her partner during his doctorate, she would not have the same safety net and thus would need to ensure that she was able to get a job after the PhD.

Chloe was aware of the demands of an academic career, having seen her partner take this career path. Her ideal post-PhD career was a post-doctoral position in Europe, as she enjoyed her experience of studying abroad during the first year of her PhD. However, Chloe recognised that this was likely to be a pipe dream, as having some caring responsibilities for her older parents would prevent her from moving too far away. She became increasingly keen on pursuing an academic career in either research or teaching as she progressed through the PhD, and was hopeful that a position would materialise in her department.

## Freija

Freija was in her mid-20s when she started her doctorate in Geography at Redbrick University. She completed an undergraduate and master's degree before working in a university for a short time after she graduated.

She applied for a PhD because she had always wanted to do further research, and had been encouraged by her undergraduate supervisor to apply for a PhD. She was engaged and co-habiting, with no caring responsibilities. She considered pursuing an academic career after the PhD but was also open to other options. Her father was an academic in another discipline, and tried to dissuade her from doing a doctorate and pursuing an academic career, due to the competitive nature of academia.

Whilst Freija was excited to start her doctorate, she recognised that her family had other priorities for her. Her parents, and her fiancée's parents, were keen for her to get married and have children, and she felt the weight of these expectations throughout her studies. Freija struggled with justifying her decision to do a PhD to her fiancée's parents, who had not been to university and were not able to understand her motivation, especially on such a relatively low stipend. Freija did not have a specific plan for her career when she began the PhD, but was hopeful that she and her partner would move abroad.

During her PhD, Freija consistently struggled with what she viewed as the conflict between the real and academic world. Whilst she enjoyed her research, she felt guilty that she was not working in a job which her family and friends would perceive as being useful. Though she was increasingly drawn to the idea of an academic career, Freija was concerned about whether academic research would enable her to have an impact on the community her work was focused on. She had a positive relationship with her supervisors, however, and perceived her lead supervisor as a non-traditional academic because of his focus on working with community groups, enabling her to view him as a positive academic role model.

As she developed stronger academic aspirations, Freija acknowledged the challenges of this career, such as the need to work under pressure to apply for funding, teach and publish work, and recognised that many academics struggled with the workload. However, she was not dissuaded by this, and viewed her PhD as an opportunity to get experience of academic life, including working in these conditions. Freija aspired to a post-doctoral position after the PhD, and was strategic in engaging in a range of activities to give herself the best chance of attaining this position, such as applying for additional small research grants and taking up a part-time research assistant post. Having seen others struggle to find work after the PhD, Freija was aware of the competition for academic jobs, and the difficulties of being employed on short-term, temporary academic contracts. However, initially this did not discourage her from this career as she felt that her desire for the stability and security of a permanent job was not as great as some of her peers. However, as Freija progressed through the PhD she started to have some doubts about pursuing an academic career which she perceived as insecure.

## Bella

Bella was in her early 20s when she started her PhD in Psychology at Modern University. Prior to this, she studied for her undergraduate degree at a different institution. She was single, with no caring responsibilities. She applied for a PhD because she felt that a doctorate would offer her the chance to do more independent research than a master's degree, and hoped to become an academic after completing the PhD. This particular career appealed because of the freedom she perceived in academia to follow her particular research interests, and to work autonomously.

Whilst Bella enjoyed her research, she found it difficult to adjust to her life as a doctoral student. She was close to her family, and found it hard to move away from them to a new city to start the PhD, having only just returned home after finishing her undergraduate degree. She also experienced anxiety during her first degree, and found that doing the PhD heightened these problems. Bella struggled with imposter syndrome during her doctorate, and found it difficult to balance her teaching with her research. Whilst she had supportive peers who she shared an office with, Bella did not have many friends in the local area and had few interests outside of her work. She also felt under pressure to demonstrate to her family that she was able to cope with the pressure of doing a PhD and that she could manage her anxiety, which meant that she often concealed the extent to which she was struggling.

During her PhD, Bella's relationship with her supervisors was difficult. She felt that they were not invested in her research and was frustrated that they were often late to supervisions. Further, early on in her studies she disclosed her anxiety to one of her supervisors after a particularly difficult supervision, and she felt that their reaction was unhelpful and dismissive. She felt that revealing her anxiety to them was a mistake and that it affected how they behaved towards her; Bella perceived that they treated her differently after this, talking to her in ways that she felt were patronising and dismissive.

Bella was keen to become an academic after the PhD, and was aware that she would need to acquire specific skills and experience to position herself for this type of role. However, she was concerned that the PhD would not be enough by itself and that she was likely to be at a disadvantage in applying for competitive academic jobs against people who had been involved in a lot of different activities during the doctorate. She hoped to work in a role which would allow her to do some research as well as teaching. During the PhD, however, Bella became somewhat unsure about her academic aspirations. She had found it difficult to move away from her family to study for her PhD, and was aware that many academic posts require individuals to be geographically mobile, meaning that she would likely have to live at a significant distance from them. These considerations made her uncertain about her likelihood of securing an academic career, but she was unsure of her other potential career options.

## Eleanor

Eleanor was in her mid-20s when she started her doctorate in English at Redbrick University. After completing her undergraduate degree, she worked in a series of low-paid jobs before self-funding a full-time master's degree at an elite UK institution. She was encouraged to apply for a PhD by a tutor, and was motivated by a strong personal interest in her topic and the possibility of pursuing a career in academia. Though she was not completely fixed on this career path, becoming an academic appealed because of the high social value placed on this role. Eleanor was in a relationship, with no caring responsibilities.

Her previous educational experiences shaped her attitude to doctoral study, and the way she considered post-PhD career options. Having studied for her masters at an elite UK university, where she was bullied by women academics and encouraged to work very long hours, she was initially wary of her female supervisor and keen to ensure that she had a better work-life balance during the PhD. Eleanor perceived the academic environment as highly competitive, and came to view the PhD as a competition with the prize being an academic job. Whilst she was critical of this, she also acknowledged her own competitive tendencies and her perception that she would feel like a failure if she was unable to secure an academic job after the PhD, which she felt stemmed from studying for her masters at a highly competitive elite institution.

For the majority of her PhD, Eleanor shared an office with her peers, which she felt made a significant, positive difference to her studies. She enjoyed her research and feeling part of her departmental community. During the PhD, she became both more enthusiastic about pursuing an academic career and also more critical of the academic environment. Her appreciation of studying at an institution with an inclusive, collegial academic environment with positive role models and supportive supervisors meant that she was keen to become an academic and continue with her research. However, she recognised that her personal circumstances would make it challenging for her to pursue this career, and was particularly concerned about the prevalence of temporary academic contracts, which she felt would be particularly problematic for her because of her class background and lack of financial security after the end of her funding period.

Though she remained keen to pursue an academic career, Eleanor was aware that aspects of this career would make her personal life more difficult. She expressed concerns that her age, gender and desire to have a family in the next few years would make it very challenging for her to become an academic, due to potential age and gender discrimination by future employers, combined with the temporary nature of many early career positions and expectations of mobility. Thus, towards the end of her second year Eleanor considered other non-academic roles including professional services roles universities, or working for a research funding body. She also considered working for organisations which would enable her to do some research but without the additional pressures of an academic career.

# 5

# Navigating Belonging Within Academic Spaces: Traversing Territories in the Humanities and Social Sciences

This chapter explores how women doctoral students in humanities and social sciences subjects attempted to develop a sense of belonging within their academic communities. Recognising literature which highlights how doctoral students in these subject areas are more likely to experience isolation than those in lab-based disciplines (Crook et al., 2021; Delamont, Atkinson, et al., 1997; Delamont et al., 2000; Phillips & Pugh, 2015), this chapter calls attention to the impact of the physical environments within which women doctoral students studied and worked. This focus on the role of physical space in participants' experiences of belonging to academic communities acknowledges that individuals' experiences always occur 'in specific places or sequences of places' (Clandinin & Connelly, 2000, p. 50). Here, spaces are understood as multidimensional, involving the perceptions of those who use them, their original intended purposes and the lived experiences of those who work within them (Lefebvre, 1991).

This chapter illuminates how women doctoral students navigated particular academic and institutional spaces during their doctorate. It explores how the culture and structure of academic environments shaped women doctoral students' ability to feel a sense of belonging, drawing on literature which examines how academic identities are shaped by disciplinary cultures (Becher, 1994; Henkel, 2004, 2005), as well as work which highlights the gendered micro-politics of academic environments (Gill, 2009; Morley, 1999). In doing so, it focuses on understanding the sites where women doctoral students felt a sense of belonging and those where they did not, as well as illuminating the factors which facilitated or precluded these feelings of belonging. Finally, this chapter explores how the encounters that participants had within these spaces, including witnessing the career experiences of other women, shaped how they imagined themselves working in these spaces in the future, as potential academics.

## Studying for a Doctorate in the Humanities and Social Sciences

Doctoral research in the humanities and social sciences takes a very different form to the traditions of doctoral study in STEM and health and related science subjects. Individuals work alone to pursue a particular research topic, which they have often selected themselves, and are supervised by either one or two academics who provide guidance and support (Phillips & Pugh, 2015). Rather than becoming socialised into their discipline by participating collaboratively in the activities of a particular research group, individuals become encultured into the disciplinary culture through their supervisors, who act as gatekeepers into the epistemic community (Delamont, Parry, et al., 1997b, 2000; Parry, 2007). Supervisors therefore exert significant influence over doctoral students in these subjects and may constitute one of their only academic role models; whilst in STEM disciplines doctoral students are likely to work with a range of senior scientists as part of wider research teams, this is not often the case for those in humanities and social sciences.

Within humanities and social sciences research, significance is more often attributed to the novelty of the doctoral research topic or approach, rather than the collective progression of a particular research problem as in STEM subjects (see Becher et al., 1994; Delamont, Parry, et al., 1997b, 2000). The processes of knowledge production, and thus the ways by which individuals learn to become legitimate members of their disciplinary community, vary between subject areas. In the arts, this may take the form of expertise demonstrated through creative performance; in the social sciences, this often relates to the completion of fieldwork; in the humanities, this relates to the production of a monograph based on secondary analysis of texts (see Delamont et al., 2000). The doctorate in the humanities and social sciences is thus most often an individualistic endeavour, lacking in the obvious opportunities for social interaction available to those working within specific research or laboratory groups. This can lead to isolation (see Delamont et al., 1997b; Golde, 2005; Hockey, 1994) and historically has been connected with poor completion and retention rates (Hockey, 1995; Lovitts, 2001; Tinto, 1993).

Whilst changes to doctoral training in the UK over the last decade have introduced a cohort approach to training delivered through specific centres or partnerships (see ESRC, 2009), the majority of doctoral students are outside of this model (Smith-McGloin & Wynne, 2022), and the dominant mode of doctoral research in the humanities and social sciences remains individualistic rather than collaborative. Interestingly, though two participants were members of doctoral training partnerships, neither of them made more than a passing reference to this, and in referring to their academic community they discussed their department and discipline. This supports the findings of research which indicates that these types of training centres have further to go in developing a sense of community identity (see Budd et al., 2018).

Given the often small numbers of doctoral students and postdoctoral researchers in humanities and social science subjects at individual institutions, it is vitally important to provide spaces which facilitate opportunities for tacit learning about academic life (see Deem & Brehony, 2000). The ability to engage in academic discussions with peers and academics in their field is critical for doctoral students' academic identity development, as this creates opportunities for them to be recognised as scholars who are able to make valuable contributions to their discipline (Jazvac-Martek, 2009; Mantai, 2019). Acknowledging literature which highlights that women doctoral students are more likely to struggle with imposter syndrome than their male counterparts (see Collett & Avelis, 2013) means that this external recognition is likely to be of greater importance to women.

Despite the tendency of these disciplines to be female-dominated at the student level, with more women than men studying for a doctorate in most non-STEM subjects in the UK (Advance HE, 2021b), this does not remain the case for those who work in these disciplines. In the UK, women constitute only about a third of professors in non-STEM subjects (Advance HE, 2021a). Further, there are differential patterns of participation by gender within sub-disciplines, with women making up around two-thirds of doctoral students in education, compared to just under half of doctoral students in business and administrative studies and historical and philosophical studies (Advance HE, 2021b). Yet research shows that doctoral students in the humanities and social sciences are more likely to want an academic career than those in STEM subjects (Higher Education Academy, 2015; The Royal Society, 2014), and that many struggle to imagine themselves in non-academic careers (Vitae, 2017).

It is therefore important to gain insight into any specific challenges that women doctoral students in these disciplines face in being able to imagine themselves as academics beyond the doctorate. This chapter explores how the spaces within which women doctoral students studied and worked affected their relationships with their peers, supervisors and other academics, and how this impacted how they imagined belonging within and beyond academic spaces. In doing so, this chapters attends to the ways in which participants traversed a number of different actual and conceptual territories, including shared and individual workspaces, departmental offices, as well as future, imagined academic communities.

## Access to Institutional Workspaces and Feeling Belonging

Existing research points to the significance of access to certain physical spaces such as offices and libraries, for positive experiences of doctoral study (Barnacle & Mewburn, 2010; Churchill & Sanders, 2007; Deem & Brehony, 2000; Gardner, 2007; Hockey, 1994). Opportunities to connect with peers and academics are essential for developing individuals' sense of belonging, as belonging requires recognition of the individual by established members of a community (May, 2013). For doctoral students, this involves feeling valued and recognised as a legitimate contributor to their academic community (White & Nonnamaker, 2008). This can be argued to be even more important for women students, who are more likely to experience imposter syndrome than their male counterparts (Collett & Avelis, 2013), and benefit from interactions with women academics who may represent role models (Curtin et al., 2016; Wladkowski & Mirick, 2019). Thus, the extent to which doctoral students are able to engage with institutional workspaces is likely to impact the ways in which they learn about academic life and feel a sense of belonging to their academic community (McAlpine & Mitra, 2015).

As full-time doctoral students, most of whom lived near their institutions, nearly all participants were regular users of on-campus institutional workspaces. Though the level of provision and the formality of the arrangements for doctoral students varied by institution and department, most had access to a desk in a shared office or workspace in their department. Though it is recognised that some groups, for example part-time doctoral students, may find accessing institutional spaces more challenging (Gardner & Gopaul, 2012; Zahl, 2015), even for full-time students, personal circumstances may affect individuals' ability to access these institutional spaces, as Martina and Chloe's experiences indicate. Both of them moved from the UK to facilitate their partners' career moves, something which literature highlights is more common for women than for men, particularly when both partners work in academia (Ackers, 2004; Tzanakou, 2017).

Martina, an international PhD student in politics at Redbrick University, moved to the UK with her partner to study full-time for her doctorate, and they lived in the city in which she studied. However, in her second year, her partner got a job in their home country, so they returned there in order to continue living together. In her final year, Martina chose to move back to the UK to write up her thesis, whilst travelling back to her home country frequently to visit her partner, friends and family. This had a significant impact on her experience of doctoral study, particularly in relation to her interactions with her peers and supervisors.

Whilst living close to her institution in her first year, Martina had been pleasantly surprised by the possibilities for social interaction with her peers. She had access to a departmental workspace shared with other doctoral students and participated in a number of structured events in her department, including weekly seminars for other first-year students, and research seminars attended by staff and students. Martina had also undertaken compulsory research methods training modules in her first year, with other students from across social science subjects, and she valued the opportunity to connect with others: "*it was actually good because I got to know other people outside my 10–12 colleagues from the department, so you get a feeling that you're part of a broader community*" (Interview 1). Her experience echoes literature which highlights how doctoral cohort training, which prioritises the learning of generic and discipline-specific skills, may be particularly helpful for international students, as it provides structured opportunities to engage with other research students (Deem & Brehony, 2000). Indeed, Martina's experience of these training modules, as well as the regular programme of events in her department, was positive, as she felt less isolated than she had expected; "*I think at least in first year, it's not as solitary as I thought it would be*" (Interview 1).

Yet even before returning to her home country in her second year, Martina anticipated feeling more isolated in the second year of her PhD, recognising that there would be fewer structured opportunities to socialise with her peers after the conclusion of her formal research training:

> I'm a bit…apprehensive…from second year onwards, how it's going to work because then I won't have any sort of routine…places to go…that doesn't sound good. I won't have any commitments that I would have to go to, for instance, apart from these seminars—but I won't have any weekly modules, so I'm a bit apprehensive of how that's going to work in terms of feeling the connection to the department and the wider university, because it will just mean that I'll be working by myself. (Interview 1)

Significantly, Martina viewed attending the weekly research training sessions as a way of feeling connected to both her department and the university itself. Having been accustomed to attending weekly sessions in order to complete research training modules, working in a more isolated manner in her second year was not appealing. Martina's views reinforce Deem and Brehony's (2000) finding that the social aspects of research training may be of vital importance to doctoral students in the social sciences, who largely work alone, as they facilitate social interactions with their peers. Further, Martina's experiences illuminate how her sense of belonging to her academic community is fostered through feeling connected to her department, which she linked to attending regular events. It is evident that Martina struggled to imagine herself belonging to her departmental community in her second year of the PhD; she uses the word "*apprehensive*" twice in quick succession to describe how she is feeling about this prospect. Understanding belonging as innately related to positive affect (Miller, 2003), it is clear that Martina envisaged facing challenges to sustaining her sense of belonging after the end of her formal research training.

Though on a number of occasions Martina described being glad to be able to work flexibly and be based in a range of locations, she also frequently acknowledged the negative aspects of spending long periods at a distance from her institution, particularly the isolation she experiences. This high level of mobility had implications for Martina's ability to feel a sense of belonging to her academic community. Indeed, for international doctoral students who have families and friends abroad, negotiating commitments in both their country of study and their home country can be challenging (Phelps, 2016). This internal struggle is reflected in two successive entries made by Martina in her research diary during the second year of her PhD, when she had returned to her home country to live with her partner. Initially, she was glad to be living back amongst her family and planned to attend a number of conferences to present her work:

05/02/2016
    I feel like I've reached a good balance at this point. I feel at peace with my choices and with what I am doing right now with my time and my life. It might have something to do with living close to my partner and also my close family, knowing in my gut that this is right where I should be at this point in my (our) life. I am sort of excited to begin my round of conference presentations about my PhD work. I like going to conferences, knowing that there are people out there who are doing such interesting stuff and to

get feedback from other academics on my work. It's a good thing to counter-balance the loneliness of PhD daily work.

Yet, in a subsequent diary entry, Martina weighs up both the costs and benefits of returning to the UK for the final year of her doctorate. Though she acknowledged that partly she "*can't wait to go back*", she recognised that there would be "*pain*" involved in leaving her partner and family:

19/04/2016
I really miss being based in [UK city]. There I could just pop in my department, have a chat with my supervisor, or go to the postgrad rooms and run some of these ideas by my colleagues to see have a second opinion on them. Part of me really can't wait to go back to [UK city] in September, although the pain of moving countries again and being away from partner and family will also be heavy.

These extracts from Martina's research diary reveal the emotional cost of her decisions about where to base herself during her doctorate. Though in the first entry she described feeling "*at peace*" with her choice to return to her home country and "*knowing in my gut*" that this was the right decision for her current life stage, this sentiment did not sustain her when she experienced the feelings of loneliness often associated with doctoral education in the humanities and social sciences (see Owler, 2010; Parry, 2007). The second, shorter diary entry 2 months later illuminates Martina's desire to work amongst colleagues once again; she describes wanting to seek others' views of her ideas, especially her supervisor's. Her need for advice and guidance from her supervisor in particular attests to the significance of the supervisory relationship for doctoral students in the social sciences (Delamont, Parry, et al., 1997b; Hockey, 1995; Phillips & Pugh, 2015), and emphasises the crucial role supervisors have in facilitating women doctoral students' belonging to their academic communities.

Martina's account highlights how belonging requires ongoing work; her sense of belonging to her academic community must be constantly renegotiated and re-established as her circumstances change (May, 2013). Her experiences reflect the findings of existing research on the experiences of international doctoral students; in her work with doctoral students in Canada, Phelps (2016) found that the high level of mobility individuals demonstrated can disrupt identity development and impede individuals' ability to develop a sense of belonging, as they are required to constantly adapt and readjust to new cultures and communities.

Despite feeling isolated during her studies, Martina demonstrated agency in attempting to sustain her connection to her wider academic community, in lieu of a close connection to her department. In the first diary entry of 2016 (see page 99), she described her excitement attending academic conferences and beginning to present her work to others. Her agency in establishing herself amongst scholars in her disciplinary community gave her a sense of being connected to others and helped her to develop a sense of belonging to her disciplinary community. She recognised that "*knowing there are people out there doing interesting stuff*" and being able to discuss her work with them could reduce some of the isolation she had experienced. Pragmatically, Martina understood that being at a distance from her department, supervisor and peers contributed to the "*loneliness of PhD daily work*", and that participating in a wider community of scholars would likely ameliorate this. She envisaged that receiving feedback from academics in her field would be helpful, and she looked forward to meeting other scholars. Martina's experiences reflect research which highlights the importance of publicly presenting oneself as a researcher for doctoral students' academic identity development (see Mantai, 2017).

Overall, Martina found studying for her PhD "*quite a lonely process*" (Interview 2). Whereas in her first year she had felt "*part of a broader community*", she recognised that not being able to access shared physical workspaces at her institutions meant that she became distanced from her peers:

> Because I'm not based in my department…physically anymore…it's easier to be out of touch with what's happening, I don't meet with…any other colleagues…so at times it may, I feel that it's a lonely experience of just focussing on my topic and not knowing exactly what everybody else is doing. (Interview 2)

This lack of ability to connect with others had a negative impact on Martina's ability to feel a sense of belonging to her academic community.

During her second year, she decided to return to the UK for the final year of her doctorate. A further diary entry from early on in her final year indicates the personal difficulties Martina faced, but also the benefits she experienced in being based near her institution once more:

25/01/2017
   First semester of third year was not easy at all, with personal changes and some health stuff making it harder to give 100%. The two most positive things were moving back to [UK city] and starting two language courses at the university, which gives me a bit of a sense of routine and some people with whom to interact on a weekly basis at least. I've just recently decided to go for an academic career, which will mean looking quite hard at grants for post-docs in the next few months and keeping an eye on adverts for early academic career posts. I want to stay in the UK as I feel this is the best place to get on my academic career.

Here, Martina acknowledged that having weekly social interactions and a "*sense of routine*" was important, despite the transition to living back in the UK having been challenging. This reimmersion within her institution was not directly linked to her decision to pursue an academic career, but acknowledging that the UK was likely to be the "*best place*" to do this, Martina recognised that she would attempt to continue belonging within this academic community after completing her PhD. Martina's experiences reveal the personal sacrifices involved in undertaking doctoral study for international students, and the cost/benefit analysis which is undertaken by individuals who are required to make difficult decisions about where to live and work.

Even for UK students, existing personal commitments could mean having to negotiate studying for their doctorate in different locations and contexts. On starting her PhD, Chloe, studying for a doctorate in social policy at Modern University—an institution with a modest number of doctoral students—was allocated a desk within a busy research centre. Chloe's partner was an early career academic, and in the first year of her PhD he was offered the opportunity to lecture at a university in Europe for a semester. In order for them to be able to continue living together, Chloe decided to move abroad for the second semester of her first year.

This is not uncommon; literature highlights the increasing number of women doctoral graduates in relationships with academics who are men, known as dual academic career relationships (Tzanakou, 2017). The resulting impact on women's careers is highly gendered, with women being less likely to relocate for an academic position than their male partners, and more likely to follow their partner and accept a job which may be less suitable to their qualifications and experience (Ackers, 2004).

For the majority of her doctorate, Chloe was based in a research centre with academics and a small number of other doctoral students. Though she had good relationships with the academics, she missed having a group of peers who she could depend on for support and advice: *"it would be nice because…you could learn from people who were in the year above you and if you are all going through tough times together"* (Interview 1). Yet as research on doctoral education indicates, there is rarely a large number of social science PhD students at individual institutions, given the comparative lack of funding in these disciplines compared to STEM subjects (see Deem & Brehony, 2000; Delamont, Parry, et al., 1997b). For Chloe, this resulted in her being the only PhD student in her subject area present on campus:

> The academics and the PhD students are all together but like there is only me, basically…because Debbie who is another PhD student is doing fieldwork, so she's out a lot. Another girl has a young kid so she sort of comes in one or two days a week and works from home the rest of the time…so there isn't a real PhD community there…it's not like there was an intake of you know 10 PhDs to [research centre] so I have got 10 PhDs on the same level as me, going through the same thing and in that way I feel a bit you know…at a disadvantage because I don't necessarily have that community. (Interview 1)

Chloe's experiences of her institutional workspace were therefore characterised by working in a very isolated manner. She described the absence of a *"real PhD community"* and expressed disappointment at not having an obvious group of peers. Though Chloe was not able to easily develop a sense of belonging through establishing connections with other students, her use of pragmatic language such as *"disadvantage"* rather than the more emotive language used by Martina indicates that this aspect of her experience was less critical to her sense of belonging. She accepted that doctoral students work flexibly and may have different preferences: "*I go in every day because everyone chooses to work wherever…you can't force everyone to come and work in the office*" (Interview 1).

The way in which Chloe approached her move abroad was highly strategic; she contacted the institution where her partner was working in a short-term academic post and secured a visiting PhD student arrangement so that she would be able to access the library and institutional workspaces. However, the initial period after she had moved abroad was quite difficult, as she struggled to make connections with anyone from her own disciplinary community:

> When I first went to [European city], I definitely had a wobble because I just felt like oh what am I doing here, but…I am a quite chatty person, so I have now made friends…but they happen to be just geographically near to me and not necessarily at all related to what I do. (Interview 1)

Yet Chloe demonstrated considerable agency in seeking support from her peers in other ways. In our first interview, she described using an online group for PhD students to share issues and support one another:

> What I have found really helpful is there is this online group on Facebook, called Postgrad study school of hard thinking. And that, that was really helpful when I had like a down point…I was saying you know I am going through a rough patch…that's been nice… even though it is like an online community of people I am never going to meet and I don't know…I have found that helpful. (Interview 1)

Being able to connect with a wider community of peers was something Chloe found "*helpful*" in the absence of a more immediate group of peers. Being able to share her experiences with others in the same situation was a positive experience, indicating the significance of opportunities to make connections with others within the academic community more widely. Chloe's experiences support findings from research which highlights how using social media and participating in online communities can help doctoral students to combat isolation, especially those working at a distance from their institution (see Vigurs, 2016)—something which may contribute positively to their sense of belonging to a wider academic community.

Though Chloe recognised the importance of forming purely social connections, she acknowledged that she would like to be able to interact more with members of her disciplinary community: "*it would have been nice in an ideal world if there was a specific person there who is doing similar research who I could sort of, have as a mentor or something*" (Interview 1). Yet, in the absence of a more formal arrangement, she attempted to build her own network. Chloe displayed considerable agency in attempting to establish herself within her local academic community by reaching out to scholars in similar disciplinary areas:

> I then decided right I'm going to be proactive and I spent ages e-mailing various people in various departments to try and find out what's going on…I'm excited because on Monday I am going for a coffee with a girl from the sociology department…she looks at masculinity and family and work / life balance so it's like similar to one part of my research area so that will be interesting to for the first time, you know speak to someone who's kind of related to what I'm doing and maybe through her I'll meet other people…like trying to build a network. (Interview 1)

Her resolve to be "*proactive*" in approaching other members of her discipline is indicative of Chloe's determination to establish herself as a valid member of her local disciplinary community and develop a sense of belonging by being recognised as a scholar in that field. The "*girl from the sociology department*" thus represents a disciplinary gatekeeper who could help Chloe to forge connections with other academics in her field. As well as offering the opportunity to be recognised as a scholar by this individual, Chloe also hoped that she could help her to build a network, which she acknowledged may have longer-term career benefits.

Though at times Chloe was frustrated that being abroad meant missing out on some opportunities such as attending specific events and engaging in undergraduate teaching, she reflected that her decision to move abroad brought benefits as well as costs. She viewed the connections she made as potentially useful for future career-related opportunities, such as engaging in collaborative work with other academics:

> I think overall it will be a good experience and it will be interesting to see how it goes talking to people who are studying a similar area to me and to see if I, you know, build connections that you know in the future you know I don't know you could work together on something or, you know so hopefully it will be you know a really useful experience. And it is good for my CV I can say I have been a visiting PhD student somewhere so… that's good. (Interview 1)

Forging connections with other academics was important for Chloe's ability to feel a sense of belonging to her disciplinary community, echoing literature which highlights the significance of social connections for individuals' belonging (Miller, 2003). Despite her positive and agentic approach to being based at a distance from her institution and the efforts she made to build relationships, a diary entry from the end of her first year indicated that Chloe was positively anticipating her return to the UK and the city where she studied, indicating that physical proximity to her academic community remained an important and valuable aspect of her doctoral experience:

> 03/08/2015
> It's my last week as a visiting PhD student abroad as I move back to the UK in 8 days, as my partner's temp contract has come to an end. Looking forward to being back in the city where I actually do my PhD!!!

Whilst Chloe's experience highlights that individuals are able to establish a sense of belonging to multiple academic communities, and that this is not necessarily predicated on regular access to institutional workspaces, it is difficult not to view the choice that she and Martina made as gendered. Literature highlights the tendency of women, particularly those with academic partners, to make migration and career decisions on the basis of their partners' careers rather than their own (Ackers, 2004; Wolf-Wendel et al., 2004), due to the social expectations on women to prioritise family over career. As well as impacting Chloe and Martina's ability to establish a sense of belonging within their academic communities at their institution during their doctorate, research highlights that decisions about mobility can have long-term implications for women's academic career progression (Ackers, 2004; Tzanakou, 2017).

## Negotiating Belonging Within Physical Workspaces

Even for those who regularly used institutional workspaces, experiences of these physical spaces varied considerably, with implications for individuals' ability to establish a sense of belonging within their academic communities. Provision of a dedicated workspace—whether a hot-desk in a shared office for doctoral students in a particular subject area, or an allocated desk within a departmental building—was not uniform across participants' experiences. Largely, individuals were given access to hot-desking within a shared space for doctoral students, with the exception of Chloe, who was given a particular desk in a research centre amongst academics, and Eleanor, a PhD student in English at Redbrick University, who was also allocated a particular desk in a shared study space for doctoral students.

Participants' experiences of belonging, or not belonging, were significantly influenced by their interactions with the physical workspaces they were given access to as well as their encounters with individuals within them. Physical workspaces provided the everyday context for the academic communities that individuals were attempting to establish themselves in. Literature on doctoral student experiences highlights that power and status are inscribed within institutional spaces (Hemer, 2012; Manathunga, 2005; Middleton, 2010), and thus it is important to attend to the micro-politics of these academic spaces and examine how physical allocations and divisions of space can either facilitate or challenge individuals' ability to feel a sense of belonging to their academic community.

There is a strong link between physical workspaces and belonging for doctoral students, who may miss out on valuable social learning opportunities if they do not utilise institutional workspaces (McAlpine & Mitra, 2015). The provision of dedicated office space for doctoral students enables informal interactions and social connections to be formed, which help to facilitate belonging (Morris & Wisker, 2011). Shared workspaces with other peers may help individuals to combat the isolation which is commonplace within experiences of doctoral study in the humanities and social sciences (Ali et al., 2007; Golde, 2005). Further, the proximity of these workspaces to the rest of the department is also of importance, as this provides opportunities for informal interactions with academics and thus may support academic identity development (see Gardner, 2007; Hockey, 1994). The physical organisation of institutional spaces can, however, reinforce existing hierarchies between staff and research students (Morris, 2021; Morris & Wisker, 2011), as Freija, a PhD student in geography at Redbrick University, experiences.

Having studied for her previous degrees at another institution, Freija found the transition to a new university challenging at first. Early on, she described how it had taken time for her to adjust to the new institution and departmental dynamics:

> I think it's taken me quite a while to settle in, because I feel like when I was at [old institution]…the final like last two years, I really started to feel like part of the department, like you'd start going to kind of seminars and you knew the lecturers and like you kind of got to know the postgrads, and… especially when I did my Masters because it was a research one, we got given desks in the postgrad office, and you just really started to feel like you knew everyone, you knew what they were doing, if you went to a seminar it was quite normal for you to like speak up and ask questions and discuss stuff, whereas I feel like maybe it's not so much to do with this university, but…I think it was quite difficult really to gauge the department and the kind of relationships between like staff and students…it just took a while to settle into that. At first, you know I felt like quite detached. (Interview 1)

Freija's comments reflect how doctoral students who have moved locations in order to undertake a PhD may feel particularly isolated, as they have had to leave their existing social and support networks (see Hockey, 1994; Mantai, 2019). Whereas during her undergraduate and master's degrees she had felt *"like part of the department"*, Freija initially felt *"detached"* from her current department. Relationships between staff and students were *"difficult to gauge"*, and she was not able to establish meaningful social connections—something which research indicates may have a negative impact on well-being (Morris & Wisker, 2011) and compromise her ability to feel a sense of belonging. Freija's experiences reveal the importance of comprehensive induction for doctoral students (see also Ali et al., 2007). However, more significantly, her experiences contradict institutional assumptions that doctoral students are experts at studying in higher education institutions because of their prior experiences, and therefore need little support in developing a sense of belonging within these spaces (White & Nonnamaker, 2008).

Significantly, Freija attributed her early feelings of detachment from the department, and her experiences of marginalisation within her academic community, to the lack of staff-student interaction. She compared this to the very different dynamic she had experienced at her previous institution, and perceived that the difference in her experience was compounded by the layout of the building:

> At [old institution] there was this big kind of like common room type thing, and it was quite normal for staff and students to have a coffee and talk, and if you were sat next to your lecturer or something, you'd just ask them like oh how was your weekend whereas when I first got here especially I felt like there was a bit more of a divide, like this is the postgrad room, this is the office, the café which is mainly used by students as well, and then the staff were all in these offices which you don't really, there's not as much interaction. At first I think I felt like that was, it was quite, I don't know, it was just harder to gauge how people interacted and the kind of relationships within the department. (Interview 1)

The physical spaces within Freija's department initially prevented her from developing a sense of belonging; her ability to make social connections with others and be accepted into the departmental community was compromised by the physical distinction between academic staff and doctoral students and the lack of common space. Freija's comments on the *"divide"* in her department shows how she perceived the provision of separate spaces for staff and students to be intentional, indicating how institutional spaces can reinforce hierarchies between staff and research students, whereas shared spaces can foster collegiality (Gardner, 2007; Morris & Wisker, 2011). This echoes literature which argues that universities are innately hierarchical institutions within which issues of power and status inform access to space, such as how contract researchers are more often allocated shared office space than permanent members of staff (Archer, 2008) and how part-time doctoral students may not be allocated workspace at their institution (Deem & Brehony, 2000). Freija's experience is not uncommon, as other research reveals; in their research with doctoral students in the social sciences in the UK, Morris and Wisker (2011) found that perceptions of themselves as low status within the academic hierarchy could lead to feelings of isolation and challenge individuals' ability to feel a sense of belonging within their academic community.

While working in close proximity to staff as well as other doctoral students may facilitate social connections and community belonging (Morris & Wisker, 2011), these opportunities can be limited due to the constraints imposed on departmental spaces. Interactions with senior colleagues are important for doctoral students' career development (Gardner, 2007), and positive relationships between doctoral students and senior academics are 'crucial in making possible and determining academic career trajectories' (Almack & Churchill, 2007, p. 105). The physical separation of staff and students within Freija's department therefore both compromised her ability to establish a sense of belonging as a doctoral student and also is not conducive to interactions which may facilitate her career development, and thus her future belonging to this academic community.

Establishing social connections with her peers was also an important aspect of Freija's ability to feel a sense of belonging within her academic community. Yet she encountered difficulties in developing these connections within her everyday workspace—the office she shared with other doctoral students—due to a lack of structured opportunities to connect with her peers. She missed out on early opportunities to develop relationships with other first-year PhD students because she had done a master's in a similar area, and so was exempt from some of the training sessions provided by the university for doctoral students. This meant that she found it difficult to establish relationships with peers: "*I remember just sitting at my desk and it'd got from about 9 o'clock to about 12 and I still hadn't… you know really interacted with anyone*" (Interview 1). There is often an assumption that doctoral students need less support in terms of induction (White & Nonnamaker, 2008), and Freija's department does not provide structured social opportunities for doctoral students, which may help to foster communities of practice (Lave & Wenger, 1991). As a key aspect of belonging is developing meaningful connections with others within a particular community and feeling at ease within the immediate social context (Miller, 2003), Freija's inability to forge these connections due to a lack of structured opportunities early on in her studies had implications for her ability to belong.

Yet taking on an academic identity in a more formalised way by starting to teach undergraduates in her second year of the PhD had a significant, positive impact on Freija's sense of belonging to her academic community. She acknowledged this directly in our second interview when asked about any differences between the first and second year of her studies: "*I think especially the teaching and getting to know staff as well as other students has made me feel more like I kind of belong in this little department which is nice*" (Interview 2). For Freija, developing meaningful relationships with peers and academics was essential to her sense of belonging. She perceived that these relationships were facilitated by her involvement in teaching:

> Getting more experience of teaching especially in the last few months has been really, really good, just because I've got to know a lot, you know met different members of staff, different PhD students and also getting to know undergrads, and Master's students, I think that whole process has just made me feel more of the department, like made me feel like part of the department more than I did before. And I think that was, even from the start quite important to me because I felt so kind of at home in my old department, where I did my undergrad and my Master's. (Interview 2)

Through delivering teaching to undergraduates alongside academics, Freija contributed to one of the department's core activities and took on responsibilities similar to academic staff, allowing her to be recognised by others in her department as a socially significant member of her academic community. Whilst literature highlights that expectations of doctoral students to engage in teaching undergraduates in an equivalent role with employed academics may contribute to a sense of uncertain status (see Rao et al., 2021), it was evident that Freija's improved sense of belonging in her second year was largely due to being able to participate as a member of her departmental teaching team and develop the social connections which she desired. This enabled Freija to feel that she both belonged and mattered within her departmental community, as she acknowledged: "*the whole process has just made me feel…like part of the department more than I did before*".

Freija's experiences resonate with literature which highlights the ways in which doctoral students often undertake similar types of academic labour as members of staff, which may have a positive impact on their academic identity development (see Jazvac-Martek, 2009). The significance of teaching for doctoral students' academic identity development has been observed by others (see Hopwood, 2010; Mantai, 2019), as the successful performance of teaching may enable doctoral students to see themselves as academics (Bansel, 2011). These experiences stand in sharp contrast to STEM participants' experiences of feeling pressured to publish, where they had not anticipated this type of academic labour and did not enjoy undertaking this work.

Like Freija, Eleanor—a PhD student in English at Redbrick University—also struggled to make connections with peers during the early stages of her PhD:

> I wasn't very happy with the desk at first…in the building I'm in, there are desks on floors 2, 3, 4 and 5. I'm on floor 4 and there aren't many other people on floor 4, and the people that are there…I think they're all from the same country…they say hello on a morning but they tend to, they all kind of swap to this language that I don't know and just talk on their own for the rest of the day…a lot of my friends are on floor five and the rest are on floor two and I was a bit like all my friends sit together without me. (Interview 1)

Though comparatively little has been written about the social relationships between international and home doctoral students in comparison to undergraduates (Leonard et al., 2006), existing research highlights that international students find participating in peer student cultures more challenging than home students (Deem & Brehony, 2000), making developing a sense of belonging within their immediate academic community difficult (Phelps, 2016). Further, a small-scale study undertaken in the UK draws attention to the lack of integration of international and home doctoral student communities, despite the desire of international students to make connections with home students (Walsh, 2010). Eleanor's inability to forge a connection with her international peers mirrors these findings and highlights that navigating cultural differences and feeling a sense of belonging are not straightforward for either home or international doctoral students.

When an opportunity arose early on in her second year for Eleanor to access a desk in an office with others working in a similar area of research, she was able to take advantage of this and move into this space. She acknowledged the significant positive impact of this on her experience and sense of belonging to her academic community:

> One of the main things that's made me kind of feel a lot more part of the community and has changed how I feel a lot is moving desks up onto the end bit of floor 5…the layout makes a difference as well…on floor 4 it's really open and people are always walking past and it doesn't feel like your space you're just always part of, very much part of the corridor and whereas my desk on floor 5 you walk to the very end of the corridor and then down here, like this bit would be our desk area so no one, there aren't offices there, no one's ever walking past, you don't go down to the end unless it's for our bit and my desk is like round the corner right next to a window…it feels more like homely instead of just like oh well you sit there next to the corridor. (Interview 2)

As with Freija, it is clear that Eleanor's experience of being allocated workspace as a doctoral student links to issues of power and status; it seems unlikely that any fully contracted academic staff would be allocated a desk which was essentially in a departmental corridor. Her comments indicate how seemingly small details of physical workspaces can have a significant, affective impact on doctoral students' experiences. This finding echoes research which highlights how doctoral students often report a perceived sense of being low status, which can create feelings of isolation and difficulties in feeling a sense of belonging (see Morris & Wisker, 2011).

In contrast, Eleanor recognised how the physical layout of her new workspace contributes to her ability to feel part of the academic community. Moving into a new office with a group of other women doctoral students enabled Eleanor to feel a sense of belonging through her day-to-day interactions with her peers in a space which they were able to make their own:

> The linguistics crowd that I sit with…it's just a big like girly office, there are 7 of us in the office, all women, we all get on really well and they have all just like decorated and it's all like flowery and nice and it's just like, it's just quite homely and…yes. I don't know. It has made a difference, but I don't, I can't fully explain why. (Interview 2)

Her description of this feminised and collegial space, which is "*decorated*", "*flowery*" and "*homely*", provides insight into the ways in which physical spaces can facilitate a sense of belonging for doctoral students, even if Eleanor did not fully understand why the change in her workspace made such a difference to her experience. This reasserts findings from other research which have highlighted how shared office spaces for doctoral students can facilitate 'informal contact, socialising, and ultimately belonging' (Morris & Wisker, 2011, p. 45). Further, beyond the atmosphere of their daily working environment, Eleanor acknowledged the value of being able to support one another on a day-to-day basis:

> We've got a WhatsApp group and everyone just says oh who is coming into the office today…it's just turning up it's just someone to have a tea break with that makes a difference…when you are really under stress it's having people around, even if they're just there and they are not saying anything it kind of, I feel like it helps a lot, the environment makes a big difference I think. (Interview 2)

Peer support can be invaluable for doctoral students, helping combat isolation (Ali et al., 2007; Lovitts, 2001), which is particularly common amongst those in the humanities and social sciences (Delamont, Parry, et al., 1997b; Phillips & Pugh, 2015). This is apparent from Eleanor's experiences; she acknowledged that casual interactions with her officemates, such as a tea break, are really valuable and that even just their presence during times of stress "*helps a lot*". These social relationships with her peers, established in a shared and supportive space, highlight how Eleanor's sense of belonging to her academic community was facilitated by the social connections she forged with others (Miller, 2003). Accessing this shared, dedicated workspace rather than her previous allocated desk had a significant impact on her well-being, which Eleanor recognised: "*I feel like I'm happier because my immediate community in like the desk world has improved*" (Interview 2). Again, Eleanor's use of language is interesting here; having described her new office as "*homely*", she subsequently commented that she was happier in "*the desk world*", indicating how significant and immersive daily workspaces may be for doctoral students, as well as demonstrating how belonging is innately affective (see May, 2013).

Exploring both Freija and Eleanor's experiences of their immediate academic environments reveals the ways in which physical workspaces may operate in multiple ways, either facilitating, challenging or, in some cases, precluding individuals' ability to feel a sense of belonging, or connection, to their academic community (Miller, 2003). The physical spaces which doctoral students are allocated within their institutions are indicative of the status and significance afforded to doctoral students as a group, something that participants intrinsically felt, even if they did not acknowledge or articulate this explicitly. Though—as in the case of Freija—they are expected to undertake academic labour such as teaching, they are rarely afforded the same status or recognised as equally valuable members of the academic community. Attending to the everyday physical environments within which women doctoral students worked enables insight into the ways in which they were able to develop a sense of belonging to their academic communities. Understanding belonging as an embodied feeling of ease with the people and places around us, involving social connections and the negotiation of power relations within our immediate social milieu, requires that we recognise the significance of space and what it represents for doctoral students—something considerably overlooked in much of the literature on doctoral student experiences.

## Imagining Future Belonging: Witnessing Gendered Careers

Beyond participants' immediate, present ability to feel belonging to their academic communities as doctoral students, their daily experiences of observing the working practices embedded in their academic environments had a significant impact on how they imagined belonging in academia in the future. For those working in largely female-dominated subject areas such as psychology (in the case of Bella), English (Eleanor) and social policy (Chloe), perceptions of academic careers were influenced by the gendered dynamics they saw within the careers of women working in these disciplines. Though they responded to this in quite different ways, each individual recognised the ways in which being a woman academic might make belonging within their disciplinary community more challenging.

Awareness of the gendered nature of academic careers varied amongst participants, along with understandings of the factors which contribute to the 'leaky pipeline' (Barinaga, 1993). Whilst Bella was aware of gendered academic career paths within her discipline—which is overwhelmingly female-dominated at undergraduate level, but male-dominated at senior academic levels—she considered that this may be simply due to individual preference and choices:

> It is quite a strange thing in Psychology I don't really know about other subjects but like, in the undergrads for instance there is a lot more females than males whereas people who are like Professors and stuff there is a lot, it is completely switched round and it kind of, it does make me think about it sometimes like, where do these people go that they disappear off and do other stuff. And I suppose, it might be a kind of difference that a lot of females maybe go and do counselling or whatever instead of sticking with the academic kind of line. (Interview 1)

Bella did not expect gender to be a factor which might affect her own academic career goals because she had not previously experienced gender to be a barrier to her achievements, and like Jane in Chap. 3, she felt that her determination to be an academic would enable her to succeed.

However, Bella did acknowledged that gender could become more of an issue for those in more senior roles, which made her reflect this could affect her future career progression:

> I think, I am quite determined and I think I am going to do it anyway…because it hasn't necessarily been a problem I have not really encountered a lot of things where it has been a problem in terms of you are a girl you can't do this…I don't know if that changes as you get to higher kind of positions…I think there is kind of this possibility of a different dynamic when you get to a different level and that, that is kind of a concern I think because I don't know what is going to happen like I don't know how that might affect me and I don't know if it would even affect me. (Interview 1)

Though it is "*kind of a concern*" as to how gender might affect her ability to develop an academic career, Bella felt that having women academic role models present in her department enabled her to envisage herself in their position one day:

> If they could do it then I can do it as well…if it was literally all just middle-aged guys that you saw it might be a bit different thinking, well those guys can do it but there isn't anyone up there that is anything like what I am like now. Or that you can imagine being in the past anything like what I am like now…I think it is good to be able to spot similarities in people that do what you want to do…ways that they are similar to you so that you can kind of think that you have something in common with those people. (Interview 1)

Bella's observations about needing to see individuals with similar characteristics succeeding in academia indicates the significance of role models for women doctoral students in enabling them to imagine themselves belonging to their academic communities in the future. Positive educational relationships form the basis of role models and can enable the construction of academic aspirations (Leondari, 2007; Rossiter, 2004), and therefore the role of academics and supervisors is crucial in helping doctoral students to see themselves as future members of the academic community. Indeed, increasing concerns about the lack of diversity in higher education—especially in academic science—have reiterated the importance of role models for individuals from all under-represented groups, including individuals who are disabled and who are from black and minority ethnic backgrounds (CRAC, 2020; The Royal Society, 2021).

Within her discipline, Eleanor also observed similar trends as to who progresses in academia. She became more aware of the gender dynamics in her department during her doctorate and noted that though there were few male PhD students in her department, there were many male lecturers, which *"means that the few men who are doing PhDs must be more likely to get jobs, and that's not very fair"* (Interview 2). She described how her supervisor, Laura, had completed her allotted period as the Head of Department and was replaced by a man:

> Last year was the last year of Laura being head of the department, and it was great that you know that there was a woman who is the head of the department and lot of the Professors are women…that is great but now…the department has been taken over by a man and one of my other supervisors is a man and the more you look around the more you think actually there are quite a lot of men here, and they are just, there just aren't as many as in the PhD and I don't know whether it's some kind of continued kind of feminist awareness so that everything around me is becoming gendered…and whether it's kind of coming in with my awareness of going to have to get a job, look at these people, they have got jobs who are the people who have got jobs? (Interview 2)

Eleanor acknowledged that her understanding of the gendered nature of academic careers informed the way in which she considered her own career options. Her observations constituted what she described as a *"feminist awareness"* where she started to feel that *"everything around me is becoming gendered"*. Eleanor, who started her doctorate with strong academic ambitions, perceived that her desire to belong to the academic community in the long-term was informed by her gender and social class:

> I feel like well you know you are a woman so you should absolutely try to be an outstanding woman it is your duty…to kind of, be a success and to show other women you can do this instead of just kind of taking a mediocre job and just having you know like a quiet family life and not being extraordinary I feel like somehow compelled to do my best to be absolutely

extraordinary and to be like I am a successful woman, other women can be successful. And that's a strange one, a hard kind of way to think about things I think. In a way that a man would never think that…also I'm from kind of like a very working-class background like the school I went, the high school I went to is currently being…it was under like special measures or something I think it's been closed down now it was like a pretty scary, rough sort of school…so I kind of feel like well you have come from that background and then you went to [Elite University] and you are doing a PhD and you are a woman you should do your best to be successful, to show other people you can do this…no Etonian has ever felt that in his life I'm sure. (Interview 2)

Eleanor's admission that as a woman from a working-class background she felt under pressure to be "*successful*", "*outstanding*" and even "*absolutely extraordinary*", resonates with literature which argues that women within the academy often feel the need to prove themselves (Acker & Armenti, 2004; Loumansky et al., 2007; Van Den Brink & Stobbe, 2009), and that belonging within the academy is more challenging for those who identify as working-class (see Hoskins, 2010; Ostrove et al., 2011; Reay, 1998). Eleanor acknowledged the gendered and classed dimensions of her aspiration to be an academic role model for others: "*no Etonian has ever felt that in his life*". It is apparent from Eleanor's experiences that the way she envisages belonging to the academic community in the future is complex. It is shaped by her awareness—even as a doctoral student—of the gendered nature of academic careers in her discipline and is informed by her understanding of working-class women as outsiders who may struggle to feel they belong in academia, and thus find the presence of role models with similar characteristics helpful.

Bella and Eleanor's accounts highlight how witnessing the gendered dynamics of their departments informed how they envisaged belonging to their disciplines in the future as academics. Having women academic role models who they could identify with helped facilitate not only to their sense of belonging in the present as doctoral students but also their ability to sustain their academic career aspirations and envisage themselves as belonging in the future. Yet beyond perceptions of departmental gender dynamics, the day-to-day experiences of women academics also significantly influenced women doctoral students' sense of imagined, future belonging.

Participants were aware not only of inequalities in relation to the representation of women within senior academic roles, but also in the ways in which their daily experiences of the academic environment differed to those of their male colleagues. Individuals observed disparities in how women academics engaged in care work, as well as examples of more overt discrimination in the workplace. Through her interactions with academics in her research centre as well as those she met through her partner James, who was an early career academic, Chloe became aware of the differences in women academics' career experiences. In her own institution, she witnessed how caring responsibilities affected individuals' ability to participate in academic activities:

> There was a seminar on from 4 till 5, loads of academics were there, and it ran over a little bit and by 5 past 5 of the, I counted, it was like 16 academics had to leave for childcare commitments to go and pick them up, and one of them was a man. So…who's doing the bulk of the domestic work? It's still women, so that has got to have an impact on your career and you know and what do you value, do you value your career or your family more because you are socially constructed that women should value family more, so it becomes less important that you are the big earner and have the big career? (Interview 1)

This small observation whilst at a departmental event led Chloe to connect the ways in which women academics with caring responsibilities participate in academic life to wider gender inequalities in academia. She perceived women academics having to leave the seminar early to collect their children as indicative of them *"doing the bulk of the domestic work"*, which she felt *"has got to have an impact on your career"*. Witnessing this made Chloe aware of how women academics are faced with what she perceived as a choice between having to *"value your career or your family more"*, and the social pressure that women are under to prioritise family over being a *"big earner"* and having a *"big career"*. The way in which Chloe phrased her reflections presents this as a question which she asks of herself, recognising that she will have to answer this if she intends to pursue an academic career in the future. Thus, observing the women academics in her department make sacrifices in order to balance their work and family lives shapes how Chloe understands the possibility of an academic career.

Chloe's concerns about the career implications of family and caring responsibilities for women academics are widely recognised in international literature on women's experience of academic life (see Acker, 1980; Lynch, 2010; Morley, 2013; Obers, 2014; Thanacoody et al., 2006; Ward & Wolf-Wendel, 2016). Research has shown how some women academics may try to conceal their caring responsibilities by deliberately not mentioning family commitments at work (see Schlehofer, 2012; Solomon, 2011). Further, Chloe's awareness of the gendered dynamics of caring reflects research which argues that the structure of modern academic careers—which require significant investment of time in activities such as attending research seminars and international conferences—discriminates against those who have caring responsibilities, who remain more likely to be women than men (see Carter et al., 2013; Kinman, 2016; Probert, 2005). Participating in these activities is increasingly a requirement for those hoping to progress their academic careers, meaning that the ability—or not—of individuals to participate in these activities can have significant implications for individuals' career progression (Lubitow & Zippel, 2014; Savigny, 2014).

Chloe related her observation of women academics in her department bearing the larger burden of caring responsibilities to her own possible academic future, seeming to consider the impact that her and her partners' choices about working patterns may have on their careers:

> I've made it clear with my partner that I would like to…if we both work 4 days a week, because we've got kids, we both have to work 4 days a week I am not working 3 or 4 days a week while he works 5 days a week…I feel like that little battle might not be as much of an issue for me, because there is no way I am going to let, but then again you say that and yeah, it's me that thinks about, I expend my brain cells thinking about oh has the hoovering been done yet and has this been done yet because I give a…crap about the house looking nice, but he doesn't so…you think well that if I had my bit of my brain freed up to just focus on work that they're not thinking about this nitty gritty stuff…I don't know. (Interview 1)

Here, Chloe envisaged a possible future where she and her partner take on similar, part-time working patterns to facilitate looking after children. Yet, whilst initially expressing confidence that this "*battle*" may not be an issue for her, she was seemingly unable to sustain this positive imagined future as she changed her train of thought to the future, wherein she realised that she was currently undertaking the majority of the domestic housework. Chloe's frustration comes across in reflecting that the "*nitty gritty*" of the domestic chores takes time and energy, and in her imagined, future negotiation of these issues, she acknowledges that she could potentially focus more on work "*if I had my bit of my brain freed up*".

This experience is commonly understood as a type of emotional labour (Hochschild, 1983), where the woman takes responsibility for managing family life, including domestic and childcare arrangements (see Toffoletti & Starr, 2016). The increased flexibility of modern academic work, such as the ability to work from home, means that the boundaries between academic and family life become blurred (Kinman, 2016). This may compound the difficulties of balancing work and family life for women academics, whose potential time to work may therefore be spent managing caring responsibilities alongside academic work within the domestic space, leaving little free time (see Rafnsdóttir & Heijstra, 2013).

Beyond her perceptions of the potential difficulties of balancing family with an academic career, Chloe learned of specific instances of gender discrimination experienced by women academics through her partner, who worked in another social science discipline. Early on, in our first interview, Chloe detailed what she described as "*quite a bad story*" about an early career woman academic, who was a colleague of his:

> Some of the academics I know who are women…there is quite a bad story actually…my partner and someone that was recruited at the very similar time to him, in a similar expertise area…they found out, because he said let's just be honest like how much do you get paid, I will tell you how much I get paid, and she gets paid less than him, so she went to complain about it, and they said it is because my partner had his thesis book out already and she didn't yet, even though she had loads of publications but she didn't have a book yet, so it was almost like they were just saying that so they weren't going to get in trouble. But it is kind of true, so she is now motor-

ing away trying to get her thesis book ready, so she can do that and then there is no reason for them to not give her the same…wage. (Interview 1)

Though research highlights the gender gap in academic publishing (Nygaard & Bahgat, 2018; Tower et al., 2007), Chloe's understanding was that the woman academic in this case has "*loads of publications*", yet she was still paid less than Chloe's partner, a male academic recruited at the same time. Despite the woman academic in this scenario being given a reason for the inequity in pay—the fact that she had not yet published a book—Chloe perceived that this was "*almost like they were just saying that so they weren't going to get in trouble*".

Within the UK higher education sector, statistics show that a range of pay inequalities persist, with women, disabled academics and BAME academics being more likely to be lower paid than their male, abled-bodied or white colleagues (see Advance HE, 2021a). In the UK, the gender pay gap remains the subject of much discussion, with recent analysis showing that the pay gap between men and women in UK universities is 15.1% (Times Higher Education, 2019). Further, Chloe's perception that the university could "*get in trouble*" for not paying this woman academic and her male colleague the same, reflects ongoing arguments that universities are not doing enough to address these inequalities in pay (MacFarlane, 2019; O'Keefe & Courtois, 2019; UCU, 2015). Though the overall gender pay gap in UK universities is considered to be significantly influenced by both the large gender pay gap amongst the professoriate and the higher proportion of women in the lowest paid roles (Pells, 2018; UCU, 2015), this anecdote indicates that even amongst early career academics with similar levels of experience, there may be differential levels of pay being offered, which may discriminate against women.

During her doctorate, Chloe developed an awareness of the disparity between the educational and career trajectory of her partner compared to her own experiences, and the career experiences of his colleagues who were women. Early on, she acknowledged that her partner, James, has had a straightforward, linear academic career trajectory, obtaining an academic job straight after his PhD and continuing in a permanent role a year later. Chloe was aware that academic careers are rarely this straightforward:

He happened to finish his PhD very quickly and to get a permanent job like on his second try…a lot of people who are above in the year above him…got their permanent jobs like a year after him so people were saying…he is…sort of a freak. (Interview 1)

Whilst James had "*always known what he wanted to do*" (Interview 1), Chloe's own educational trajectory involved a second attempt at an undergraduate degree, as well as a combination of part-time study and work which eventually led to a master's degree and an application for PhD funding. She acknowledged that she found the ease of his career progression frustrating; "*he has just flown through it…it seems like almost like everything has just been easy…for him*" (Interview 1). Chloe recognised that James' comparatively straightforward career progression and success affected how she viewed her own journey: "*that's really hard because I'm always probably going to be comparing myself to his timescales*" (Interview 1). This comparison links with literature which indicates how women doctoral students are more likely to start their PhD later in life than men, and more often have a non-linear educational trajectory (Bagilhole & White, 2013; Brown & Watson, 2010; Leonard, 2001). Whereas James' career conformed to a traditional linear academic career path and his progression appeared to happen with some degree of ease, research shows that this is more usual for men than for women (see Cabrera, 2007; Doherty & Manfredi, 2006; White, 2013). Yet, as Chloe noted in the way that she compared her own progress unfavourably with his, there are still 'masculinised expectations of an academic career' (Ollilainen & Solomon, 2014, p. 34), meaning that Chloe and others with a less traditional career path may feel less legitimate within the academy and thus feel less able to develop a sense of belonging within their academic communities.

Witnessing the experiences of women academics, whose career experiences appeared to differ to those of their male colleagues even at an early stage, led to Chloe becoming somewhat disillusioned with academia and struggling to envisage herself belonging within this community. Initially, she had a positive view of universities and their values, having previously worked in the private sector: "*I sort of idealise this place and universities as like this you know, amazing gender equal place to work and then so it is funny to see that it isn't…while it might be a lot nicer here, than where I used to work, it's not perfect*" (Interview 2). These expectations of the academy mean that Chloe's disappointment with what she encounters is more significant, something also experienced by other participants who returned to academia from other employment sectors, such as Jessie.

During her PhD, Chloe learned that universities can also be unequal workplaces, particularly for those from marginalised groups. Even at an early stage in her studies, she observed the lack of ethnic diversity amongst academics and the lack of women in senior roles:

> I feel like we're the enlightened ones, apparently so you know…we should be doing, we should be setting the example there should be more women in, you know management roles, especially in academia it should be, and you know, and there should be more you know, people from the BME community…because that's atrocious as well, you know there is just…you go to conferences and look around…you know, you know there might be more women now, although they will probably not be in as high positions but there is hardly any black people. (Interview 1)

Though she does not refer to her own minority ethnic background, Chloe's feeling that the higher education sector should be "*setting the example*" in terms of the representation of ethnic minorities and women in academic roles may be connected to her own identity as a woman of colour. It is interesting that as the only participant in this study who was not white, Chloe was the only one who notes the under-representation of BAME academics in UK universities. Her observation that the lack of individuals from the BAME community in academia is "*atrocious*" reflects research which highlights how BAME academics are less likely to progress to senior roles (Alexander & Arday, 2015; Bhopal, 2014) and the racial discrimination experienced by BAME academics (see Bhopal et al., 2015; Rollock, 2019). In this context, envisaging herself belonging within the academy as a BAME academic is unlikely to be straightforward for Chloe, particularly given that as a woman of colour, she is in the minority as a doctoral student (Bradbury, 2013; Mattocks & Briscoe-Palmer, 2016).

## Summary

This chapter has outlined how women doctoral students in the humanities and social sciences navigated belonging within a range of academic spaces: the broader, institutional environment; physical, everyday workspaces; as well as imagined, conceptual future spaces within the academy. It has demonstrated how belonging could be felt and negotiated within and outside departmental communities, showing how participants demonstrated agency in finding ways to belong to their broader disciplinary communities when they struggled to access more immediate peer or academic communities. This involved connecting with peers within online spaces and engaging in undergraduate teaching.

For those who lived at a significant distance from their institution, who did not have the opportunity to connect frequently with peers and academics in their department, belonging could be established by participating in conferences and by seeking out connections with other scholars who worked more locally. All of these activities helped individuals to enact academic identities, though for individuals who lived at a distance from their institution, developing this sense of belonging to their academic communities was more challenging. Both participants who had moved abroad during their PhD found that returning to live in the city where they studied helped them to feel more connected to their peers. It appeared that decisions about mobility, which can be viewed as gendered choices, did therefore have some impact on women's ability to feel a sense of belonging to their academic communities.

Whilst feelings of isolation are known to be higher amongst those studying for a doctorate in the humanities and social sciences (Delamont et al., 2000; Morris & Wisker, 2011; Parry, 2007), it was evident that some institutions and departments were able to facilitate peer communities through the provision of dedicated spaces for doctoral students. The contrast between the experiences of Freija and Eleanor highlights the positive impact that institutional spaces can have on women doctoral students' experiences, when they are organised in ways which offer opportunities to connect with academics and peers. Indeed, the physical workspaces which doctoral students are allocated within their institutions are indicative of the status and significance afforded to doctoral students as a group—something that participants were keenly aware of, even if this was not explicitly stated. Interestingly, despite literature which highlights the significance of the supervisors for the enculturation of doctoral students in the arts and humanities (see Becher et al., 1994; Delamont, Parry, et al., 1997b, 2000), this chapter indicates that for participants in this study, their supervisor was not necessarily the most important influence in helping them to feel a sense of belonging within their academic community. Only Martina, Chloe and Eleanor specifically discussed the impact of their supervisors on their experiences at all, and only Martina acknowledged her need for his acceptance and recognition as a legitimate scholar in her field. Thus, this chapter makes an original contribution to literature on disciplinary communities within doctoral experiences, indicating that connections with peers and the presence of role models more generally may be more significant for individuals' belonging.

For individuals who worked closely alongside academics, it was apparent that witnessing other women's career experiences shaped their awareness of the gendered dynamics of their disciplinary and departmental communities. Participants' observations, often derived from casual interactions and encounters, informed the ways in which they understood academic life as different for women academics than for men, and this had an impact on their sense of belonging in the present, and also in their imagined, future belonging. Witnessing how women academics' daily lives and careers were shaped by managing caring responsibilities and instances of discrimination, along with a developing awareness of the lack of women in senior roles in their own departments, had a significant and negative impact on how participants understood the possibility of pursuing an academic career as a woman. This was compounded for those who were members of groups already marginalised in academic spaces, such as working-class women and BAME women. Despite their initial academic aspirations on starting the PhD, these observations had an impact on the ease with which participants could envisage themselves belonging as an academic in the future. The doctorate therefore appears to be a key opportunity wherein individuals assess whether they are able to imagine belonging in academic spaces in the longer term.

# References

Acker, S. (1980). Women, the other academics. *British Journal of Sociology of Education, 1*(1), 81–91.

Acker, S., & Armenti, C. (2004). Sleepless in academia. *Gender and Education, 16*(1), 3–24. https://doi.org/10.1080/0954025032000170309

Ackers, L. (2004). Managing relationships in peripatetic careers: Scientific mobility in the European Union. In *Women's Studies International Forum* (Vol. 27, No. 3, pp. 189–201). Pergamon.

Advance HE. (2021a). Equality in higher education: Staff statistical report 2021.

Advance HE. (2021b). Equality in higher education: Student statistical report 2021.

Alexander, C., & Arday, J. (2015). *Aiming higher: Race, inequality and diversity in the academy*. Runnymede Perspectives.

Ali, A., Kohun, F., & Levy, Y. (2007). Dealing with social isolation to minimize doctoral attrition—A four stage framework. *International Journal of Doctoral Studies, 2*(1), 33–49. https://doi.org/10.28945/3082

Almack, K., & Churchill, H. (2007). Power and the PhD Journey: 'Getting in' and 'Getting on'. In *Power, knowledge and the academy* (pp. 36–52). Palgrave Macmillan.

Archer, L. (2008). The new neoliberal subjects? Young/er academics' constructions of professional identity. *Journal of Education Policy, 23*(3), 265–285. https://doi.org/10.1080/02680930701754047

Bagilhole, B., & White, K. (2013). *Generation and gender in academia*. Palgrave Macmillan.

Bansel, P. (2011). Becoming academic: A reflection on doctoral candidacy. *Studies in Higher Education, 36*(5), 543–556. https://doi.org/10.1080/03075079.2011.594592

Barinaga, M. (1993). Science education: The pipeline is leaking women all the way along. *Science, 260*(5106), 409–411. https://doi.org/10.1126/science.260.5106.409

Barnacle, R., & Mewburn, I. (2010). Learning networks and the journey of 'becoming doctor'. *Studies in Higher education, 35*(4), 433–444. https://doi.org/10.1080/03075070903131214

Becher, T. (1994). The significance of disciplinary differences. *Studies in Higher education, 19*(2), 151–161.

Becher, T., Henkel, M., & Kogan, M. (1994). *Graduate education in Britain* (Vol. 108). Higher Education Policy Series 17.

Bhopal, K. (2014). *The experiences of BME academics in higher education: Aspirations in the face of inequality*. Leadership Foundation for Higher Education Stimulus Papers.

Bhopal, K., Brown, H., & Jackson, J. (2015). *Academic flight: How to encourage black and minority ethnic academics to stay in UK higher education*. Equality Challenge Unit.

Bradbury, J. (2013, May 3). Black, female and postgraduate: Why I cannot be the only one. *The Guardian*. Retrieved from https://www.theguardian.com/higher-education-network/blog/2013/may/03/black-postgraduate-university-diversity-recruitment

Brown, L., & Watson, P. (2010). Understanding the experiences of female doctoral students. *Journal of further and Higher Education, 34*(3), 385–404. https://doi.org/10.1080/0309877X.2010.484056

Budd, R., O'Connell, C., Yuan, T., & Ververi, O. (2018). *The DTC Effect: ESRC doctoral training centres and the UK social science doctoral training landscape*. Liverpool Hope University Press.

Cabrera, E. F. (2007). Opting out and opting in: Understanding the complexities of women's career transitions. *Career Development International, 12*(3), 218–237. https://doi.org/10.1108/13620430710745872

Carter, S., Blumenstein, M., & Cook, C. (2013). Different for women? the challenges of doctoral studies. *Teaching in Higher Education, 18*(4), 339–351. https://doi.org/10.1080/13562517.2012.719159

Churchill, H., & Sanders, T. (2007). *Getting your PhD: A practical insider's guide*. Sage.

Clandinin, D. J., & Connelly, F. M. (2000). *Narrative inquiry: Experience and story in qualitative research*. Sage.

Collett, J. L., & Avelis, J. (2013). *Family-friendliness, fraudulence, and gendered academic career ambitions*. American Sociological Association Annual Meeting.

CRAC. (2020). Qualitative research on barriers to progression for disabled scientists. Retrieved from https://www.crac.org.uk/Media/Default/files/Qualitative%20research%20on%20barriers%20to%20progression%20of%20disabled%20scientists.pdf

Crook, R., Gooding, P., Whittaker, C., Edge, D., Faichnie, C., Westwood, M., & Peters, S. (2021). Student, academic and professional services staff perspectives of postgraduate researcher well-being and help-seeking: a mixed-methods co-designed investigation. *Studies in Graduate and Postdoctoral Education, 12*(1), 113–130.

Curtin, N., Malley, J., & Stewart, A. J. (2016). Mentoring the next generation of faculty: Supporting academic career aspirations among doctoral students. *Research in Higher Education, 57*(6), 714–738.

Deem, R., & Brehony, K. J. (2000). Doctoral students' access to research cultures-are some more unequal than others? *Studies in Higher Education, 25*(2), 149–165. https://doi.org/10.1080/713696138

Delamont, S., Atkinson, P., & Parry, O. (1997). *Supervising the PhD: A Guide to Success*. Open University Press.

Delamont, S., Atkinson, P., & Parry, O. (2000). *The doctoral experience: Success and failure in graduate school*. Routledge.

Delamont, S., Parry, O., & Atkinson, P. (1997b). Critical mass and pedagogic continuity: Studies in academic habitus. *British Journal of Sociology of Education, 18*(4), 533–549.

Doherty, L., & Manfredi, S. (2006). Women's progression to senior positions in English universities. *Employee Relations, 28*(6), 553–572. https://doi.org/10.1108/01425450610704498

ESRC. (2009). *ESRC postgraduate training and development guidelines 2009 for the accreditation of doctoral training centres and doctoral training units*. ESRC.

Gardner, S. K. (2007). I heard it through the grapevine: Doctoral student socialization in chemistry and history. *Higher Education, 54*(5), 723–740.

Gardner, S. K., & Gopaul, B. (2012). The part-time doctoral student experience. *International Journal of Doctoral Studies, 7*(12), 63–78.

Gill, R. (2009). Breaking the silence: The hidden injuries of neo-liberal academia. In R. Ryan-Flood & R. Gill (Eds.), *Secrecy and silence in the research process: Feminist reflections* (pp. 228–244). Routledge.

Golde, C. M. (2005). The role of the department and discipline in doctoral student attrition: Lessons from four departments. *The Journal of Higher Education, 76*(6), 669–700.

Hemer, S. R. (2012). Informality, power and relationships in postgraduate supervision: Supervising PhD candidates over coffee. *Higher Education Research & Development, 31*(6), 827–839. https://doi.org/10.1080/07294360.2012.674011

Henkel, M. (2004). Current science policies and their implications for the formation and maintenance of academic identity. *Higher Education Policy, 17*(2), 167–182.

Henkel, M. (2005). Academic identity and autonomy in a changing policy environment. *Higher Education, 49*(1), 155–176. https://doi.org/10.1007/s10734-004-2919-1

Higher Education Academy. (2015). *Postgraduate research experience survey*. Retrieved from https://www.heacademy.ac.uk/knowledge-hub/postgraduate-research-experience-survey-2015

Hochschild, A. (1983). *The managed heart: Commercialization of human feeling*. University of California Press.

Hockey, J. (1994). New territory: Problems of adjusting to the first year of a social science PhD. *Studies in Higher Education, 19*(2), 177–190. https://doi.org/10.1080/03075079412331382027

Hockey, J. (1995). Getting too close: A problem and a possible solution in social science PhD supervision. *British Journal of Guidance and Counselling, 23*(2), 199–210.

Hopwood, N. (2010). Doctoral experience and learning from a sociocultural perspective. *Studies in Higher Education, 35*(7), 829–843.

Hoskins, K. (2010, March). The price of success? The experiences of three senior working class female academics in the UK. In *Women's Studies International Forum* (Vol. 33, No. 2, pp. 134–140). Pergamon.

Jazvac-Martek, M. (2009). Oscillating role identities: The academic experiences of education doctoral students. *Innovations in Education and Teaching International, 46*(3), 253–264. https://doi.org/10.1080/14703290903068862

Kinman, G. (2016). *Managing the work-home interface: The experience of women academics. Exploring resources, life-balance and well-being of women who work in a global context* (pp. 127–144). Springer.

Lave, J., & Wenger, E. (1991). *Situated learning: Legitimate peripheral participation*. Cambridge University Press.

Lefebvre, H. (1991). *The production of space*. Blackwell.

Leonard, D. (2001). *A woman's guide to doctoral studies*. Open University Press.

Leonard, D., Metcalfe, J., Becker, R., & Evans, J. (2006). *Review of literature on the impact of working context and support on the postgraduate research student learning experience*. The Higher Education Academy.

Leondari, A. (2007). Future time perspective, possible selves, and academic achievement. *New Directions for Adult and Continuing Education, 2007*(114), 17–26. https://doi.org/10.1002/ace.253

Loumansky, A., Goodman, S., & Jackson, S. (2007). Women and work/life balance. In P. Cotterill, S. Jackson, & G. Letherby (Eds.), *Challenges and negotiations for women in higher education* (pp. 223–240). Springer.

Lovitts, B. E. (2001). *Leaving the ivory tower: The causes and consequences of departure from doctoral study*. Rowman & Littlefield.

Lubitow, A., & Zippel, K. (2014). Strategies of academic parents to manage work-life conflict in research abroad. In V. Demos, C. W. Berheide, & M. T. Segal (Eds.), *Gender transformation in the academy* (pp. 63–84). Emerald Group.

Lynch, K. (2010). Carelessness: A hidden doxa of higher education. *Arts and Humanities in Higher Education, 9*(1), 54–67. https://doi.org/10.1177/1474022209350104

MacFarlane, B. (2019, June 5). Women professors, pay, promotion, and academic housekeeping. WonkHE. Retrieved from https://wonkhe.com/blogs/women-professors-pay-promotion-and-academic-housekeeping/

Manathunga, C. (2005). The development of research supervision: "Turning the light on a private space". *International Journal for Academic Development, 10*(1), 17–30.

Mantai, L. (2017). Feeling like a researcher: Experiences of early doctoral students in Australia. *Studies in Higher Education, 42*(4), 636–650.

Mantai, L. (2019). "Feeling more academic now": Doctoral stories of becoming an academic. *The Australian Educational Researcher, 46*(1), 137–153.

Mattocks, K., & Briscoe-Palmer, S. (2016). Diversity, inclusion, and doctoral study: Challenges facing minority PhD students in the United Kingdom. *European Political Science, 15*, 476–492.

May, V. (2013). *Connecting self to society: Belonging in a changing world*. Macmillan International Higher Education.

McAlpine, L., & Mitra, M. (2015). Becoming a scientist: PhD workplaces and other sites of learning. *International Journal of Doctoral Studies, 10*(2), 111–128. https://doi.org/10.28945/2112

Middleton, S. (2010). Rhythms of place Time and space in the doctoral experience. In *The Routledge doctoral supervisor's companion* (pp. 203–214). Routledge.

Miller, L. (2003). Belonging to country—A philosophical anthropology. *Journal of Australian Studies, 27*(76), 215–223.

Morley, L. (1999). *Organising feminisms: The micropolitics of the academy*. Palgrave Macmillan.

Morley, L. (2013). The rules of the game: Women and the leaderist turn in higher education. *Gender and Education, 25*(1), 116–131.

Morris, C. (2021). "Peering through the window looking in": Postgraduate experiences of non-belonging and belonging in relation to mental health and wellbeing. *Studies in Graduate and Postdoctoral Education*. https://doi.org/10.1108/SGPE-07-2020-0055

Morris, C., & Wisker, G. (2011). *Troublesome encounters: Strategies for managing the wellbeing of master's and doctoral education students during their learning processes*. HEA ESCalate Subject Centre Report.

Nygaard, L. P., & Bahgat, K. (2018). What's in a number? how (and why) measuring research productivity in different ways changes the gender gap. *Journal of English for Academic Purposes, 32*, 67–79.

Obers, N. (2014). Career success for women academics in higher education: Choices and challenges: Part 2: HELTASA 2012 special section. *South African Journal of Higher Education, 28*(3), 1107–1122.

O'Keefe, T., & Courtois, A. (2019). 'Not one of the family': Gender and precarious work in the neoliberal university. *Gender, Work & Organization, 26*(4), 463–479.

Ollilainen, M., & Solomon, C. R. (2014). Carving a "Third path": Faculty parents' resistance to the ideal academic worker norm. In V. Demos, C. W. Berheide, & M. T. Segal (Eds.), *Gender transformation in the academy* (pp. 21–39). Emerald Group.

Ostrove, J. M., Stewart, A. J., & Curtin, N. L. (2011). Social class and belonging: Implications for graduate students' career aspirations. *The Journal of Higher Education, 82*(6), 748–774.

Owler, K. (2010). A 'problem' to be managed? Completing a PhD in the arts and humanities. *Arts and Humanities in Higher Education, 9*(3), 289–304.

Parry, S. (2007). *Disciplines and doctorates*. Springer.

Pells, R. (2018). Gender pay gap: How much less are women paid at your university? *Times Higher Education*, 6 April. Available at: https://www.timeshighereducation.com/news/gender-pay-gap-how-much-less-are-women-paid-your-university

Phelps, J. M. (2016). International doctoral students' navigations of identity and belonging in a globalizing university. *International Journal of Doctoral Studies, 11*(1), 1–14.

Phillips, E., & Pugh, D. (2015). *How to get a PhD: A handbook for students and their supervisors* (6th ed.). Open University Press.

Probert, B. (2005). 'I just couldn't fit it in': Gender and unequal outcomes in academic careers. *Gender, Work & Organization, 12*(1), 50–72. https://doi.org/10.1111/j.1468-0432.2005.00262.x

Rafnsdóttir, G. L., & Heijstra, T. M. (2013). Balancing work–family life in academia: The power of time. *Gender, Work & Organization, 20*(3), 283–296.

Rao, N., Hosein, A., & Raaper, R. (2021). Doctoral students navigating the borderlands of academic teaching in an era of precarity. *Teaching in Higher Education, 26*(3), 454–470.

Reay, D. (1998). Surviving in dangerous places: Working-class women, women's studies and higher education. *Women's Studies International Forum, 21*(1), 11–19. https://doi.org/10.1016/s0277-5395(97)00087-3

Rollock, N. (2019). *Staying power: The career experiences and strategies of UK Black female professors*. UCU.

Rossiter, M. (2004). Educational relationships and possible selves in the adult undergraduate experience. *The Cyril O'Houle Scholars in Adult and Continuing Education Program Global Research Perspectives, 4,* 138–155. https://doi.org/10.1002/ace.259

Savigny, H. (2014). Women, know your limits: Cultural sexism in academia. *Gender and Education, 26*(7), 794–809. https://doi.org/10.1080/09540253.2014.970977

Schlehofer, M. (2012). Practicing what we teach? An autobiographical reflection on navigating academia as a single mother. *Journal of Community Psychology, 40*(1), 112–128.

Smith-McGloin, R., & Wynne, C. (2022). *Structures and strategy in doctoral education in the UK and Ireland*. UK Council for Graduate Education.

Solomon, C. R. (2011). "Sacrificing at the altar of tenure": Assistant professors' work/life management. *The Social Science Journal, 48*(2), 335–344. https://doi.org/10.1016/j.soscij.2010.11.006

Thanacoody, P. R., Bartram, T., Barker, M., & Jacobs, K. (2006). Career progression among female academics: A comparative study of Australia and Mauritius. *Women in Management Review, 21*(7), 536–553. https://doi.org/10.1108/09649420610692499

The Royal Society. (2014, December). *Doctoral students' career expectations principles and responsibilities*. The Royal Society.

The Royal Society. (2021). STEM sector must step up and end unacceptable disparities in Black staff and students academic progression and success. Retrieved from https://royalsociety.org/news/2021/03/stem-ethnicity-report/

The Universities and Colleges Union (UCU). (2015). The gender pay gap in higher education. Retrieved from https://www.ucu.org.uk/media/8620/The-gender-pay-gap-in-higher-education-201516%2D%2D-full-report-May-17/pdf/ucu_2015-16genderpaygapreort_full_may17.pdf

Times Higher Education. (2019, April 8). Gender pay gap: UK universities report slow progress. Retrieved from https://www.timeshighereducation.com/news/gender-pay-gap-uk-universities-report-slow-progress

Tinto, V. (1993). *Leaving college: Rethinking the causes and cures of student attrition*. University of Chicago Press.

Toffoletti, K., & Starr, K. (2016). Women academics and work–life balance: Gendered discourses of work and care. *Gender, Work & Organization, 23*(5), 489–504.

Tower, G., Plummer, J., & Ridgewell, B. (2007). A multidisciplinary study of gender-based research productivity in the worlds best journals. *Journal of Diversity Management (JDM), 2*(4), 23–32.

Tzanakou, C. (2017). Dual career couples in academia, international mobility and dual career services in Europe. *European Educational Research Journal, 16*(2–3), 298–312.

Van Den Brink, M., & Stobbe, L. (2009). Doing gender in academic education: The paradox of visibility. *Gender, Work & Organization, 16*(4), 451–470. https://doi.org/10.1111/j.1468-0432.2008.00428.x

Vigurs, K. (2016). Using Twitter to Tackle Peripherality? Facilitating networked scholarship for part-time doctoral students within and beyond the university. *Fusion Journal, 1*(008), 1–18.

Vitae. (2017). *One size does not fit all: Arts and humanities doctoral and early career researchers' professional development survey.* The Careers Research and Advisory Centre (CRAC) Limited.

Walsh, E. (2010). A model of research group microclimate: Environmental and cultural factors affecting the experiences of overseas research students in the UK. *Studies in Higher Education, 35*(5), 545–560.

Ward, K., & Wolf-Wendel, L. (2016). Academic motherhood: Mid-Career perspectives and the ideal worker norm. *New Directions for Higher Education, 2016*(176), 11–23. https://doi.org/10.1002/he.20206

White, J., & Nonnamaker, J. (2008). Belonging and mattering: How doctoral students experience community. *NASPA Journal, 45*(3), 350–372.

White, K. (2013). An outsider in academia. In B. Bagilhole & K. White (Eds.), *Generation and gender in academia* (pp. 103–126). Palgrave Macmillan.

Wladkowski, S. P., & Mirick, R. G. (2019). Mentorship in doctoral education for pregnant and newly parenting doctoral students. *Journal of Women and Gender in Higher Education, 12*(3), 299–318.

Wolf-Wendel, L., Twombly, S. B., & Rice, S. (2004). *The two-body problem: Dual-career-couple hiring practices in higher education.* JHU Press.

Zahl, S. (2015). The impact of community for part-time doctoral students: How relationships in the academic department affect student persistence. *International Journal of Doctoral Studies, 10*, 301.

# 6

# Reflecting on Women Doctoral Students' Belonging: Struggles, Strategies and Successes

This chapter draws together the findings of earlier chapters, which have illuminated the various ways in which women doctoral students across disciplines attempted to belong within their academic communities. In the first half of the chapter, I reflect on the struggles that participants faced in trying to belong, their strategies for attempting to do so and the extent to which these were successful. In doing so, I highlight different types of belonging which emerged from their experiences, the various sites where belonging was felt, as well as the spaces in which this was more challenging. In this chapter, I examine the commonalities from across participants' experiences, but also highlight key areas of difference which were apparent between disciplinary areas.

Belonging necessitates the recognition of individuals as legitimate contributors to a community by more powerful members (Lave & Wenger, 1991; May, 2013); in reflecting on this, I draw attention to how far women doctoral students were able to feel like legitimate members of their academic communities, and the impact of their relationship with peers, academics and supervisors on their ability to do so. In the latter half of this chapter, I consider how experiences of belonging during the doctorate affected women's post-PhD decisions and career destinations, and particularly the ways they perceived an academic career. I conclude by reflecting on the implications of struggling to belong within academia as a woman doctoral student for individuals and their identities, as well as for academic institutions and the higher education sector as a whole.

## Sites of Belonging for Women Doctoral Students

In analysing women's experiences of doctoral study, it was apparent that some individuals were able to establish a sense of belonging in some particular contexts, spaces, and situations. Doctoral students participate in multiple communities during their studies, from international disciplinary communities to specific lab groups, as well as communities at institutional, disciplinary and departmental levels. The interplay of these 'nested communities' (White & Nonnamaker, 2008, p. 350) creates a unique academic environment within which students need to establish themselves (Baker & Lattuca, 2010). However, the departmental community is particularly significant for PhD students, as it often is the site of students' everyday workspaces and thus constitutes the physical context for the development of relationships with peers and colleagues (White & Nonnamaker, 2008). Physical workspaces and peer groups were key aspects of participants' departmental communities, and I focus on them in my subsequent analysis. Acknowledging the physical, conceptual and experiential nature of academic communities (Kogan, 2000; Lefebvre, 1991), I draw attention to the sites where some participants were able to feel they belonged, whilst also highlighting the spaces and situations where individuals faced barriers to belonging. The circumstances within which belonging may be felt are highly individual, yet there were clear parallels and commonalities between women's experiences.

### Belonging Within Institutional Spaces

As might be expected, for those studying at a considerable distance from their institution—as was the case for Martina and Chloe, who both lived outside the UK for a significant proportion of their doctorate—feeling a sense of belonging to their institutional academic community was challenging. Without easy opportunities to connect with peers and academics, both women struggled to gain recognition from others within their disciplinary community and thus establish a sense of legitimacy. The nature of their doctoral research in the social sciences compounded this; feelings of isolation are more common amongst those working in these disciplines, who usually have little access to the social opportunities offered by working within a specific research group (Delamont et al., 1997, 2000; Phillips & Pugh, 2015). It was clear that for both women, moving back to the UK to live in the city where they studied had a positive impact on their sense of belonging to their academic communities. Despite this upheaval—and sacrifice for Martina, who chose to live in another country to be with her partner—the sense of feeling connected to their institution contributed to improved well-being and facilitated academic identity development.

Yet simply living somewhere where there is easy access to institutional spaces was by no means a guarantee of belonging. Academic hierarchies were visible in the way in which institutions designed and allocated workspaces, with individuals such as Freija and Liz unable to make connections with academics due to the separation of doctoral student workspaces from academics' offices in their departments. There were several instances where it was apparent that individuals felt marginalised within their academic communities by being designated workspaces which were entirely separate from those used by academics in their department. These experiences contributed to perceptions of doctoral students as low status, with a negative impact on well-being and precluding feelings of belonging. Research shows how the interactions that doctoral students have with academics are key in facilitating academic identity development (Jazvac-Martek, 2009; Mantai, 2019), as they enable individuals to understand what is involved in academic life and provide opportunities for doctoral students to form connections with key members of their academic communities and establish their academic legitimacy (Golde, 2005; Manathunga, 2014; Rossiter, 2004). Having informal opportunities to interact with academics is therefore a crucial part of developing a sense of belonging to their academic community in the present (McAlpine & Mitra, 2015), and the networks that doctoral students establish during their studies may also prove critical in facilitating post-PhD career opportunities (see Denicolo & Becker, 2008; Dever et al., 2008; Wisker, 2007).

Further, though literature indicates the importance of opportunities to connect with peers for doctoral students' well-being (Ali et al., 2007; Deem & Brehony, 2000; Morris & Wisker, 2011), not all participants were easily able to interact with other doctoral students. It is often assumed that doctoral students do not need any support in developing a sense of belonging within institutional communities due to their prior experiences of higher education (see White & Nonnamaker, 2008). However, many participants struggled to establish this sense of belonging, particularly in the first year of their studies. Whilst research training sessions could be valuable for individuals, providing early, structured opportunities to meet and connect with peers, these were not widely available. For some, missing out on these sessions made it difficult to develop meaningful connections with peers, meaning that establishing a sense of belonging within their academic community was more challenging. Institutional efforts to provide formal and structured opportunities for doctoral students to meet and connect with peers could be vital for supporting feelings of belonging.

Access to institutional workspaces where individuals could work alongside their peers was also highly variable, with implications for their ability to develop a sense of belonging within their communities. For Liz, who lived at some distance from her institution, despite the difficulty of the journey and challenges around parking, there were clear and distinct benefits to working alongside her peers in a shared workspace, which helped her to feel a sense of belonging. However, for others such as Chloe, who did not have easy access to a group of peers, it was more difficult to feel a sense of belonging, though this was ameliorated to some extent by accessing support through online peer communities (see Vigurs, 2016). Even for those who were assigned space within buildings where other doctoral students worked, the ways in which workspaces were designed and allocated could have a significant impact on individuals' ability to feel they belonged. For Eleanor, who was originally allocated a desk in a corridor space on a floor with students who often spoke in another language, this meant that she felt unable to develop meaningful connections with her peers and felt isolated within her everyday working environment. Being able to move into a dedicated office space with other UK students during her second year had a hugely positive impact on her well-being, and, by her own admission, enabled her to feel a sense of belonging within her academic community. This highlights the significance of allocating appropriate workspaces for doctoral students and the importance of facilitating the integration of international and home doctoral student communities (Walsh, 2010).

## Belonging Within Disciplines

Despite the increased participation of women in STEM at undergraduate and postgraduate levels, and significant policy focus on creating a more inclusive culture within academic STEM, women doctoral students in these subjects faced inherent challenges to feeling a sense of belonging within their disciplinary communities. For participants in this study, though they had already studied one or more scientific degrees prior to the PhD, establishing a sense of belonging within their disciplinary community was not straightforward. For those studying engineering, they had been accustomed to feeling 'other' within their subject area for some time prior to the doctorate, due to the traditionally male-dominated nature of the discipline. Their increased visibility as women (Van Den Brink & Stobbe, 2009) made seeking advice and support during the doctorate challenging, with implications for individuals' well-being (Chakraverty, 2019; Handforth, 2022). These findings reinforce other research which has highlighted how women in STEM disciplines have less access to guidance and support during the doctorate than their male peers (see Etzkowitz & Gupta, 2006; Etzkowitz et al., 2000; Royal Society of Chemistry, 2018).

Women doctoral students in STEM subjects experienced the culture of their disciplinary communities as marginalising, making developing a sense of belonging extremely challenging. For Pepper in particular, there was a perception of the culture of academic engineering as hostile and gendered, due to negative interactions with her male supervisor and other male academics. Even at events intended to provide a supportive and constructive environment for women doctoral students—such as the one

Jane attended at the start of her doctorate which focused on overcoming implicit bias—sexist and discriminatory attitudes were encountered, which contributed to feelings of marginalisation and otherness. Further, Harriet's experience of being treated differently to her male peer, and perceiving that expectations of her scientific abilities were based on gendered stereotypes, also indicate how participants felt othered within their disciplinary communities. All of these experiences represent a wider culture of discrimination within STEM disciplines and provide evidence of an ongoing 'chilly climate' (Britton, 2017), within which women doctoral students find it very difficult to establish a sense of belonging.

For some participants in other disciplines, there were key instances where they were able to connect with scholars in their disciplinary community, which helped facilitate feelings of belonging. Literature highlights how networking has historically been more challenging for women due to the persistence of 'boy's clubs' which marginalise women academics (Van den Brink & Benschop, 2014; Barnard et al., 2010; Fisher & Kinsey, 2014), and how women are less likely than men to have access to the most prestigious networks which may lead to opportunities for career advancement (Heffernan, 2021). Yet for some women doctoral students who were able to establish connections with academics beyond their institution, this was an important way in which they were able to develop a sense of academic legitimacy. For Martina, Chloe and Jessie, either making connections with academics at conferences or having ongoing communications with individuals working in similar areas, enabled them to be recognised as legitimate members of their disciplinary areas by other senior members of the community. Research highlights the importance of academics helping to enculture doctoral students into the discipline (Emmioglu et al., 2017; Parry, 2007), and especially for those working at a distance from their institution, making these connections helped them feel like a valuable member of their disciplinary community.

Yet there were also situations in which women doctoral students' efforts to belong within their disciplinary communities were compromised by the actions of more powerful members of the academic community. For Jessie, though her experience of working with a senior academic at another institution during her PhD helped her to feel like a valid and valuable member of her disciplinary community, other experiences with academics in her subject area were less positive, such as encountering sexist attitudes from the keynote speaker at an academic conference. Further, institutional mechanisms intended to support doctoral students could fail and instead undermine women's ability to feel a sense of belonging, with negative implications for their well-being. Whilst doctoral supervisors have a responsibility to actively facilitate the enculturation of doctoral students into the discipline (Manathunga, 2014), some did not take opportunities to support women doctoral students to belong. For Sally, her supervisors' failure to either invite her to the meeting they held with her co-authors on an academic paper or introduce her to them undermined her sense of legitimacy as a member of her disciplinary community, as she was not able to establish a sense of connection to her colleagues or be recognised as a valuable contributor. This experience highlights the liminal position of doctoral students within the academic hierarchy, where their contributions to academic work are sought but are not recognised as being equally valuable as work undertaken by academics.

## Belonging within Departmental Communities

Perhaps more significant was the ability of individuals to feel a sense of belonging within their departments, as these often represented the immediate physical and intellectual environments within which participants worked and studied. Departmental communities provide opportunities for social interaction and enculturation into a particular discipline (Henkel, 2004; Parry, 2007), and thus represent key communities for women doctoral students to establish a sense of belonging within. For Freija, who initially struggled to forge relationships with academics and peers in her department, starting to teach alongside academics in her second year of the PhD made a considerable difference to her ability to feel a sense of departmental belonging. From feeling isolated and unable to make meaningful connections with others in her first year, being involved in this core academic activity and being recognised as a member of a teaching team were critical to her feeling 'at home' in her department. Whilst literature highlights that expectations of doctoral students to engage in teaching alongside employed academics have the potential to become exploitative (see Rao et al., 2021), it was clear that Freija's sense of belonging was enabled by the opportunity to engage in teaching, and also by the positive reception of Freija onto the departmental teaching team by other academics. This highlights how significant the behaviours of other academics, as well as supervisors, can be in facilitating doctoral students' belonging.

Conversely, where individuals found themselves in situations where their personal values directly conflicted with those being performed by those around them, it was much more difficult to establish a sense of belonging. For those who experienced the pressure to publish academic work during the doctorate, such as Jane, Liz and Harriet—all of whom were resistant to doing so due to concerns about their well-being and capacity to complete the thesis within funding periods—this pressure had negative implications for their ability to feel they belonged within their departmental communities. Where participants perceived supervisors and academics working to excess, individuals struggled both with not feeling they belonged within this culture and also in attempting not to succumbing to these cultural pressures, which they felt would lead to a poor work-life balance.

Beyond experiencing some cultural working practices as exclusionary, establishing a sense of belonging within departmental communities was challenging for women doctoral students in situations where supervisors and academics reinforced traditional hierarchies. For those who had had successful careers prior to the PhD, being treated as low-status members of the academic community was difficult, particularly for Jessie who had previous research experience. Her attempts to contribute to academic research activities beyond her thesis, and to engage in the departmental community by helping to organise a symposium to showcase doctoral students' research, were refuted by academics in her department who did not attend the event or invite her to become involved in other research projects. These actions kept Jessie on the periphery of her departmental community and prevented her from forging meaningful connections with academics in her department, contributing to a disempowering experience (Lave & Wenger, 1991). These actions show how the actions of senior academics can maintain the peripheral and liminal status of doctoral students within academic hierarchies.

## Belonging in Everyday Academic Spaces

Whilst opportunities to connect with peers and academics were clearly valuable and important in facilitating academic identities and feelings of belonging, not all interactions within academic spaces were positive. As McAlpine and Mitra (2015) observe, not all institutional spaces are conducive to positive experiences of workplace learning, and for some women doctoral students, academic workspaces including offices and labs were viewed negatively due to local practices and behaviours. Literature highlights how academic institutions are shaped by traditional hierarchies of power and status (Hemer, 2012; Manathunga, 2005; Middleton, 2010), and micro-politics which marginalise individuals from minority groups (see Gill, 2009; Hoskins, 2010; Morley, 1999; Pittman, 2010; Reay, 1998; Rollock, 2019; Valentine & Wood, 2010). Thus, even everyday sites where women doctoral students conducted their research could be uncomfortable spaces within which to study and work, due to the actions of other students and academics.

Participants from across disciplinary areas encountered lad culture in their everyday workspaces and within their daily working relationships with peers and academics. For Harriet, working in a STEM subject which required lab work, the atmosphere of her lab made her and her female colleague uncomfortable due to their male colleagues' collective behaviour. Without the presence of her female colleague, Harriet acknowledged that she did not feel comfortable within this space, or feel able to challenge their behaviour. This experience indicates how women continue to be marginalised within academic STEM, and highlights the challenges to belonging faced by women doctoral students. Yet there were other, similarly gendered experiences for participants in non-STEM subjects too. For Sally, she recognised at an early stage of her studies that her relationship with her male supervisors was not equivalent to the relationship that her male peer had with them, and that she was not able to engage in the same "banter". This affected her ability to share her concerns about her work and challenges she encountered in her personal life, with negative implications for her well-being. Sally's experiences indicate the complicity of academics in perpetuating lad culture, as other research has shown (see Jackson & Sundaram, 2020).

Beyond experiences of lad culture in everyday academic workspaces, in Jane's case—which involved weeks of fieldwork in another country as part of her research—she also encountered more extreme sexist behaviour. Being both the victim of sexual harassment and witnessing the harassment of younger women students by a lecturer in her department whilst on fieldwork was a deeply uncomfortable experience, which she acknowledged put her in a difficult position both at the time and on her return to her institution. Research highlights that this type of behaviour is not uncommon within higher education institutions (see Nature, 2019; Page et al., 2019), and that reporting of incidents is low due to concerns that women will not be believed or that no action will be taken by institutions—an assumption which appears well-founded (Tutchell & Edmonds, 2020). Clearly, if women doctoral students do not feel safe either on campus or in any spaces where they interact with male academics, there is little hope of being able to establish feelings of belonging within these communities.

In reflecting on the sites where women doctoral students found belonging more or less challenging, establishing a sense of belonging was more difficult for those working at a distance from their institution and department, for those in traditionally male-dominated disciplines, for those who encountered very hierarchical attitudes within their departments and for those who worked with supervisors and other academics who failed to recognise them as legitimate contributors to their academic communities. The sites in which belonging was easier for women doctoral students to establish were those in which access to peer communities and support were more straightforward, and where women were able to work in shared spaces with other doctoral students. However, even these spaces were not always experienced as positive, with lad culture affecting some women's ability to feel comfortable in their working environment. Further, being recognised as a valuable contributor to the academic community by more senior individuals was key to women doctoral students' ability to feel a sense of belonging. Other key factors which helped to facilitate their belonging were support mechanisms which could be provided by institutions: having dedicated societies or departmental committees for doctoral students provided opportunities for social interactions with peers, opportunities to engage in departmental activities such as research opportunities and teaching, as well as pragmatic mechanisms such as providing individuals access to a staff member with pastoral responsibilities for doctoral students, who was not their supervisor.

## Claiming Legitimacy and Developing Strategies for Belonging

Beyond examining the sites where belonging was, and was not, felt, understanding the barriers women faced in developing a sense of belonging generated insight into the strategies that they developed to try and overcome these challenges. Individuals demonstrated considerable agency in attempting to establish feelings of legitimacy, validity and, ultimately, belonging; but their ability to successfully enact these strategies was variable due to the culture of some academic communities.

For those who had felt marginalised within their departmental communities, forging strong connections with peers was a key to establish feelings of belonging during their doctorate. For Harriet, who struggled with the power dynamics of her supervisory relationship and the pressure of her workload within the lab, connecting with peers through her departmental postgraduate society was vital for her well-being during her PhD and also enabled her to establish a strong peer group within her academic community, and thus develop a sense of belonging. For Eleanor, too, accessing peer support made a significant impact on her ability to feel a sense of belonging within her departmental community. Having initially felt isolated by being allocated a desk in a corridor, Eleanor's strategic decision to approach her Head of Department and request a more suitable workspace facilitated her connections with a small group of women with whom she shared an office for the rest of her studies. This enabled her to create her own peer support network within her department, which had a positive impact on her well-being and her ability to feel a sense of belonging.

Other participants also attempted to forge stronger connections with peers by engaging in departmental activities, such as organising research seminars and taking on additional roles representing postgraduate students. For Liz, who lived at a distance to her institution and was conscious that she was older than the majority of her peers, making efforts to connect with her peers through organising a departmental student symposium was a positive and affirming experience. This strategy helped her to establish a sense of belonging to her academic community in her second year, which enabled her to continue with her studies; she had considered leaving her PhD in her first year. However, not all participants had the same level of success in their attempts to engage in their departmental community. For Jessie, who volunteered to become a student representative and help organise a symposium designed to showcase PhD students' work, this strategy was less successful. Academics appeared disinterested, and Jessie became frustrated with the hierarchical nature of her departmental community, perceiving that her input was not recognised or valued.

A further strategy undertaken by participants in order to establish a sense of belonging was to seek connections with academics outside their own institution, especially when their own departmental culture was either unwelcoming or inaccessible. For Jessie, forging a connection with an academic from another university who she sought advice from throughout her studies helped her to claim legitimacy within her disciplinary community, as she felt recognised and valued as a contributor to her discipline by a senior member of the community. For Martina and Chloe, this was a more pragmatic strategy, enacted out of necessity, due to living at a distance from their institution.

For others, who struggled with the power dynamics of their supervisory relationships, another strategy was to learn how to manage these relationships to secure the outcomes that they wanted. For Liz, this meant subverting the traditional academic hierarchy by seeking support from an academic who had pastoral responsibility for doctoral students, who was able to speak to her supervisors directly, enabling Liz to circumvent the difficulties inherent in directly resisting her supervisors' expectations around her publishing work. For others, such as Harriet and Jane, their attempts to resist what they perceived as unreasonable expectations of their supervisors around working practices were enacted more subtly, for example, by refusing to work on evenings and weekends. However, it took time for individuals to build the confidence to be able to enact these strategies, and not all were able to do so successfully, as Pepper's experience of leaving her studies indicates.

Despite encountering structural, cultural and gendered barriers to belonging within their academic communities, women doctoral students demonstrated considerable agency in trying to find their own ways to belong within the academy. Strategies included developing strong peer communities, engaging in departmental activities, attempting to resist what they perceived as unreasonable expectations in relation to working practices and subverting traditional academic hierarchies within supervisory relationships. These strategies represent a desire for a more collegial, inclusive and supportive academic environment which enables individuals to prioritise well-being over productivity, as well as indicating some resistance to neoliberalised expectations of academic labour. However, some strategies for facilitating belonging were more successful than others, and some individuals were more able to enact these strategies than others.

Further, not all strategies that participants developed in order to try and belong within their academic communities can be viewed in such a positive light. For those who encountered lad culture, at either a lower or a more extreme level, it was apparent that women doctoral students were not able to fully acknowledge or recognise the impact of these experiences on their ability to feel a sense of belonging within the academy. Indeed, Harriet and Sally both downplayed the role of lad culture on their daily life, though it was clear that they had felt isolated and marginalised on multiple occasions due to the behaviour of academics and peers.

These findings mirror those of other studies, which highlight how women in the academic environment may downplay experiences of discrimination as an unconscious self-protection strategy, enabling them to resist viewing their academic environment as sexist and thus more challenging for them to progress within (see Van Den Brink & Stobbe, 2009; Hughes et al., 2017). For Jane, who both experienced and witnessed sexual harassment during her studies, fully acknowledging this was difficult due to the feelings of shame and guilt that resulted from this experience. She was unsure both whether to, and how to, report this, recognising that as a PhD student she would be taking a risk in doing so, and that her position as a PhD student made her feel disempowered. Jane's experience indicates how academic hierarchies can compound the existing power differentials implicit in sexual harassment and make it more difficult for victims to report these behaviours (see Ahmed, 2021; Bull & Page, 2021; Tutchell & Edmonds, 2020).

## Post-PhD Futures: Considering Long-Term Belonging in Academia

The different levels of success that women doctoral students had in accessing institutional support mechanisms, and in devising strategies to try and develop feelings of belonging, had a significant impact on how they envisaged their post-PhD futures. Interactions with peers, supervisors and other academics, and individuals' encounters with local and wider academic cultures, all shaped how women experienced the doctorate in the present, and how they perceived their possible post-PhD career options. For some, establishing a sense of belonging within their academic communities in the short term, during their PhD, was straightforward, but constructing viable, long-term academic identities where they could envision belonging to this community beyond the PhD was more difficult. For others, this future identity construction was possible, though it required them to engage in some element of compromise.

In total, four different typologies of present and/or future imagined belonging emerged from analysis of participants' experiences. Firstly, there were those who had really struggled to establish a sense of belonging within their academic community as doctoral students, who could not imagine themselves belonging in the future as academics. Secondly, those who did manage to establish some feelings of belonging to their academic community as doctoral students, after initial difficulties, but struggled to envisage feeling this belonging in the future. Thirdly, some who felt a sense of belonging as doctoral students could imagine themselves belonging in the future, though this involved making certain compromises in order to do so. The fourth typology relates to those who, despite some initial struggles, had felt the sense belonging to their academic community, and thus were able to imagine themselves belonging within academia relatively unproblematically. These typologies enable insight into the temporal dimensions of belonging and reinforce how belonging is an ongoing accomplishment which must be constantly renegotiated (May, 2013).

Though all participants struggled to establish feelings of belonging to their academic community at different stages of their doctorate, some did experience these feelings during their studies and were able to envisage belonging to this community in the longer term. However, this was by no means the case for all participants. Whilst participants' feelings of belonging shifted and were not fixed across the various stages of their PhD, the ways in which they did, or did not, experience feelings of belonging during their doctorate had a direct impact on how able they were to imagine becoming academics in the future. These findings support those of other research which has found that the PhD is a critical stage wherein women's academic identities are either forged or rejected (see Guest et al., 2013; Mason et al., 2009; Royal Society of Chemistry, 2008; Wellcome Trust, 2013).

Within this study, four key typologies relating to women doctoral students' present and future belonging within academic communities were identified. Firstly, and perhaps unsurprisingly, there were those who had really struggled to ever establish a sense of belonging within their academic community as doctoral students, who could not imagine themselves belonging in the future as academics. For Pepper and for Sally, their experiences of the academic environment were largely negative; each of them had felt marginalised by the actions of both supervisors and other academics in their department. Post-PhD, they instead envisaged themselves working in sectors which they perceived to be less hierarchical, and which would be more conducive to their well-being.

Secondly, other participants—Eleanor and Liz—did manage to establish some feelings of belonging to their academic community as doctoral students even after some initial difficulties, but they struggled to envisage feeling this belonging in the future. For Eleanor, this largely related to her perceptions of academic careers as insecure, and often requiring individuals to demonstrate considerable mobility to take up temporary posts, especially during the early career stage. Her working-class background and lack of financial security, combined with her perception that balancing an academic career with having children would be difficult, meant that she could not easily imagine herself belonging to her academic community beyond the PhD. For Liz—who also identified as working-class—her difficulties with supervisors and experiences of imposter syndrome, combined with her admission that her husbands' career was likely to take priority over her own post-PhD career, meant that though she had established a sense of belonging during the latter stages of her studies, being able to envisage herself as belonging to her academic community in the longer-term was not straightforward.

For others—who had also been able to feel a sense of belonging within their academic community at some stage as doctoral students—it was possible to imagine themselves belonging in the future, though this involved making certain compromises in order to do so. For Harriet, Jessie, Chloe and Jane, whose experiences fell within this third typology of belonging, each were able to envisage a future where they could belong within their academic communities, but they acknowledged that this would come at some kind of personal cost. Harriet and Jessie could both imagine being academics but acknowledged that in order to do so they would need to prioritise the publication of first-authored papers above all other types of academic work—something neither of them ideally wanted to do—in order to be viewed as legitimate and successful academics. For Chloe, being able to imagine herself as an academic would necessitate her working part-time and being able to secure an agreement with a partner to share future childcare. For Jane, the compromise she envisaged having to make to belong in academia was being willing to adopt a more traditionally masculine approach to career progression and engage in self-promotion and pursuing publications above all other activities.

Yet for all of these women, it was clear that there were limitations on their willingness to make these, and other compromises, to try and belong within academia. For Harriet and Jane, who had concerns about the impact of cultural expectations of total dedication to work within academic STEM on their well-being, they were unwilling to make this effort to belong within academia if it were to come at the expense of their personal happiness. For Chloe and Jessie, they recognised that there were geographical limitations on their ability to belong within their academic community in the future due to existing caring commitments.

Finally, there were some participants—again who, despite some initial struggles, had managed to establish feelings of belonging to their academic community as doctoral students—who were able to imagine themselves belonging within academia relatively unproblematically. Despite each of them having at times struggled to establish a sense of belonging, Bella, Martina and Freija were able to envisage belonging to their academic communities in the future, without detailing any of the kinds of compromises that others imagined having to make. Possible factors which shaped their ability to establish this sense of belonging were access to female academic role models, which appeared to be of critical importance for Bella; seeing women in senior academic roles in her department enabled her to visualise herself as being similarly able to successfully forge an academic career path. For Martina, making efforts to connect with other scholars outside her institution by attending academic conferences, and moving back to the UK so that she could engage regularly with academics and peers in her departmental community at seminars, training and other events appeared to be key in facilitating her sense of belonging. For Freija, too, having regular opportunities to connect with other academics seems to have been vital for her ability to envisage herself belonging within her academic community in the future, particularly being able to work alongside them in a teaching role which enabled her to perform an academic identity (Bansel, 2011; Hopwood, 2010; Mantai, 2019).

The emergence of these four typologies of present/future belonging experienced by women doctoral students reveals the types of factors which made it more difficult for individuals to imagine themselves belonging within academia in the longer term. For those working in practice-based disciplines, including health-related disciplines and engineering, there was significant frustration with the hierarchical nature of academia, which individuals perceived made it more difficult to undertake research which could have a direct impact on the communities they hoped to help. This perceived clash between the values held by individuals and those espoused within academic life meant that some participants struggled to reconcile this conflict and found it difficult to envisage belonging within their academic community.

Concern around individuals' future well-being as potential academics was also a significant issue which challenged participants' ability to imagine belonging within academia. Many perceived that the pressure to publish work, as well as cultural expectations of total dedication to academic work, particularly in STEM subjects, was off-putting, even as PhD students. However, the possibility of remaining within this culture in the long term and working in ways that individuals perceived as unhealthy in order to succeed was unappealing to many. Though there was evidence of some participants trying to resist these pressures during their PhD, it was clear that most perceived that they would need to compromise their work-life balance in order to be successful academics, as both Harriet and Jane acknowledge.

For some, witnessing the gendered nature of women academics' career experiences was particularly discouraging, especially for those who witnessed discrimination and therefore expected that they too could face this if they were to pursue an academic career, although some felt that they would be able to overcome this successfully. For Harriet and Jane, though, viewing the experiences of other women scientists, particularly those who had struggled to combine family life with an academic career, made it very difficult to sustain a long-term positive academic identity, indicating a lack of positive role models for women in STEM.

It was evident that being able to envisage this long-term belonging in academia was harder for some women than for others. The prevalence of gendered stereotypes and discrimination against other women scientists meant that imagining belonging in academia beyond the PhD was more challenging for women doctoral students in STEM subjects, such as Jane, Harriet and Pepper. However, imagining long-term belonging in academia was also more difficult for those from working-class backgrounds, such as Eleanor and Liz, or those who had caring responsibilities, like Jessie and Chloe. For these women, it was more challenging to envisage belonging to a community within which careers were often insecure, and which would necessitate geographical mobility.

## Implications of (Not) Belonging for Individuals, Identities, Institutions and the Sector

In this chapter, I have drawn attention to the ways in which women doctoral students in this study attempted to establish feelings of belonging within their academic communities and the extent to which their strategies were successful. I have highlighted the spaces and situations in which establishing a sense of belonging was more (or less) challenging, and the types of factors which could facilitate or preclude these feelings of belonging. This chapter has also provided new understandings of how feelings of belonging during the doctorate shaped women's ability to forge long-term academic identities. Four key typologies of present/future belonging emerged, revealing the extent to which personal characteristics such as social class and caring responsibilities affected how women were able to envisage belonging in academia in the longer term. Here, I draw together the implications of women doctoral students' struggle to belong within academic communities, examining this for individuals and their identities, as well as considering the implications for higher education institutions and the sector as a whole.

Undertaking a doctorate has been referred to as a 'high risk activity' (Delamont et al., 2000) for individuals, in that it requires the dedication of a significant amount of time and effort for an outcome which is not guaranteed (Brailsford, 2010; Golde, 2005; Lovitts, 2001; Wellcome Trust, 2013). Indeed, there is an expectation that doctoral study will be challenging—not just academically but also emotionally. Even for individuals who completed their doctorate a number of years ago, the memories of their PhD can still be painful: 'the vast majority of academics bear the scars of their postgraduate research' (Delamont et al., 2000, p. 32). The content of guidance literature aimed at new and current doctoral students is particularly revealing in this respect; there is often focus on addressing the isolation that students are likely to feel, with chapters addressing the difficulties of managing supervisors, coping with stress, staying sane and dealing with discrimination. The overall implication is that though there may be future rewards, doctoral study is an experience which requires careful negotiation of structural challenges. Further, the language often used to describe doctoral study in blogs, media articles and guidance literature for doctoral candidates positions doctoral study as an ordeal to be endured or "survived" (see Karp, 2009; Leonard, 2001; Matthiesen & Binder, 2009; Phillips & Pugh, 2015; Rugg & Petre, 2010; von Weitershausen, 2014).

For the women in this study, there were various aspects of their doctoral experience which were painful. Whilst Pepper was the only participant to leave her PhD, Liz and Sally both strongly considered it due to the difficulties they encountered and the negative impact on their wellbeing. For Pepper, her experience of working with industry during her PhD led her to understand that working in this environment, rather than in academia, was likely to be the best decision for her future. Encountering barriers to belonging during their PhD not only shaped participants' career aspirations—and for the vast majority, dissuaded them from their initial desire to pursue an academic career—but it also had a wider impact on how they viewed the academic environment. Several participants acknowledged that they had previously not been aware of the gendered nature of academic careers, and that until they became PhD student, they had not recognised the types of barriers, including discrimination, that women academics faced. This was particularly the case for those in humanities and social sciences disciplines, whose experiences until that point were of their female-dominated subject areas, both in terms of the student body and the staff teaching them. However, as they started to develop academic identities during the doctorate and became further encultured into the academic environment, they began to notice differences in women academics' career trajectories and experiences. Many directly witnessed, or experienced, gender discrimination, and felt marginalised within academic spaces.

Thus, whilst some women were able to maintain their academic aspirations, though acknowledging that they would need to compromise in order to do so, others had different responses to struggling to belong in academia. Some participants experienced significant conflict about their career aspirations and strategies for achieving their goals. Whilst initially Jane envisages trying to "*act a little bit more like a man, but not too much more*" in progressing her academic career, later in her studies she instead decided to aim for a postdoctoral position after the PhD as a short-term strategy to gain academic legitimacy in her field, before stepping into the policy world. Other strategies included taking up an ambivalent position towards the possibility of pursuing an academic career, as Jessie and Eleanor did. Maintaining ambivalence about this career path enabled them to be open to any academic opportunities which arose after the PhD, but also allowed them to fully recognise the difficulties inherent in this career and to envisage other possible career choices. A further strategy was to explore alternative career options during doctorate, with some undertaking an industry placement during their studies, which enabled them to consider routes out of academia. However, particularly for those in STEM, it was evident that there was a lack of appropriate guidance for those considering careers outside of academia, reinforcing the findings of other research which has highlighted the need for improved careers advice for doctoral students (see Nature, 2019; Vitae, 2017). Beyond this, one final strategy enacted by participants as a result of encountering barriers to belonging during the doctorate was to reject the possibility of an academic career altogether—a response which existing research has suggested is common and innately gendered (see Royal Society of Chemistry, 2008; Wellcome Trust, 2013).

In terms of participants' identities, the impact of struggling to belong within academia was significant. For those who had started the PhD with academic aspirations and had begun to formulate an academic identity, the realisation that their personal values may clash with those they would need to take on as academics was problematic and posed the multiple possible identities that participants wanted to take on as conflicting, rather than compatible. Other research has highlighted the difficulties inherent in academic identity construction for doctoral students (see Austin, 2002; Emmioglu et al., 2017; Mantai, 2017; McAlpine et al., 2010; Wisker, 2010), and how this may be more challenging for those from marginalised groups (Baker & Lattuca, 2010).

While a small number of participants appeared able to imagine themselves taking on longer-term academic identities relatively unproblematically, the majority found this a much more difficult prospect, and for some this was an impossibility. Significantly, experiences of not belonging within their academic community during the doctorate made maintaining desired long-term academic identities challenging, requiring individuals to envisage making significant compromises to personal values in order to sustain these academic identities. For those who considered ways in which they could attempt to embody the neoliberalised values they saw enacted in academia, such as attempting to publish as many first-authored papers as possible, they recognised that there would likely be a cost to their own well-being in order to do so. Thus, the desire to engage in academic identity development was in direct conflict with individuals' desire to maintain their future well-being.

Existing research indicates how women doctoral students may feel required to compartmentalise aspects of their lives in order to be successful in their studies, which can lead to a fragmented sense of identity (Araújo, 2005; Byers et al., 2015), something that may cause significant distress (Jazvac-Martek, 2009). Continuing to compartmentalise other important facets of their identity, or compromise personal values in the long term, may protract this process of fragmentation and contribute to poor well-being. This argument is reinforced by studies which have found that those who pursued academic research careers after their PhD were actually less satisfied than those who went on to have careers in other sectors (UK Council for Science and Technology, 2007; Diamond et al., 2014; Vitae, 2013).

Academic identities were understood by the majority of women doctoral students in this study as existing in opposition to other desired identities. The nature of academic careers, involving considerable competition for largely insecure, temporary jobs for which geographical mobility would likely be expected, along with significant pressure to publish work, was discouraging to those who wanted to start a family in the future or who already had caring responsibilities. Many participants, and particularly those in STEM, were simply unable to reconcile taking on an academic identity with the identity of becoming a mother. As Harriet reflects: *"it's like…how do you be a good mum and…do all your research?"*. Her experience of witnessing the challenges encountered by her female postdoc colleague who has children, leaves her unable to resolve this conflict. This perception of incompatibility between these two identities presents women doctoral students who want a family with a choice which appears binary, particularly if there are no positive role models to support the idea that it is possible to reconcile these identities (see Mason & Goulden, 2004; Mason et al., 2013; Royal Society of Chemistry, 2008; Wellcome Trust, 2013).

Embodying academic identities was not straightforward for the majority of participants. This study adds rich new findings to existing research which highlights that the experience of undertaking doctoral study can discourage women students from pursuing an academic career (Guest et al., 2013; Hatchell & Aveling, 2008). Perceived conflict of the values inherent within academic work with their own personal values, as well as perceptions of academic life as being incompatible with motherhood, meant that, for most, they were not easily able to imagine belonging within academia beyond the end of their PhD. It became clear that the doctorate operated as a site of formative experience for women doctoral students, wherein career aspirations were constructed and reconstructed, and within which academic identities were formulated, renegotiated and, in some cases, abandoned altogether.

The challenges that women doctoral students faced in feeling belonging within their academic communities also have significant long-term implications for higher education institutions. Research indicates that women are less likely than men to progress to doctoral study (Wakeling & Hampden-Thompson, 2013), and those women that do are more likely to take longer to complete their doctorate (Thune et al., 2012). Further, other studies highlight how women doctoral students are more likely than men to report mental health issues (Levecque et al., 2017), to struggle with imposter syndrome during their studies (Collett & Avelis, 2013) and to experience gender stereotyping, discrimination and harassment (Bull & Rye, 2018; Hughes et al., 2017; Nature, 2019; De Welde & Laursen, 2011). The implications of this inequality extend beyond individuals themselves, with multiple potentially damaging consequences for higher education institutions. Morley (2013) draws attention to the role that higher education institutions play in perpetuating exclusionary structures, processes and practices and the way in which this undermines social justice. Beyond the business case for addressing the 'lower' end of what has been called the 'leaky pipeline' (Barinaga, 1993) in terms of retaining talent within the academic workforce, Morley (2013) highlights the social justice implications for the higher education sector of not changing structures and practices which marginalise individuals from certain groups. Not only will the sector continue to lose talented researchers, but existing social inequalities will become further entrenched.

Researchers have argued that universities have failed to take action to make higher education spaces safe for women students and staff, despite their duty of care (Ahmed, 2021; Jackson & Sundaram, 2020; Page et al., 2019; Tutchell & Edmonds, 2020). Allowing academic cultures to persist which marginalise doctoral students from under-represented groups, including women, ethnic minorities, those from low socioeconomic backgrounds and those who have disabilities, means that universities are reinforcing social inequalities and are complicit in perpetuating cultures which cause harm to particular groups. Further, given existing inequalities in access to doctoral provision for those in these groups (see Advance HE, 2021b; Wakeling & Hampden-Thompson, 2013), universities have a moral responsibility to create inclusive academic cultures which recognise the potential discrimination that individuals will face, and act to make these spaces safe and possible for all to feel a sense of belonging within.

For the higher education sector, the implications of women doctoral students' inability to feel a sense of belonging within academic communities are similarly serious. Whilst it is important to note that the intention of all doctoral students is not to secure an academic career—and indeed those intentions would not be realised, given the significant competition for few academic posts (Vitae, 2013)—an academic career remains the most common aspiration amongst doctoral students internationally (Nature, 2019). Yet, with women doctoral students being less likely than men to be encouraged to engage in activities related to developing an academic career (Dever et al., 2008), and less likely to be introduced to useful networks (Asmar, 1999; Giles et al., 2009; Kemelgor & Etzkowitz, 2001), it is evident that there remain clear gender differences in the experiences of doctoral students, and that this shapes who is able to succeed in academia. Despite ongoing calls to increase the diversity of the academic workforce, unless serious attention is paid to making academic communities more inclusive from the early career stage, it is likely that little will change.

A significant part of women doctoral students' inability to envisage longer-term belonging in academia was due to the types of practices they saw were necessary to enact in order to succeed as academics. Expectations of complete dedication to work, including considerable pressure to publish work and to demonstrate geographical mobility, were discouraging to many, especially for those with existing caring responsibilities or who hoped to start a family. The impact on the academic workforce of these neoliberalised working practices is significant, and existing research has drawn attention to the well-being crisis amongst academics internationally (Loveday, 2018; Morrish, 2019; Wray & Kinman, 2021), something which is echoed amongst the doctoral student population (Havergal, 2017; Hazell et al., 2020; Levecque et al., 2017). The sector should recognise that this is not sustainable, particularly in the context of the Covid-19 pandemic which has generated additional pressures in relation to workload, work-life balance and working practices (Creaton, 2021; Levine & Rathmell, 2020; Vitae, 2020; Woolston, 2020; Wray and Kinman, 2021). In addition, despite a range of international initiatives to further the case for gender equality in higher education over the last three decades, it appears that the sector remains some way off making academic careers appear both possible and desirable to women doctoral students who are, or intending to become, mothers. Evidently, this excludes a significant proportion of the potential workforce.

In order to address these damaging consequences for individuals, their academic identities, as well as for institutions and the sector as a whole, I explore some potential solutions in the next chapter. This focuses on how institutions and academic communities—and the individuals who work within them—can facilitate women's belonging and academic identity development through the creation of inclusive academic cultures, and disciplinary and departmental strategies which aim to support belonging.

## References

Advance HE (2021b). Equality in higher education: Student statistical report 2021. Accessed from: https://www.advance-he.ac.uk/knowledge-hub/equality-higher-education-statistical-report-2021

Ahmed, S. (2021). *Complaint!* Duke University Press.

Ali, A., Kohun, F., & Levy, Y. (2007). Dealing with social isolation to minimize doctoral attrition- A four stage framework. *International Journal of Doctoral Studies, 2*(1), 33–49. https://doi.org/10.28945/3082

Araújo, E. R. (2005). Understanding the PhD as a phase in time. *Time & Society, 14*(2–3), 191–211. https://doi.org/10.1177/0961463X05055133

Asmar, C. (1999). Is there a gendered agenda in academia? The research experience of female and male PhD graduates in Australian universities. *Higher Education, 38*(3), 255–273.

Austin, A. E. (2002). Preparing the next generation of faculty: Graduate school as socialization to the academic career. *The Journal of Higher Education, 73*(1), 94–122.

Baker, V. L., & Lattuca, L. R. (2010). Developmental networks and learning: Toward an interdisciplinary perspective on identity development during doctoral study. *Studies in Higher Education, 35*(7), 807–827. https://doi.org/10.1080/03075070903501887

Bansel, P. (2011). Becoming academic: A reflection on doctoral candidacy. *Studies in Higher Education, 36*(5), 543–556. https://doi.org/10.1080/03075079.2011.594592

Barinaga, M. (1993). Science education: The pipeline is leaking women all the way along. *Science, 260*(5106), 409–411. https://doi.org/10.1126/science.260.5106.409

Barnard, S., Powell, A., Bagilhole, B., & Dainty, A. (2010). Researching UK women professionals in SET: A critical review of current approaches. *International Journal of Gender, Science and Technology, 2*(3), 362–381.

Brailsford, I. (2010). Motives and aspirations for doctoral study: Career, personal, and interpersonal factors in the decision to embark on a history PhD. *International Journal of Doctoral Studies, 5*, 15–27.

Britton, D. M. (2017). Beyond the chilly climate: The salience of gender in women's academic careers. *Gender & Society, 31*(1), 5–27.

Bull, A., & Page, T. (2021). Students' accounts of grooming and boundary-blurring behaviours by academic staff in UK higher education. *Gender and Education, 33*(8), 1057–1072.

Bull, A., & Rye, R. (2018). *Silencing students: Institutional responses to staff sexual misconduct in UK higher education*. The 1752 Group and University of Portsmouth, Portsmouth, UK.

Byers, V. T., Smith, R. N., Angrove, K. E., McAlister-Shields, L., & Onwuegbuzie, A. J. (2015). Experiences of select women doctoral students: A feminist standpoint theory perspective. *International Journal of Education, 7*(1), 266–304. https://doi.org/10.5296/ije.v7i1.6982

Chakraverty, D. (2019). Impostor phenomenon in STEM: Occurrence, attribution, and identity. *Studies in Graduate and Postdoctoral Education., 10*(1), 2–20.

Collett, J. L., & Avelis, J. (2013). *Family-friendliness, fraudulence, and gendered academic career ambitions*. American Sociological Association Annual Meeting.

Creaton, J. (2021). Addressing the mental health crisis. *Nature Reviews Cancer, 21*(1), 1–2.

De Welde, K., & Laursen, S. (2011). The glass obstacle course: Informal and formal barriers for women PhD students in STEM fields. *International Journal of Gender, Science and Technology, 3*(3), 571–595.

Deem, R., & Brehony, K. J. (2000). Doctoral students' access to research cultures-are some more unequal than others? *Studies in Higher Education, 25*(2), 149–165. https://doi.org/10.1080/713696138

Delamont, S., Atkinson, P., & Parry, O. (1997). *Supervising the PhD: A guide to success.* Open University Press.

Delamont, S., Atkinson, P., & Parry, O. (2000). *The doctoral experience: Success and failure in graduate school.* Routledge.

Denicolo, P., & Becker, L. (2008). The supervision process and the nature of the research degree. In G. Hall & J. Longman (Eds.), *The postgraduate's companion* (pp. 123–143). Sage.

Dever, M., Laffan, W., Boreham, P., Behrens, K., Haynes, M., Western, M., & Kubler, M. (2008). *Gender differences in early post-PhD employment in Australian universities: The influence of PhD experience on women's academic careers: Final report.*

Diamond, A., Roberts, J., Vorley, T., Birkin, G., Evans, J., Sheen, J., & Nathwani, T. (2014). UK Review of the provision of information about higher education: advisory study and literature review: report to the UK higher education funding. Accessed from: https://core.ac.uk/download/pdf/20090196.pdf

Emmioglu, E., McAlpine, L., & Amundsen, C. (2017). Doctoral students' experiences of feeling (or not) like an academic. *International Journal of Doctoral Studies, 12,* 73–91.

Etzkowitz, H., & Gupta, N. (2006). Women in science: A fair shake? *Minerva, 44*(2), 185–199.

Etzkowitz, H., Kemelgor, C., & Uzzi, B. (2000). *Athena unbound: The advancement of women in science and technology.* Cambridge University Press.

Fisher, V., & Kinsey, S. (2014). Behind closed doors! Homosocial desire and the academic boys club. *Gender in Management: An International Journal, 29*(1), 44–64.

Giles, M., Ski, C., & Vrdoljak, D. (2009). Career pathways of science, engineering and technology research postgraduates. *Australian Journal of Education, 53*(1), 69–86. https://doi.org/10.1177/000494410905300106

Gill, R. (2009). Breaking the silence: The hidden injuries of neo-liberal academia. In R. Ryan-Flood & R. Gill (Eds.), *Secrecy and silence in the research process: Feminist reflections* (pp. 228–244). Routledge.

Golde, C. M. (2005). The role of the department and discipline in doctoral student attrition: Lessons from four departments. *The Journal of Higher Education, 76*(6), 669–700.

Guest, M., Sharma, S., & Song, R. (2013). *Gender and career progression in theology and religious studies*. Durham University.

Handforth, R. (2022). Feeling "stupid": Considering the affective in women doctoral students' experiences of imposter 'syndrome'. In *The Palgrave handbook of imposter syndrome in higher education* (pp. 293–309). Palgrave Macmillan.

Hatchell, H., & Aveling, N. (2008). Gendered disappearing acts: Women's doctoral experiences in the science workplace. In *Australian Association for Research in Education Conference* (vol. 30), Brisbane.

Havergal, C. (2017, April 13). *Universities can do more to support PhD students' mental health*. Times Higher Education. Retrieved from https://www.timeshighereducation.com/opinion/universities-can-do-more-support-phd-students-mental-health.

Hazell, C. M., Chapman, L., Valeix, S. F., Roberts, P., Niven, J. E., & Berry, C. (2020). Understanding the mental health of doctoral researchers: A mixed methods systematic review with meta-analysis and meta-synthesis. *Systematic Reviews, 9*(1), 1–30.

Heffernan, T. (2021). Academic networks and career trajectory: 'There's no career in academia without networks. *Higher Education Research & Development, 40*(5), 981–994.

Hemer, S. R. (2012). Informality, power and relationships in postgraduate supervision: Supervising PhD candidates over coffee. *Higher Education Research & Development, 31*(6), 827–839. https://doi.org/10.1080/07294360.2012.674011

Henkel, M. (2004). Current science policies and their implications for the formation and maintenance of academic identity. *Higher Education Policy, 17*(2), 167–182.

Hopwood, N. (2010). Doctoral experience and learning from a sociocultural perspective. *Studies in Higher Education, 35*(7), 829–843.

Hoskins, K. (2010, March). The price of success? The experiences of three senior working class female academics in the UK. In *Women's studies international forum* (vol. 33, no. 2, pp. 134–140). Pergamon.

Hughes, C. C., Schilt, K., Gorman, B. K., & Bratter, J. L. (2017). Framing the faculty gender gap: A view from STEM doctoral students. *Gender, Work and Organization, 24*(4), 398–416.

Jackson, C., & Sundaram, V. (2020). *Lad culture in higher education: Sexism, sexual harassment and violence*. Routledge.

Jazvac-Martek, M. (2009). Oscillating role identities: The academic experiences of education doctoral students. *Innovations in Education and Teaching International, 46*(3), 253–264. https://doi.org/10.1080/14703290903068862

Karp, J. R. (2009). *How to survive your PhD: The Insider's guide to avoiding mistakes, choosing the right program, working with professors, and just how a person actually writes a 200-Page paper*. Sourcebooks, Inc.

Kemelgor, C., & Etzkowitz, H. (2001). Overcoming isolation: Women's dilemmas in American academic science. *Minerva, 39*(2), 153–174.

Kogan, M. (2000). Higher education communities and academic identity. *Higher Education Quarterly, 54*(3), 207–216.

Lave, J., & Wenger, E. (1991). *Situated learning: Legitimate peripheral participation*. Cambridge University Press.

Lefebvre, H. (1991). *The production of space*. Blackwell.

Leonard, D. (2001). *A woman's guide to doctoral studies*. Open University Press.

Levecque, K., Anseel, F., De Beuckelaer, A., Van der Heyden, J., & Gisle, L. (2017). Work organization and mental health problems in PhD students. *Research Policy, 46*(4), 868–879. https://doi.org/10.1016/j.respol.2017.02.008

Levine, R. L., & Rathmell, W. K. (2020). COVID-19 impact on early career investigators: A call for action. *Nature Reviews Cancer, 20*(7), 357–358.

Loveday, V. (2018). The neurotic academic: Anxiety, casualisation, and governance in the neoliberalising university. *Journal of Cultural Economy, 11*(2), 154–166.

Lovitts, B. E. (2001). *Leaving the ivory tower: The causes and consequences of departure from doctoral study*. Rowman & Littlefield.

Manathunga, C. (2005). The development of research supervision: "Turning the light on a private space". *International Journal for Academic Development, 10*(1), 17–30.

Manathunga, C. (2014). *Intercultural postgraduate supervision: Reimagining time, place and knowledge*. Routledge.

Mantai, L. (2017). Feeling like a researcher: Experiences of early doctoral students in Australia. *Studies in Higher Education, 42*(4), 636–650.

Mantai, L. (2019). "Feeling more academic now": Doctoral stories of becoming an academic. *The Australian Educational Researcher, 46*(1), 137–153.

Mason, M. A., & Goulden, M. (2004). Marriage and baby blues: Redefining gender equity in the academy. *The Annals of the American Academy of Political and Social Science, 596*(1), 86–103. https://doi.org/10.1177/0002716204596000104

Mason, M. A., Goulden, M., & Frasch, K. (2009). Why graduate students reject the fast track. *Academe, 95*(1), 11–16.

Mason, M. A., Wolfinger, N. H., & Goulden, M. (2013). *Do babies matter? Gender and family in the ivory tower.* Rutgers University Press.

Matthiesen, J. K., & Binder, M. (2009). *How to survive your doctorate: What others don't tell you.* Open University Press.

May, V. (2013). *Connecting self to society: Belonging in a changing world.* Macmillan International Higher Education.

McAlpine, L., Amundsen, C., & Jazvac-Martek, M. (2010). Living and imagining academic identities. In L. McAlpine & G. Akerlind (Eds.), *Becoming an academic: International perspectives* (pp. 129–149). Palgrave Macmillan.

McAlpine, L., & Mitra, M. (2015). Becoming a scientist: PhD workplaces and other sites of learning. *International Journal of Doctoral Studies, 10*(2), 111–128. https://doi.org/10.28945/2112

Middleton, S. (2010). Rhythms of place time and space in the doctoral experience. In *The Routledge doctoral Supervisor's companion* (pp. 203–214). Routledge.

Morley, L. (1999). *Organising feminisms: The micropolitics of the academy.* Palgrave Macmillan.

Morley, L. (2013). The rules of the game: Women and the leaderist turn in higher education. *Gender and Education, 25*(1), 116–131.

Morris, C., & Wisker, G. (2011). *Troublesome encounters: Strategies for managing the wellbeing of master's and doctoral education students during their learning processes.* HEA ESCalate Subject Centre Report.

Morrish, L. (2019). *Pressure vessels: The epidemic of poor mental health among higher education staff.* Higher Education Policy Institute.

Nature. (2019). *Nature PhD survey 2019: Report by shift learning.* Retrived from: https://figshare.com/s/74a5ea79d76ad66a8af8

Page, T., Bull, A., & Chapman, E. (2019). Making power visible: "Slow activism" to address staff sexual misconduct in higher education. *Violence Against Women, 25*(11), 1309–1330.

Parry, S. (2007). *Disciplines and doctorates.* Springer.

Phillips, E., & Pugh, D. (2015). *How to get a PhD: A handbook for students and their supervisors* (6th ed.). Open University Press.

Pittman, C. T. (2010). Race and gender oppression in the classroom: The experiences of women faculty of color with white male students. *Teaching Sociology, 38*(3), 183–196.

Rao, N., Hosein, A., & Raaper, R. (2021). Doctoral students navigating the borderlands of academic teaching in an era of precarity. *Teaching in Higher Education, 26*(3), 454–470.

Reay, D. (1998). Surviving in dangerous places: Working-class women, women's studies and higher education. *Women's Studies International Forum, 21*(1), 11–19. https://doi.org/10.1016/s0277-5395(97)00087-3

Rollock, N. (2019). *Staying power: The career experiences and strategies of UK black female professors.* UCU.

Rossiter, M. (2004). Educational relationships and possible selves in the adult undergraduate experience. *The Cyril O'Houle Scholars in Adult and Continuing Education Program Global Research Perspectives, 4*, 138–155. https://doi.org/10.1002/ace.259

Royal Society of Chemistry. (2008). The chemistry PhD: The impact on women's retention. *A Report for the UK Resource Centre for Women in SET and the Royal Society of Chemistry*, 1–38.

Royal Society of Chemistry. (2018). *Breaking the barriers: Women's retention and progression in the chemical sciences.* Retrieved from: http://www.rsc.org/campaigning-outreach/campaigning/incldiv/inclusion%2D%2Ddiversity-resources/womens-progression/s.

Rugg, G., & Petre, M. (2010). *The unwritten rules of PhD research.* McGraw-Hill Education (UK).

Thune, T., Kyvik, S., Sörlin, S., Olsen, T. B., Vabø, A., & Tømte, C. (2012). *PhD education in a knowledge society: An evaluation of PhD education in Norway.* Retrieved from: https://kudos.dfo.no/files/5b5/5b53171090a43ba55e3eb128b2c6a98fc30ac57609e09d6a74c19527cc06a660/NIFUrapport2012-25.pdf

Tutchell, E., & Edmonds, J. (2020). *Unsafe spaces: Ending sexual abuse in universities.* Emerald Group Publishing.

UK Council for Science and Technology. (2007). *Pathways to the future: The early careers of researchers in the UK.* Council for Science and Technology.

Valentine, G., & Wood, N. (2010). *The experiences of lesbian, gay and bisexual staff and students in higher education.* Equality and Human Rights Commission research summary 39. Retrieved from: https://www.equalityhumanrights.com/sites/default/files/research-summary-39-experiences-of-lesbian-gay-bisexual-higher-education.pdf

Van den Brink, M., & Benschop, Y. (2014). Gender in academic networking: The role of gatekeepers in professorial recruitment. *Journal of Management Studies, 51*(3), 460–492.

Van Den Brink, M., & Stobbe, L. (2009). Doing gender in academic education: The paradox of visibility. *Gender, Work and Organization, 16*(4), 451–470. https://doi.org/10.1111/j.1468-0432.2008.00428.x

Vigurs, K. (2016). Using Twitter to tackle peripherality? Facilitating networked scholarship for part-time doctoral students within and beyond the university. *Fusion Journal, 1*(008), 1–18.

Vitae. (2013). *What do researchers do? Early career progression of doctoral graduates.* The Careers Research and Advisory Centre (CRAC) Limited.

Vitae. (2017). *One size does not fit all: Arts and humanities doctoral and early career researchers' professional development survey.* The Careers Research and Advisory Centre (CRAC) Limited.

Vitae. (2020). *The impact of the Covid-19 pandemic on researchers in universities and research institutes.* Retrieved from: https://www.vitae.ac.uk/impact-and-evaluation/the-impact-of-the-covid19-pandemic%20on-researchers-in-universities-and-research-institutes

von Weitershausen, I. (2014, March 20). *How to stay sane through a PhD: Get survival tips from fellow students.* The Guardian. Retrieved from https://www.theguardian.com/higher-education-network/blog/2014/mar/20/phd-research-mental-health-tips.

Wakeling, P., & Hampden-Thompson, G. (2013). *Transition to higher degrees across the UK: An analysis of national, institutional and individual differences. HEA research series.* Higher Education Academy.

Walsh, E. (2010). A model of research group microclimate: Environmental and cultural factors affecting the experiences of overseas research students in the UK. *Studies in Higher Education, 35*(5), 545–560.

Wellcome Trust. (2013). *Risks and rewards: How PhD students choose their careers.* Ipsos MORI.

White, J., & Nonnamaker, J. (2008). Belonging and mattering: How doctoral students experience community. *NASPA Journal, 45*(3), 350–372.

Wisker, G. (2007). *The postgraduate research handbook: Succeed with your MA, MPhil, EdD and PhD.* Palgrave Macmillan.

Wisker, G. (2010). The 'good enough'doctorate: Doctoral learning journeys. *Acta Academica: Critical Views on Society, Culture and Politics, 1,* 223–242.

Woolston, C. (2020). Pandemic darkens postdocs' work and career hopes. *Nature, 585*(7824), 309–312.

Wray, S., & Kinman, G. (2021). *Supporting staff wellbeing in higher education: A report for education support.* Retrieved from: https://www.educationsupport.org.uk/media/x4jdvxpl/es-supporting-staff-wellbeing-in-he-report.pdf

# 7

# Facilitating Belonging and Academic Identities: Addressing Barriers Faced by Women Doctoral Students

This chapter sets out some practical and constructive suggestions, based on the findings of this study, for how institutions, departments and individuals might work to remove the barriers that women doctoral students face to belonging within academic communities. These strategies would support women doctoral students to connect with peers and academics; feel safe, valued and legitimate within academic spaces; and facilitate their academic identity development. Recent research has illustrated the discrimination and harassment experienced by doctoral students during their studies, indicating the urgent need for improvements in this area; an international survey undertaken in 2019 found that a fifth of respondents had experienced this, with gender and racial discrimination being the most common forms of discrimination encountered (Nature, 2019).

It is important to note that it is not just women doctoral students who need support in finding ways to belong within the academy. Developing a sense of belonging is not straightforward for individuals whose identities have traditionally been marginalised within society and in academic spaces. Throughout this book I have argued that these feelings of marginalisation are compounded for doctoral students, who occupy a liminal position within the academic hierarchy (Handforth, 2022). Yet PhD students with disabilities, those from BAME backgrounds, from working-class backgrounds and the LGBTQ+ community face additional barriers to belonging in academia (see Acker & Haque, 2015; Arday, 2017; English & Fenby-Hulse, 2019; Hannam-Swain, 2018; Hastie, 2021; Ostrove et al., 2011), with particular challenges for individuals whose identities intersect across these groups (see Crumb et al., 2020; Mattocks & Briscoe-Palmer, 2016).

There is a clear need for higher education institutions and those who work within them to better support individuals who have traditionally been under-represented and discriminated against within the academy. In this chapter, I draw on my research to highlight the structural barriers to belonging that women doctoral students encountered during their studies, and consider how academic institutions and individuals working in these spaces can create more inclusive academic cultures. These insights have international relevance for those considering doctoral study, as well as current doctoral students, institutions, supervisors and others involved in doctoral education and support.

## Addressing Barriers to Belonging: Institutional Responsibilities

In the face of increasing evidence that higher education institutions may not be safe spaces for women students (see Bull & Page, 2021; NUS, 2010; Page et al., 2019; Phipps & Young, 2015; Phipps, 2018; Tutchell & Edmonds, 2020), addressing the issue of sexual harassment should be the first priority for all institutions. Given the inherently affective nature of belonging, clearly the basic need to feel safe in academic spaces is a prerequisite for women to feel a sense of belonging within academic communities. Women doctoral students are more likely than men to both experience and witness gender-based bullying and harassment (Nature, 2019; Wellcome Trust, 2020), as well as be subject to gender stereotyping and discrimination (Bull & Rye, 2018; Hughes et al., 2017; De Welde & Laursen, 2011). Yet internal processes to report incidents of sexual harassment and discrimination within higher education institutions are often unclear and ineffective in addressing the behaviour of perpetrators (The 1752 Group and McAllister Olivarius, 2020). Further, it is apparent that many universities seek to use non-disclosure agreements (NDAs) to keep incidents confidential (Page et al., 2019; Weale & Batty, 2016; Whitley & Page, 2015), to the detriment of victims' well-being (see Bull & Rye, 2018). Thus, despite increasing evidence published over the last decade which reveals the systemic nature of sexual harassment within higher education institutions (Australian Human Rights Commission, 2017; Cantor et al., 2019; NUS, 2010; Phipps & Young, 2015), perhaps unsurprisingly, reporting of incidents remains low, at around 10% in the UK (NUS, 2018).

If women are to feel safe to both study and work within academic spaces, higher education institutions must act to address the lower-level attitudes and behaviours which contribute to sexual harassment and violence. This study found that participants had often encountered 'lad culture', which was perpetuated by both students and staff. This culture of 'laddism', manifested in sexist comments often described as "*banter*", as well as aggressive behaviours directed at women, operates at various levels to exclude, undermine and marginalise women students and members of staff. Unless seemingly low-level behaviours—which may be dismissed as "laddism" by some—are challenged, this enables a climate within which sexual harassment and violence become normalised (Phipps & Young, 2015). Universities should therefore develop policies which address lad culture by defining and giving examples of sexist behaviour and discrimination, sexual harassment, bullying and violence, making reporting processes transparent as well as outlining how incidents will be dealt with.

Universities must take action to improve processes for dealing with staff sexual misconduct, including making reporting systems for incidents of harassment clear and accessible to students, and ensuring that any individual associated with an accusation is not involved in the decision-making process. In the UK, the 1752 Group [1] has developed guidance for the sector on how institutions can address staff sexual misconduct, including recommended procedures relating to reporting, investigation and decision-making (the 1752 Group and McAllister Olivarius, 2020). Yet with no direct action from bodies with regulatory

---

[1] A UK-based research, consultancy and campaign organisation dedicated to ending staff sexual misconduct in higher education.

responsibilities for setting guidelines for institutions, there is considerable work still to do to improve these processes. In addition to improving reporting and complaints processes, after investigating incidents appropriately, it is vital that institutions take action to punish perpetrators rather than attempting to conceal these incidents. A significant aspect of this relates to not silencing victims of sexual harassment; a global campaign called '*Can't Buy My Silence*' [2] is attempting to get universities to stop using NDAs as a way of dealing with complaints about sexual harassment, bullying and other forms of misconduct. Currently, 14 UK institutions have pledged to stop using NDAs for this purpose, at the time of writing.

Beyond making efforts to improve the safety of all academic spaces for women students and staff, higher education institutions could be proactive in finding ways to support women's belonging, such as facilitating inclusive women's networks which recognise the barriers that women doctoral students face to belonging in academia. Research indicates how the persistence of 'boy's clubs' in academia contributes to gender inequality by marginalising women, particularly in STEM subjects (De Welde & Laursen, 2011), and by facilitating men's interests in relation to progression and promotion (Barnard et al., 2010; Fisher & Kinsey, 2014). The importance of access to useful networks for doctoral students' academic career development is well understood (Denicolo & Becker, 2008; Heffernan, 2021; Wisker, 2007), yet women are less likely than men to have access to these networks during their doctorate (Dever et al., 2008; Giles et al., 2009; Kemelgor & Etzkowitz, 2001). Thus, by providing opportunities for self-identifying women doctoral students to network with academics, and by funding appropriate events and activities for women academics, universities could facilitate the development of a supportive and inclusive academic community.

Evidently, there are a range of actions that higher education institutions could take to address the barriers to belonging faced by women doctoral students. These centre around ensuring that at the most basic level, academic spaces and communities are safe for women. Feminist academic Diana Leonard highlighted that sexual harassment 'serves either

---

[2] https://cantbuymysilence.com/universities-pledge-list/

to drive us out of the organisation, or at least to stress our lack of fit' (Leonard, 2001, p. 221), showing how these behaviours shape women's ability to belong to academic communities both in the short and long term. It is disappointing that so little appears to have changed over the last two decades.

There is an urgent need for universities to address the culture of sexual harassment present in higher education institutions, ensuring that victims have clear reporting procedures and that complaints processes are followed consistently, and enacted with empathy and sensitivity by individuals who are not connected with any accusations. Institutions should take actions which address gender discrimination in all its various forms, including tackling sexual harassment and lad culture. However, universities should also work to support and build networks for women, being mindful of the need to make these welcoming and inclusive for women of all backgrounds, as well as to those in more precarious positions within the academic hierarchy, such as doctoral students and early career academics.

## Facilitating Academic Identities: Creating Inclusive Academic Cultures

This study has shown how developing a sense of belonging may be a complex endeavour for women, something not fully understood by institutions and those working with doctoral students (White & Nonnamaker, 2008; Wisker et al., 2010). Belonging is affective, involving forging connections with others and negotiating power relations in order to be accepted and recognised as a legitimate member of the community (May, 2013; Miller, 2003). Academic cultures were often experienced as marginalising for women in this study, in relation to both the gender discrimination they encountered personally (or witnessed others experience) and the working practices that they saw embedded within their academic communities. In order to enable women doctoral students to feel a sense of belonging within these spaces, it is vital that institutions, academics and those with responsibilities for doctoral education and support work to create more inclusive academic cultures.

Academic careers continue to present challenges for women who plan to start a family, due to gender discrimination, expectations of mobility, the prevalence of temporary contracts, and perceived conflict between the demands of family and work. Indeed, having children, as well as other care commitments, is one of the main issues known to contribute to the 'leaky pipeline' (van Anders, 2004; Mason et al., 2013; Royal Society of Chemistry, 2008). Participants in this study struggled to align an academic identity with the identity of becoming a mother, and lacked positive role models to offer visibility to a future in which these identities were shown as compatible. These findings reinforce those of other studies, which indicate the significance of academic role models for women considering careers in academia, particularly in STEM disciplines (see Fagan & Teasdale, 2021; Mason et al., 2009; Royal Society of Chemistry, 2018; Wladkowski & Mirick, 2019).

For these perceptions of academic careers to change, and in order to prevent successive generations of women choosing to leave academia after the PhD, it is critical that the academy becomes more family-friendly, both in relation to the terms and conditions of employment and also in relation to cultural expectations of women and academic labour. In relation to this first factor, this necessitates making part-time and flexible working more possible, particularly for those in STEM subjects where career success is often dependent on external grant funding, which is often not offered on a flexible basis (see Royal Society of Chemistry, 2018; Wellcome Trust, 2013). Enabling women to take up funding, employment and fellowship opportunities flexibly—and part-time where this is desired—will be an important step in facilitating women's career progression, along with initiatives which aim to make academic events and conferences more accessible to those with young families (see Bos et al., 2019).

Beyond structural changes, though, it is vital that institutions, individuals and the sector work to challenge discriminatory attitudes towards women and care work. There are double standards in the ways in which men and women academics with children are perceived, with evidence of a 'motherhood penalty' which is not experienced by men (Benard &

Correll, 2010; Hughes et al., 2017). Perhaps unsurprisingly, some women academics try to conceal their caring responsibilities by deliberately not mentioning family commitments at work (see Schlehofer, 2012; Solomon, 2011). Further, even where part-time, flexible options are available for women academics to take up, these are often linked to a type of discrimination known as 'flexibility stigma' (Williams, 2000), based on assumptions that women employed on this basis are less committed to work (see Cech & Blair-Loy, 2014). It is therefore important that those working in academic spaces, particularly those in senior roles, challenge these discriminatory attitudes when they are encountered. Further, if more men were to take up parental leave and flexible working options, these working practices would become normalised, with a reduction in stigma (see Royal Society of Chemistry, 2018; Sallee et al., 2016).

Linked to this, the other main factor which challenged women's ability to take on a long-term academic identity was the perception of academic careers as requiring total dedication to work. The impact of neoliberalised working practices on women doctoral students was felt through their participation in a culture wherein they witnessed supervisors and academics working very long hours, being under significant pressure to publish work and in some cases demanding presenteeism on campus during weekends and holidays. It appears that doctoral students have become inculcated into these ways of working; an international survey of doctoral students found that a quarter of respondents reported working over 50 hours a week on their research (see Nature, 2019). Further, a recent report in the UK found that expectations of long working hours and presenteeism had a greater negative impact on women's mental health and well-being than men's (Wellcome Trust, 2020). This report also highlighted that doctoral students perceived that there was little focus on support for academics' well-being within higher education institutions (ibid, 2020).

Over the last decade, there has been increasing evidence that doctoral students struggle with poor mental health and well-being (see Guthrie et al., 2018; Hazell et al., 2020; Levecque et al., 2017; Nature, 2019). Historically, institutional funding has focused almost exclusively on the well-being of undergraduates, who have very different needs to doctoral students (Vitae, 2018). Yet funding pressures, concerns around future careers, poor relationships with supervisors and significant workload contribute to poor levels of well-being amongst doctoral student populations (see Guthrie et al., 2018). Further, women doctoral students, those from lower socio-economic backgrounds and those from minority ethnic backgrounds are more likely to experience a decline in their mental health during the PhD (Gonzalez et al., 2021), with experiences of racial discrimination particularly contributing to lower levels of well-being (see Arday, 2018; Posselt, 2021). In the UK, whilst there has been some recognition of the scale of the issue of poor well-being amongst doctoral students within the sector (see Vitae, 2018, 2020), there is a clear need to ensure that tailored mental health and well-being support is available to doctoral students.

Institutions and departments should make efforts to promote healthy attitudes to work, which recognise the pressures on academics but also support individuals to establish an appropriate work-life balance. Clearly, this must sit alongside efforts from the sector to shift the research culture away from the current intense focus on productivity, and towards one which focuses on upholding ethical standards for research, as well as diversity and inclusion (see Wellcome Trust, 2020). This would require a significant push back against the neoliberalisation discourse within higher education, which has dominated for over two decades. Departments should ensure that supervisors are aware of their influence on doctoral students, particularly in relation to the impact of their working practices on those that they supervise; participants in this study reported either implicit or explicit expectations to work long hours and be present on campus, which had a negative impact on their well-being and sense of belonging. Supervisors and academics should encourage doctoral students to develop a healthy work-life balance during their studies, and they should recognise the particular challenges faced by those with caring responsibilities and their need for additional support. Further, it was apparent that having access to advice beyond their supervisor was of value for women doctoral students, enabling them to seek pastoral support and help when encountering difficulties with their supervisory relationship. Departments should ensure that all doctoral students have access to a senior member of staff who is able to resolve these difficulties where they arise.

In order to create more inclusive academic cultures, institutions, departments and individuals working within them should ensure that appropriate and effective student support services are in place for doctoral students. It is vital that departments ensure that doctoral students are aware of how to access specialist student support services including counselling, and that supervisors and academics are knowledgeable about student support services and can effectively recommend and signpost students towards relevant services. Further, all staff should recognise the additional challenges faced by those from marginalised groups and make efforts to provide appropriate support. Providing targeted and well-funded activities which support mental health and well-being is therefore a key method through which institutions, supervisors and those involved in supporting doctoral students can facilitate inclusive academic cultures, which support women's ability to belong within academic communities.

Considering the long-term inclusivity of academic cultures, it is also important to consider how academic careers can be perceived as accessible to all. Though statistics highlight that many doctoral students who do aspire to become academics will ultimately be unsuccessful, due to the disparity between the numbers of doctoral students and opportunities for academic employment (see Vitae, 2012), if academic careers are to become truly meritocratic then all students should be supported in their academic identity development. Of course, the PhD is no longer an 'academic passport' (Noble, 1994, p. 2), and arguably should not be conceived of as such. It is known that doctoral students struggle to access career guidance and may need support in developing career goals pertaining to careers beyond academia (Vitae, 2018). Further, supervisors should be encouraged to conceive of the PhD as a professional development opportunity rather than an academic apprenticeship. Institutions should provide dedicated career advisors for doctoral students, and embed opportunities for doctoral students to seek career advice and support throughout their studies, acknowledging that career aspirations are likely to shift during this time. Departments and supervisors can play a crucial role in encouraging doctoral students to consider their career options at an early stage rather than just in the final year of their doctorate, and promoting opportunities for students to connect with employers, such as placements.

Yet despite the increased focus on the 'leaky pipeline', it remains the case that more women are dissuaded from an academic career than men, and that this occurs during their time as doctoral students (see Guest et al., 2013; Royal Society of Chemistry, 2008; Wellcome Trust, 2013). There is evidence, supported by the findings of my research, to suggest that women are less likely than their male counterparts to be encouraged to gain relevant experience and access useful networks which can facilitate academic employment (see Curtin et al., 2016; Dever et al., 2008). Thus, whilst the contemporary doctorate is now far from purely an academic apprenticeship, and the odds of long-term academic employment are low, given that a significant proportion of those who undertake doctoral study aspire to academic careers, it is important that all those who have these aspirations are supported to secure relevant experience and knowledge they need to pursue this career, should they wish to.

## Thinking to the Future: Disciplinary and Departmental Strategies to Support Belonging

This study has illustrated the significance of both disciplinary and departmental communities for women doctoral students, with each offering possibilities for establishing a sense of belonging within. Here, I draw out possible strategies which these communities could develop to support women doctoral students' belonging, in recognition of the barriers which this research has revealed.

Firstly, making efforts to clarify the role of doctoral students within departments would help to address a significant issue which arose within this research; it was apparent that their liminal status was a challenging aspect of most participants' experiences during their PhD. The ways in which they were perceived by academics varied by institution and discipline, but also appeared to be highly dependent on the culture of individual departments. Many felt that they were viewed as low status, despite being expected to undertake additional academic labour to their thesis, such as teaching, supervising or acting as a research assistant on other academics' research projects. Yet in other settings, individuals were treated like members of staff and felt valued as such. Thus, formalising the role of doctoral students and recognising the value of their academic labour within the departmental community would help to facilitate feelings of belonging.

Clarifying the specific role, responsibilities, and expectations of doctoral students, where these are absent, would also help in recruiting future doctoral candidates, helping to provide clear guidelines as to what individuals should expect. For example, outlining how there will be opportunities during the doctorate to engage in teaching, supervising and publishing academic work, but being clear that this is not a requirement or expectation, would help address some of the concerns expressed in this study by participants, who felt under undue pressure to engage in these activities, often to the detriment of their own research, and in many cases to their well-being. Outlining clear expectations of doctoral students and their contributions to academic communities would support feelings of belonging, and thus support individuals' well-being (Vitae, 2020). Academics and supervisors working with doctoral students who do undertake these additional activities should make efforts to recognise their efforts appropriately, ascribing equal credit for doctoral students' labour as with the labour of other academics. Further, within the recruitment process, departments should attend to the experiences that candidates have accrued prior to the PhD, recognising that many women especially are likely to come to doctoral study later in life, and therefore will already have existing experience and expertise which can be drawn on.

Secondly, fostering supportive doctoral student communities which enable individuals to access peer support would make a significant, positive impact to women doctoral students' experiences. Where developing a cohort identity has been undertaken more deliberately, for example in professional doctoral programmes, there is some evidence that this has helped to combat feelings of isolation and contributed to feelings of belonging (see Dos Santos & Lo, 2018; Fenge, 2012), though more formalised doctoral training partnerships in the UK appear to have had only limited success with this (see Budd et al., 2018). Given the link between doctoral students' belonging and retention (Lovitts, 2001), and the importance of peer networks for individuals' well-being (Morris & Wisker, 2011), departments should take actions to facilitate supportive communities for doctoral students. This could take the form of providing regular opportunities for doctoral students to meet and form peer networks, or more formalised peer mentoring systems which have been found to be effective in fostering a sense of community, across disciplines (see Paolucci et al., 2021). A further way of supporting doctoral student communities would be the provision of appropriate spaces where individuals can work together, alongside academics.

Strategies to support doctoral students' belonging could involve developing a coordinated programme of events, targeted to focus on key stages of the doctorate, such as induction, the confirmation process and viva preparation. Particular emphasis should be given to providing opportunities for individuals to meet and network with peers during the first few weeks and months of doctoral programmes. This study highlighted how enabling individuals to make connections with peers at an early stage of their studies helped them to develop a supportive network of peers which can help to sustain motivation throughout the challenges of the doctorate. The provision of (optional) opportunities which allow doctoral students to work with academics and contribute to their departmental communities, such as representative roles on committees and organisational roles for research events, are a key way in which departments can value doctoral students' contributions and facilitate feelings of belonging. Further, supporting, funding and promoting specific networks for doctoral students would allow peers to make connections outside of their immediate workspaces and lab groups, which might be preferable. Initial research which evaluates the impact of PhD support groups run by institutions has shown a positive impact on individuals' well-being (see Panayidou & Priest, 2021).

Whilst the research reported in this book was undertaken before the Covid-19 pandemic, it is evident that many of the challenges that women doctoral students faced in belonging within their academic communities will have been compounded by the pandemic and related lockdowns. A key aspect of doctoral experiences which emerged from this research was individuals' access to institutional and departmental spaces, an issue which has been particularly pertinent during the last two years of the pandemic, as doctoral students reported increased isolation, poor home working environments and a sense of dislocation from their academic communities (see Jackman et al., 2021). It was evident that being allocated appropriate workspaces where individuals could base themselves during their studies, and network with other doctoral students and academics, often contributed significantly to participants' well-being, with participants in this study who had lived abroad temporarily choosing to return to be closer to their institutions.

For participants who had access to shared workspaces where they could work alongside their peers, this largely facilitated positive interactions and helped to foster a sense of community belonging. Further, for those who worked with academics within these spaces, the opportunities to make connections were perceived as valuable. However, it is important to note that for those in STEM subjects, the culture of these shared workspaces could be problematic, with academics and supervisors in some cases perpetuating 'laddish' cultures or performing unhealthy working habits. Departments and institutions should consider the types of spaces which are most appropriate for doctoral students, recognising the impact that this allocation can have on perceived status (see Morris, 2021), and the potential benefits for individuals' sense of belonging to an academic community. However, care should be taken to ensure that the working cultures enacted within these spaces are inclusive and promote healthy working practices. In addition, efforts should be made to support those living at a distance from their institution to find ways to connect with other scholars in their area, and to engage in their departmental community virtually, in order to facilitate a sense of belonging.

Finally, institutions and departments which hold equality and diversity focused events targeting women doctoral students should ensure that the messages and advice being delivered to attendees are constructive. This study highlighted how individuals, particularly for those in STEM subjects, were often made to feel that the issues they were likely to face as women in academia were due to individual shortcomings, such as failing to make their CVs look 'masculine', or failing to 'sell themselves' enough to get an academic job, rather than relating to the structural nature of gender discrimination within the academy. It is clear that initiatives designed to support women in male-dominated academic disciplines should be carefully considered and thoughtfully delivered, in a way which does not entrench existing stereotypes or present a model of academic success based on masculine ideals of career progress.

## Final Thoughts

This study has demonstrated that the failure of academic cultures and communities to facilitate women doctoral students' belonging must be addressed by universities and all who work within them, if women are to succeed in academia. In 2001, Diana Leonard argued that 'women are made to feel not quite first-class citizens in the academic community' (p. 161), and little appears to have changed. Without any action from the sector, or from individual institutions, many women doctoral students will continue to struggle to belong within their academic communities and find it difficult to envisage themselves as academics. This has clear ramifications for the future of the higher education sector, which will continue to lose out on the talents of highly qualified individuals (Morley, 2013). Failing to address the issues outlined above will also contribute to the persistence of inequality in the academy. The serious challenges that women face to belonging in academic spaces during their doctorate—a prerequisite for an academic career—must be addressed.

## References

Acker, S., & Haque, E. (2015). The struggle to make sense of doctoral study. *Higher Education Research & Development, 34*(2), 229–241.

Arday, J. (2017). *Exploring black and minority ethnic (BME) doctoral students' perceptions of an academic career.* Universities and Colleges Union.

Arday, J. (2018). Understanding mental health: What are the issues for black and ethnic minority students at university? *Social Sciences, 7*(10), 196.

Australian Human Rights Commission. (2017). Change the course: National report on sexual assault and sexual harassment at Australian universities. *Redress, 26*(2), 27–29.

Barnard, S., Powell, A., Bagilhole, B., & Dainty, A. (2010). Researching UK women professionals in SET: A critical review of current approaches. *International Journal of Gender, Science and Technology, 2*(3), 362–381.

Benard, S., & Correll, S. J. (2010). Normative discrimination and the motherhood penalty. *Gender & Society, 24*(5), 616–646.

Bos, A. L., Sweet-Cushman, J., & Schneider, M. C. (2019). Family-friendly academic conferences: A missing link to fix the "leaky pipeline"? *Politics, Groups, and Identities, 7*(3), 748–758.

Budd, R., O'Connell, C., Yuan, T., & Ververi, O. (2018). The DTC Effect: ESRC doctoral training centres and the UK social science doctoral training landscape. Liverpool Hope University Press, Liverpool.

Bull, A., & Page, T. (2021). Students' accounts of grooming and boundary-blurring behaviours by academic staff in UK higher education. *Gender and Education, 33*(8), 1057–1072.

Bull, A., & Rye, R. (2018). *Silencing students: Institutional responses to staff sexual misconduct in UK higher education*. The 1752 Group and University of Portsmouth, Portsmouth, UK.

Cantor, D., Fisher, B., Chibnall, S., Harps, S., Townsend, R., Thomas, G., Lee, H., Kranz, V., Herbison, R., & Madden, K. (2019). *Report on the AAU campus climate survey on sexual assault and misconduct*. The Association of American Universities.

Cech, E. A., & Blair-Loy, M. (2014). Consequences of flexibility stigma among academic scientists and engineers. *Work and Occupations, 41*(1), 86–110.

Crumb, L., Haskins, N., Dean, L., & Avent Harris, J. (2020). Illuminating social-class identity: The persistence of working-class African American women doctoral students. *Journal of Diversity in Higher Education, 13*(3), 215.

Curtin, N., Malley, J., & Stewart, A. J. (2016). Mentoring the next generation of faculty: Supporting academic career aspirations among doctoral students. *Research in Higher Education, 57*(6), 714–738.

De Welde, K., & Laursen, S. (2011). The glass obstacle course: Informal and formal barriers for women PhD students in STEM fields. *International Journal of Gender, Science and Technology, 3*(3), 571–595.

Denicolo, P., & Becker, L. (2008). The supervision process and the nature of the research degree. In G. Hall & J. Longman (Eds.), *The postgraduate's companion* (pp. 123–143). Sage.

Dever, M., Laffan, W., Boreham, P., Behrens, K., Haynes, M., Western, M., & Kubler, M. (2008). *Gender differences in early post-PhD employment in Australian universities: The influence of PhD experience on women's academic careers: Final report*. University of Queensland.

Dos Santos, L. M., & Lo, H. F. (2018). The development of doctoral degree curriculum in England: Perspectives from professional doctoral degree graduates. *International Journal of Education Policy and Leadership, 13*(6), n6.

English, R., & Fenby-Hulse, K. (2019). Documenting diversity: The experiences of LGBTQ doctoral researchers in the UK. *International Journal of Doctoral Studies, 14*(1), 403–430.

Fagan, C., & Teasdale, N. (2021). Women professors across STEMM and non-STEMM disciplines: Navigating gendered spaces and playing the academic game. *Work, Employment and Society, 35*(4), 774–792.

Fenge, L. A. (2012). Enhancing the doctoral journey: The role of group supervision in supporting collaborative learning and creativity. *Studies in Higher Education, 37*(4), 401–414.

Fisher, V., & Kinsey, S. (2014). Behind closed doors! Homosocial desire and the academic boys club. *Gender in Management: An International Journal, 29*(1), 44–64.

Giles, M., Ski, C., & Vrdoljak, D. (2009). Career pathways of science, engineering and technology research postgraduates. *Australian Journal of Education, 53*(1), 69–86. https://doi.org/10.1177/000494410905300106

Gonzalez, J. A., Kim, H., & Flaster, A. (2021). *Transition points: Well-being and disciplinary identity in the first years of doctoral studies.* Studies in Graduate and Postdoctoral Education.

Guest, M., Sharma, S., & Song, R. (2013). *Gender and career progression in theology and religious studies.* Durham University.

Guthrie, S., Lichten, C. A., Van Belle, J., Ball, S., Knack, A., & Hofman, J. (2018). Understanding mental health in the research environment: A rapid evidence assessment. *Rand Health Quarterly, 7*(3), 2.

Handforth, R. (2022). Feeling "stupid": Considering the affective in women doctoral students' experiences of imposter 'syndrome'. In *The Palgrave handbook of imposter syndrome in higher education* (pp. 293–309). Palgrave Macmillan.

Hannam-Swain, S. (2018). The additional labour of a disabled PhD student. *Disability & Society, 33*(1), 138–142.

Hastie, A. (2021). Class act: Reflections on a working-class academic sense of self as a graduate teaching assistant. *Postgraduate Pedagogies, 1*(1), 27–47.

Hazell, C. M., Chapman, L., Valeix, S. F., Roberts, P., Niven, J. E., & Berry, C. (2020). Understanding the mental health of doctoral researchers: A mixed methods systematic review with meta-analysis and meta-synthesis. *Systematic Reviews, 9*(1), 1–30.

Heffernan, T. (2021). Academic networks and career trajectory: 'There's no career in academia without networks'. *Higher Education Research & Development, 40*(5), 981–994.

Hughes, C. C., Schilt, K., Gorman, B. K., & Bratter, J. L. (2017). Framing the faculty gender gap: A view from STEM doctoral students. *Gender, Work and Organization, 24*(4), 398–416.

Jackman, P. C., Sanderson, R., Haughey, T. J., Brett, C. E., White, N., Zile, A., et al. (2021). The impact of the first COVID-19 lockdown in the UK for doctoral and early career researchers. *Higher Education*, 1–18. https://doi.org/10.1007/s10734-021-00795-4

Kemelgor, C., & Etzkowitz, H. (2001). Overcoming isolation: Women's dilemmas in American academic science. *Minerva, 39*(2), 153–174.

Leonard, D. (2001). *A woman's guide to doctoral studies*. Open University Press.

Levecque, K., Anseel, F., De Beuckelaer, A., Van der Heyden, J., & Gisle, L. (2017). Work organization and mental health problems in PhD students. *Research Policy, 46*(4), 868–879. https://doi.org/10.1016/j.respol.2017.02.008

Lovitts, B. E. (2001). *Leaving the ivory tower: The causes and consequences of departure from doctoral study*. Rowman & Littlefield.

Mason, M. A., Goulden, M., & Frasch, K. (2009). Why graduate students reject the fast track. *Academe, 95*(1), 11–16.

Mason, M. A., Wolfinger, N. H., & Goulden, M. (2013). *Do babies matter? Gender and family in the ivory tower*. Rutgers University Press.

Mattocks, K., & Briscoe-Palmer, S. (2016). Diversity, inclusion, and doctoral study: Challenges facing minority PhD students in the United Kingdom. *European Political Science, 15*, 476–492.

May, V. (2013). *Connecting self to society: Belonging in a changing world*. Macmillan International Higher Education.

Miller, L. (2003). Belonging to country—A philosophical anthropology. *Journal of Australian Studies, 27*(76), 215–223.

Morley, L. (2013). The rules of the game: Women and the leaderist turn in higher education. *Gender and Education, 25*(1), 116–131.

Morris, C. (2021). "Peering through the window looking in": Postgraduate experiences of non-belonging and belonging in relation to mental health and wellbeing. Studies in Graduate and Postdoctoral Education.

Morris, C., & Wisker, G. (2011). *Troublesome encounters: Strategies for managing the wellbeing of master's and doctoral education students during their learning processes*. HEA ESCalate Subject Centre Report.

National Union of Students. (2010). *Hidden marks: A study of women students' experiences of harassment, stalking, violence and sexual assault*. NUS.

National Union of Students. (2018). *Power in the academy: Staff sexual misconduct in UK higher education*. NUS.

Nature. (2019). *Nature PhD survey 2019: Report by shift learning*. Retrived from: https://figshare.com/s/74a5ea79d76ad66a8af8

Noble, K. A. (1994). *Changing doctoral degrees: An international perspective*. SRHE/Open University Press.

Ostrove, J. M., Stewart, A. J., & Curtin, N. L. (2011). Social class and belonging: Implications for graduate students' career aspirations. *The Journal of Higher Education, 82*(6), 748–774.

Page, T., Bull, A., & Chapman, E. (2019). Making power visible: "Slow activism" to address staff sexual misconduct in higher education. *Violence Against Women, 25*(11), 1309–1330.

Panayidou, F., & Priest, B. (2021). *Enhancing postgraduate researcher wellbeing through support groups*. Studies in Graduate and Postdoctoral Education.

Paolucci, E. O., Jacobsen, M., Nowell, L., Freeman, G., Lorenzetti, L., Clancy, T., & Lorenzetti, D. L. (2021). *An exploration of graduate student peer mentorship, social connectedness and well-being across four disciplines of study*. Studies in Graduate and Postdoctoral Education.

Phipps, A. (2018). 'Lad culture' and sexual violence against students. In *The Routledge handbook of gender and violence* (pp. 171–182). Routledge.

Phipps, A., & Young, I. (2015). Neoliberalisation and 'lad cultures' in higher education. *Sociology, 49*(2), 305–322.

Posselt, J. (2021). *Discrimination, competitiveness, and support in US graduate student mental health*. Studies in Graduate and Postdoctoral Education.

Royal Society of Chemistry. (2008). The chemistry PhD: The impact on women's retention. *A Report for the UK Resource Centre for Women in SET and the Royal Society of Chemistry*, 1–38.

Royal Society of Chemistry. (2018) Breaking the barriers: Women's retention and progression in the chemical sciences. Retrieved from: http://www.rsc.org/campaigning-outreach/campaigning/incldiv/inclusion--diversityresources/womens-progression/s.

Sallee, M., Ward, K., & Wolf-Wendel, L. (2016). Can anyone have it all? Gendered views on parenting and academic careers. *Innovative Higher Education, 41*(3), 187–202.

Schlehofer, M. (2012). Practicing what we teach? An autobiographical reflection on navigating academia as a single mother. *Journal of Community Psychology, 40*(1), 112–128.

Solomon, C. R. (2011). "Sacrificing at the altar of tenure": Assistant professors' work/life management. *The Social Science Journal, 48*(2), 335–344. https://doi.org/10.1016/j.soscij.2010.11.006

The 1752 Group, and McAllister Olivarius. (2020). *Sector guidance to address staff sexual misconduct in UK higher education: Recommendations for reporting, investigation and decision-making procedures relating to student complaints of staff sexual misconduct*. Retrieved from: https://1752group.files.wordpress.com/2020/03/the-1752-group-and-mcallister-olivarius-sector-guidance-to-address-staff-sexual-misconduct-in-uk-he-1.pdf.

Tutchell, E., & Edmonds, J. (2020). *Unsafe spaces: Ending sexual abuse in universities*. Emerald Group Publishing.

Van Anders, S. M. (2004). Why the academic pipeline leaks: Fewer men than women perceive barriers to becoming professors. *Sex Roles, 51*(9–10), 511–521. https://doi.org/10.1007/s11199-004-5461-9

Vitae. (2018). *Exploring wellbeing and mental health and associated support services for postgraduate researchers*. Retrieved from: https://www.vitae.ac.uk/doing-research/wellbeing-and-mental-health/HEFCE-Report_Exploring-PGR-Mental-health-support/view

Vitae. (2020). *Programme evaluation of HEFCE Catalyst Fund: Supporting mental health & wellbeing for postgraduate research students*. Retrieved from: https://www.vitae.ac.uk/vitae-publications/catalyst-fund-supporting-mental-health-and-wellbeing-for-postgraduate-research-students

Vitae. (2012). *What do researchers want to do? The career intentions of doctoral researchers*. The Careers Research and Advisory Centre (CRAC) Limited.

Weale, S., & Batty, D. (2016, October 21). *University sex abuse report fails to tackle staff attacks on UK students*. The Guardian. Retrieved from https://www.theguardian.com/society/2016/oct/21/university-sex-abuse-report-fails-staff-attacks-students.

Wellcome Trust. (2013). *Risks and rewards: How PhD students choose their careers*. London: Ipsos MORI.

Wellcome Trust. (2020). *What researchers think about the culture they work in*. Retrieved from: https://cms.wellcome.org/sites/default/files/what-researchers-think-about-the-culture-they-work-in.pdf

White, J., & Nonnamaker, J. (2008). Belonging and mattering: How doctoral students experience community. *NASPA Journal, 45*(3), 350–372.

Whitley, L., & Page, T. (2015). Sexism at the Centre: Locating the problem of sexual harassment. *New Formations, 86*(86), 34–53.

Williams, J. C. (2000). *Unbending gender: Why family and work conflict and what to do about it*. Oxford University Press.

Wisker, G. (2007). *The postgraduate research handbook: Succeed with your MA, MPhil, EdD and PhD*. Palgrave Macmillan.

Wisker, G., Morris, C., Cheng, M., Masika, R., Warnes, M., Trafford, V., & Lilly, J. (2010). *Doctoral learning journeys: Final report.* Higher Education Academy. Retrieved https://www.heacademy.ac.uk/system/files/doctoral_learning_journeys_final_report_0.pdf

Wladkowski, S. P., & Mirick, R. G. (2019). Mentorship in doctoral education for pregnant and newly parenting doctoral students. *Journal of Women and Gender in Higher Education, 12*(3), 299–318.

# Index

Academic communities, 4, 6, 7, 9, 10, 15, 17, 19, 20, 33, 38, 40–44, 48–52, 75–78, 81, 85, 86, 90, 93, 94, 97, 99, 101, 103–106, 108–112, 114, 116, 117, 135, 138, 140–150, 152–154, 156, 158, 160, 162, 163, 165, 167, 168, 183, 185–187, 189–192, 194–197, 199–209, 214, 216, 217, 227–232, 234, 236–245, 247, 249–251, 259, 260, 262, 263, 267, 269–272

Academic conferences, 6, 149, 154, 191, 233, 243

Academic cultures, 4, 9, 14, 20, 33, 42, 44–48, 50, 78, 84, 96, 98, 101, 108, 135, 144, 147, 155, 160, 240, 249–251, 260, 263–268, 272

Academic hierarchies, 19, 33, 48, 52, 135, 138, 141, 144, 146, 167, 168, 200, 229, 233, 234, 238–240, 259, 263

Academic identity, 1–23, 35, 41, 42, 48, 49, 77, 85, 86, 88–90, 108, 110–112, 143, 145–147, 149, 153, 157, 158, 183, 185, 191, 198, 201, 202, 216, 229, 235, 240, 241, 243–249, 251, 259–272

Academic labour, 10, 13, 36, 37, 45, 47, 48, 51, 108, 117, 164, 202, 205, 239, 264, 268, 269

Academic values, 153–158

Academic working practices, 135, 158

Academic workspaces, 235, 236

Athena SWAN, 3, 37, 43, 76, 85

# Index

BAME academics, 213, 215
BAME doctoral students, 49
Belonging, v, vi, 3, 4, 6, 7, 9, 10, 13, 14, 16–20, 33–52, 75–117, 135–169, 183–217, 227–251, 259–272
Bullying, 76, 79, 260–262

Career guidance, 12, 267
Caring responsibilities, 7, 8, 20–23, 35, 37, 38, 86, 168, 210–212, 217, 244, 245, 248, 250, 265, 266
Chilly climate, 37, 38, 83, 232
Competition for academic jobs, 10, 12

Departmental communities, 44, 94, 135, 138, 140, 141, 148, 149, 166, 167, 189, 199, 202, 216, 217, 228, 233–234, 237, 238, 243, 268–271
Disciplinary communities, 3, 43, 44, 48, 75, 78, 81, 83, 93, 95, 104, 106, 109, 141, 145, 146, 149, 158, 168, 185, 191, 194–196, 206, 216, 217, 228, 229, 231–233, 238
Distance learners, 189, 191–193, 195
Doctoral completion rates, 6, 15, 76
Doctoral student attrition, 78
Doctoral student retention, 48
Doctoral supervision, 77
Doctoral supervisors, 41, 75, 233
Doctoral training, 105, 185, 269

Enculturation, 48, 78, 144, 217, 233
Exploitation of PhD students, 78

Female role models, 76, 243
Feminization of higher education, 34
Flexibility stigma, 265
Flexible working, 76, 264, 265

Gatekeepers, 19, 41, 75–117, 137, 141–144, 168, 184, 195
Gendered academic cultures, 3, 16, 52, 76, 84–109, 135
Gendered careers, 206–215
Gendered expectations, 37, 51, 80, 84, 88, 93, 95, 109, 117, 150
Gendered institutions, 35
Gendered patterns of progression, 76, 79
Gender in supervision, 149–152, 168
Gender pay gap, 213
Geographical mobility, 49, 76, 244, 248, 250

Ideal workers, 35, 47
Implicit bias, 85, 232
Imposter syndrome/imposterism, 8, 18, 33, 44, 49, 50, 81, 147, 152, 163, 168, 185, 187, 242, 249
Isolation, 3, 6, 13, 17, 78, 81, 138, 152, 166, 183, 185, 189, 191, 195, 198, 200, 204, 216, 229, 245, 269, 270

Lab groups, 103, 228, 270
Lad culture, 19, 39, 50, 51, 84, 96, 98, 117, 135, 151, 235, 236, 239, 261, 263
Leaky pipeline, 1, 2, 16, 52, 76, 206, 249, 264, 268
Legitimacy, 3, 10, 16, 18, 19, 39–43, 46, 51, 135–169, 229, 232, 233, 237–240, 246
Legitimate peripheral participation, 33, 40–42, 135

Male networks, 81, 92, 232, 262
Marginalisation, 3, 8, 33, 50, 51, 77, 81, 84, 93, 95, 97, 103, 117, 135, 145–147, 149, 152, 163, 168, 199, 232, 259
Mature learners, 147
Mental health, 8, 46, 49, 111, 112, 159, 161, 249, 265–267
Micro-politics, 19, 44, 146, 184, 197, 235
Motherhood penalty, 91, 264

Neoliberal academy, 35, 110, 162
Neoliberalisation, 10, 107, 117, 162, 266
Neoliberal working practices, 19, 101, 250, 265
Networking, 142, 147–149, 232

Part-time work, 20, 76, 212, 214, 242, 264
Peer communities, 6, 117, 166, 216, 230, 236, 239
Peer groups, 19, 77, 106, 166, 228, 237
Post-doctoral careers, 10–14
Postdoctoral scientists, 77
Power dynamics, 15, 19, 50, 77, 100, 102, 104, 106, 109, 113, 137, 144, 151, 152, 160, 237, 238
Presenteeism, 52, 101, 113, 265
Pressure to publish, 10, 49, 106, 158–167, 234, 243, 248, 250, 265
Principal investigators (PI), 75, 77, 94, 95, 102–104, 113, 116
Professional doctorates, 136
Publication rates, 37

Racial discrimination, 51, 215, 259, 266
Research Excellence Framework (REF), 45, 156, 159, 162
Role models, 52, 77, 93, 150, 184, 187, 207, 209, 217, 244, 248, 264

Safety of campus spaces, 100, 262
Sexism, 38, 51, 79, 80, 88
Sexual harassment, 3, 38, 39, 50, 79, 98–100, 117, 236, 239, 240, 260–263

Teaching as doctoral students, 36, 48, 49, 202, 233, 234, 237

Teaching Excellence Framework (TEF), 46, 162

Well-being, 6, 37, 40, 42, 46, 48–50, 81, 85, 86, 98, 100, 110, 111, 144, 153–155, 158–167, 199, 205, 229–231, 233–235, 237, 239, 241–243, 246–248, 250, 261, 265–267, 269–271

Women in STEM, 2, 8, 36, 43, 51, 76, 78–80, 84, 86, 88, 93, 96, 116, 117, 159, 231, 244, 262, 264

Women professors, 2, 3, 137, 186, 208, 213

Women's participation, 3, 18, 33, 34, 79

Working-class background, 38, 147, 168, 209, 241, 244, 259

Work-life balance, 47, 110, 111, 114, 139, 155, 165, 234, 244, 251, 266

Milton Keynes UK
Ingram Content Group UK Ltd.
UKHW020123231123
433084UK00006B/329

9 783031 119491